Hefner

HEFNER

By FRANK BRADY

MACMILLAN PUBLISHING CO., INC.

NEW YORK

The author and publisher wish to thank the following for their kind permission to reprint material:

My Fellow Americans by Malcolm Boyd. Copyright © 1970 by Malcolm Boyd. Reprinted by permission by Holt, Rhinehart and Winston, Inc.

Who Lost an American by Nelson Algren. © Nelson Algren 1960, 1961, 1962, 1963. Courtesy Macmillan Publishing Co., Inc.

"The Sage and Serious Doctrine of Hugh Hefner" by M. J. Sobran, Jr. *National Review*, February 1, 1974. Courtesy *National Review*, 150 East 35th Street, New York, N.Y. 10016.

"The Pubic Hair Papers" by Anthony Haden-Guest. From *Rolling Stone* Issue #150, December 20, 1973. © 1973 by Straight Arrow Publishers Inc. All Rights Reserved. Reprinted by Permission.

Reprinted from *Eternal Fire* by Calder Willingham by permission of the publisher, Vanguard Press, Inc. Copyright © 1963, 1962, by Calder Willingham.

The Presidential Papers by Norman Mailer. © 1960, 1961, 1962, 1963 by Norman Mailer. Courtesy G. P. Putnam's Sons.

S.T.P. A Journey Through America with the Rolling Stones by Robert Greenfield. Copyright © 1974 by Robert Greenfield. Reprinted by permission of the publishers, Saturday Review Press/E. P. Dutton & Co., Inc.

"Can You Bare It?" Reprinted by permission of *Forbes Magazine* from the March 1, 1971 issue.

"Playboy and the Preachers" by Theodore Peterson. Reprinted by permission of *Columbia Journalism Review* from the Spring 1966 issue.

"Richard Cory" is reprinted by permission of Charles Scribner's Sons from *The Children of the Night* by Edwin Arlington Robinson.

Front cover of first issue of *Playboy*, © 1953, *Playboy*.
Photograph of Marilyn Monroe, © 1953, *Playboy*.

Macmillan Publishing Co., Inc.
866 Third Avenue, New York, N.Y. 10022
Collier-Macmillan Canada Ltd.

First Printing 1974

Printed in the United States of America

Library of Congress Cataloging in Publication Data

Brady, Frank.
  Hefner.

  1. Hefner, Hugh Marston, 1926–
Z473.H44B7   070.5'092'4 [B]   74–13739
ISBN 0–02–514600–9

TO MAX

Hefner

CHAPTER 1

"I'm in the center of the world."

FROM the beginning months of 1963 to mid-1965, Hugh Marston Hefner left his fabled mansion a grand total of nine times. As a result of his hermetic ways, he began to establish a reputation for being almost as reclusive as Howard Hughes, prompting new journalist Tom Wolfe to christen "Hef" the "King of the Status Dropouts."

Hef responded: "I don't *need* to leave here. Why should I? I've got more right here now inside this house than most people ever find in a lifetime!"

In 1960 he had purchased an imposing four-storied brick mansion, trimmed with gray stone, located at 1340 North State Parkway in one of Chicago's most fashionable sections. The original price was $400,000 and he immediately invested another $350,000 redecorating it. Since then he has spent an additional $740,000 on structural changes, wings, and decorations. Today the entire mansion contains over 100 rooms.

Hefner combined this realty venture with his business, displaying his talents as a master manipulator when it came to his pleasure-oriented life. Hefner's then parent corporation, the HMH Publishing Co., was the actual purchaser of the house, since the building was to be used as a set for photo shootings, a center for entertaining advertisers and other businessmen, a guest house for special writers, artists, and photographers in Chicago doing work for *Playboy*, and eventually as a home for some two dozen Playboy Bunnies and other permanent and semipermanent guests. At first it was called "The Playboy Guest House."

Deep in the innards of the manse Hefner had constructed a mammoth, contemporary, windowless "apartment," totally sealed off from the rest of the house when he wanted privacy, accessible at other times through several entrances. It is here that he has lived for over fourteen years.

When he first moved into the mansion, and while it was being redecorated, Hefner still traveled each day by chauffeur-driven limousine the eight or ten blocks to the Playboy offices, as he had done in the past. Should he grow bored during the journey, he could watch color television, have a drink from the bar, listen to his favorite recordings, make an international telephone call, or read either *The Wall Street Journal*, the *Chicago Tribune*, or *Chicago Sun-Times*, all in his $30,000 custom-built Mercedes limousine with HMH-1340 Illinois license plate. For a short period, whenever Hefner rode in the car the chauffeur would hoist two small orange flags with Playboy's corporate symbol, the rabbit head, emblazoned on them as though Hefner were a head of state or a foreign diplomat displaying his country's colors. As the car drove down Lake Shore Drive, Chicagoans would gape, expecting to see Mayor Richard Daley or Senator Charles Percy. "Too pretentious," was Hefner's eventual comment, and he instructed that the flags be removed.

4

In time, though, Hefner came to question the necessity of even this short trip. He ordered a suite of offices and a conference room constructed in the Mansion, connected directly to his quarters by a spiral staircase, and he moved in a staff of personal secretaries and assistants. For a short period, he used both offices alternately, but early in 1963 he closed his personal office at 232 East Ohio Street, bequeathing it to a Playboy executive and his secretary. Hefner's adjoining bachelor apartment was converted into storage area and another office. From that day until the present—fourteen years—Hefner has journeyed to his corporate offices, now housed in the Playboy skyscraper just three minutes away by car, less than five times.

In 1967, Hefner had moved the bulk of the Playboy offices into what was formerly the Palmolive Building, one of Chicago's most attractive and prestigious office structures. Though he had signed a ninety-nine-year lease and expended millions of dollars in redecorating the interior of the building, he did not get around to visiting it until nearly a year later. Around three o'clock one morning he had the unaccustomed desire to get some fresh air. He emerged from his protective million-dollar cocoon to discover that it was dark out and a light rain was falling. Wrapping his thin coat around him, unshaven, slightly chilled, wondering where to go now that he was out, he decided to walk the few blocks to Michigan Avenue and have his first look at his skyscraper headquarters.

"It turned out the guard didn't know who I was and wouldn't admit me," Hefner recalled wryly. "But he finally let me in."

Hefner quietly visited all the deserted, plush-carpeted floors of the building and examined all of his executives' offices, the awed security guard padding silently after him. In my office he spied a layout for a forthcoming feature on the Lake Geneva Playboy Hotel and stopped to examine it. He decided it needed some corrections; the next morning

5

I received a memo about it that began, "Late last night I happened to be in the Playboy Building. . . ." Though the thirty-seven-story building houses thousands of employees, it is Hefner's mansion that is the true vertex of the Playboy kingdom.

Hefner had the interior of the Mansion designed so that it would be "more than just a pleasure palace; it's a place in which I can work and play without unnecessary interruptions and inconvenience." Though he has no specific routine, he might on a typical day go to sleep at 8 or 9 A.M., arise at 3 or 4 in the afternoon (or later), and then begin work.

"At first people didn't understand the house wasn't a typical house," Hefner once explained to the Reverend Malcolm Boyd. "The rhythm of the house is the rhythm of the people living inside it, not of the sun and the moon and the world outside. It's a world unto itself and within itself. You see, man is the only creature who can control his environment. Other men are already doing the same thing I am in different ways, and more will in the future. I control the clock with a twenty-four-hour staff. Audiovisual equipment collects data for me to review later. Nothing says the day has to have twelve, sixteen, or twenty-four hours, or begin at 7 A.M., 3 P.M., or midnight. The hours can function as an extension of a man instead of committing him to do certain things at certain times. For example, most men work in the daytime."

In order to maintain this sense of timelessness, virtually all of the windows of the Mansion are heavily shaded and draped. Some are also paneled over so that no beam of sunshine, no bit of rain, no night, no day can be detected from the inside. The temperature is always kept the same: pleasantly temperate. It is the ultimate tomb.

The house was originally built in 1906 for Dr. George S. Isham, a socially and civically prominent turn-of-the-century physician whose family helped found what is now the Northwestern University College of Medicine. Dr. Isham secured the services of a noted architect, James Gamble Rogers, from Paris to design it.

When Teddy Roosevelt came to Chicago he would usually stay at the house, as would Admiral Robert Peary. It was considered to be one of the most posh, showplace homes in the city of Chicago.

When Dr. Isham died in 1926 the house was sold and part of it broken up into apartments. Hefner had the place restored to its Victorian elegance and added a contemporary touch that makes 1340 North State as beautiful today as it was a half-century ago.

The entrance hall contains the electronic equivalent of a medieval moat and drawbridge: a closed-circuit TV system with a camera that scans all who seek entrance. When a visitor is recognized, one of Hefner's servants presses a button and a giant, iron-grille inner door swings open in true Ali Baba fashion. If the visitor, however, is *not* known to the one who buzzes, the sesame remains inviolably closed until a conversation, similar to the following typical one, ensues:

"Who's calling please?" says a loud, harsh voice, cut with piercing radio static.

"Frank Brady," says the visitor, feeling somewhat self-conscious, knowing that he's being electronically scrutinized but unable to rescrutinize his scrutinizer as he stretches his neck toward the Cyclopean TV camera located above the seven-foot door.

"Who?" the voice demands.

"Frank Brady," he repeats sheepishly.

A long silence follows while the servant checks a daily typewritten list of visitors and guests expected at the Mansion and, not finding the given name there, then scans a master list of "friends" who are to gain immediate access without a prior appointment, such as Aristotle Onassis, Leonid Brezhnev, and the Queen of England.

Voice tries again, dumbly:

"*Who's* calling?"

7

"I said 'Frank Brady,'" replies person, getting louder.

"I'm sorry but your name is not on the list."

"I have an appointment with Mr. Hefner. I'm writing his biography. I've flown here from New York."

There is more silence. Perhaps five minutes of it. Finally, "We're checking."

Eventually the buzzer sounds, the huge door swings open, and a liveried butler dressed in black and white, as if in an *opera bouffe*, formally greets the visitor. "I'm terribly sorry, Mr. Brady," he says obsequiously. "We didn't recognize you because of the beard, and I guess Mr. Hefner failed to inform us that you were arriving."

Once inside the *sanctus sanctorum* the inefficient rudeness of the entrance barrier immediately vanishes and the visitor is afforded the pleasures of what Norman Mailer calls "one of the most extraordinary houses in America."

The reception hall is decorated in gleaming white stone and marble and is dominated by a heroically proportioned seven-foot abstract bronze sculpture of "modern woman" by Abbott Pattison. One flight up a large oaken staircase covered with a thick red carpet is a starkly white door, locked, bearing a small brass plaque carrying the inscription, "*Si Non Oscillas, Noli Tintinnare,*" which means "If You Don't Swing, Don't Ring." Often guests are met here by another butler, sometimes the same one who was responsible for guarding the front entrance.

Through this white door, down a long hallway decked with paintings by Jackson Pollock, Willem de Kooning, and other great contemporary artists, a pair of ceiling-high French doors open on the main room of the Mansion, a cavernous and seignorial hall-of-a-room, sixty feet long, thirty feet wide and twenty-two feet high, culminating in a walk-in Italian marble fireplace at the far end, the hearth of which is the size of a small stage. The room is reached by a broad stairway flanked by two medieval suits of armor with lances at the ready. A splendid, large black-and-white abstract by

8

Franz Kline reigns violently over one wall. Columnist Herb Caen told his *San Francisco Chronicle* readers that the room was "a huge and magnificent drawing room as grand (and no smaller than) the St. Francis lobby."

The walls are oak paneled. Four stately oak pillars flank the entranceway, the beamed ceiling is inlaid with flowered frescoes, and the floor is inlaid oak.

Though the structure and shell of the room have been completely restored to look exactly the same as they did when the original Rough Rider strode across its floors, the furnishings are totally modern, with long sofas, oversized armchairs, lamps of abstract design, and cocktail table-benches. Picasso's classic *Nude Reclining*, valued at $275,000, hangs majestically over the fireplace; major portions of the remaining walls are hung with other famous works of art.

In the center of the room, acting as a stunted room divider, is a fifteen-foot-long, freestanding stereo console with enough electronic equipment to service a small radio station. Hefner has a record library of over 3,000 LPs, most of them jazz and pop, with an extensive inventory of two of his favorites, Frank Sinatra and Peggy Lee.

Hefner is an inveterate lover of the movies; so behind a pair of paneled doors are two 35-mm professional motion picture projectors capable of showing either standard or wide-screen movies. A full cinemascope-sized screen can be lowered from a hidden compartment in the ceiling by the touch of a button. First-run movies and other feaures are shown at least once a week when Hefner is in Chicago.

The room also contains a fourteen-foot table which seats sixteen for formal dining, but it is more often used as an informal buffet service.

Off the main room are several opulently appointed guest chambers known somewhat ostentatiously as the Red Room, the Blue Room, etc. Also adjoining the main room are a smallish dining—or breakfast—room, two bars, and Hefner's famous twenty-four-hour kitchen, which is capable of providing for the gastronomic needs of a major hotel. As Mailer discovered, "one had been able to get the equivalent of any drink made at any bar at any hour of the world, one could have chili at 4 A.M. or ice cream at 10." The kitchen staff works round the clock in shifts, ready to provide one with any gustatory whim. Guests can have breakfast in bed every morning if they wish. In fact, they can have every meal in bed, every day—and often do.

The top floors of the house contain offices for Hefner's and the Mansion's staff, small apartments and rooms for guests and friends, and a dormitory for the two dozen Bunnies who regularly live there. The servants number forty-six.

Downstairs, at basement level, is a regulation bowling alley with automatic pinsetter in addition to the full-size swimming pool, with poolside decorations made to resemble a South Sea island, complete with thatched huts and a cascading waterfall that looks like a honeymoon retreat for Jon Hall and Dorothy Lamour. Behind the waterfall—and reachable only by swimming under it—is a cave furnished with many waterproof cushions, soft lights and, usually, music. On the same level as the pool is a game room that contains a pool table, pinball machines, a roulette table, and a miniature Grand Prix racecourse. There are also several steam rooms.

Underneath the pool is, of course, the underwater bar, which can be reached either by sliding down a fireman's pole or by descending a stone-walled staircase which resembles the entrance to a Parisian underground cafe. The bar is cozy, cushioned and has a picture window that looks —aquarium-like—into the pool.

Shortly after moving into the Mansion, Hefner began having huge parties every Friday night, starting at about midnight and often ending around noon the next day. Telegrams of invitation were wired to virtually every celebrity who happened to be in Chicago that night, and many came.

10

These guests were joined by Playboy staffers and a large group of Beautiful People from advertising agencies (to whom Hefner tried to sell ad space), modeling agencies, publishing, airlines, and show business. The hoped-for impression was of a Rabelaisian orgy, and most of the invitees seemed to wish it would become one. Almost every Chicago Bunny was there (in civilian dress); approximately five hundred guests attended each week. The parties, even for Hefner, were prohibitively expensive—well over $5,000. In addition to the drinks, an elaborate buffet and a breakfast for those who stayed long enough, there was the cost of the salaries of over two dozen employees, including bartenders, cooks, coat checkers, and guards. Recently, when I asked Hefner about the cost of these parties, he seemed annoyed: "There is no truth whatsoever in the statement that I gave up those Friday night parties because of the expense. The cost was insignificant. Uninvited people began crashing the parties because they knew they were always held on Fridays, so when we gave a party we switched it to another night. But the real reason I gave up the parties is simple: They bored me!"

On the same level as the main hall, Hefner's personal quarters—like a plush time capsule locked safely in the center of a spaceship—are covered with white, ankle-deep, wall-to-wall vicuña carpeting.

"I'm afraid you'll have to remove your shoes," he says graciously to his rare personal visitors. "We do that to keep the carpet clean."

His study, an elegant room, has a fireplace flanked by ceiling-high bookcases containing works he considers pertinent to the editing of *Playboy* and many volumes of his favorite novelists: Fitzgerald, Hemingway, Nabokov, and Lawrence. Every piece of furniture—chairs, tables, desks—is custom-made. The floor is an obstacle course of papers, photos, envelopes, folders, memos, transparencies, and books. Piles and stacks are everywhere. For the most part they

11

relate to his current editorial work, but they also concern his many other business ventures. Though the appearance is one of hopeless confusion, Hefner claims he knows where everything is and can put his hands on anything he wants in a matter of seconds. Whenever the carpet is shampooed, he demands that his secretaries chart a "map" of each island of paperwork so that it can be precisely replaced in his free-form filing system. He sometimes works at a large L-shaped desk above which hangs an original cartoon from *The Realist* depicting a fiendish *grafittieur* scrawling across a wall, "Hugh Hefner is a virgin."

Most of Hefner's work, however, is done in his bedroom, which is a miniature version of the main drawing room with the same oak-paneled walls and beamed ceiling.

Symbolically, he spends a huge amount of time working in his now-famous Brobdingnagian circular bed, which Tom Wolfe described in the *New York Herald Tribune* as "a bed and a half . . . the biggest, roundest bed in the history of the world." It's eight and a half feet in diameter and fits into a bank of curved cabinets that are equipped with a refrigerator, bar, dictaphone, and remote-control switching for radio, stereo, and television. A Rapidial phone, programmed with 200 telephone numbers that can be "dialed" by pressing a single button, is also built into the cabinet. Motorized controls are an important part of its equipment; Hefner can set the bed vibrating or rotate it to change, in effect, his immediate environment. It goes a full 360 degrees in either direction, "33⅓, 45, and 78," explains Hefner with a smile. Once asked by an interviewer where one bought round sheets for a round bed, Hefner answered charmingly, "I haven't the vaguest idea."

An Ampex television camera resides in the bedroom, and it is usually aimed at the bed, with a setup for instantaneous transmission into a TV screen set into the wall. Wolfe wondered why, and his question elicited the following:

12

Hefner: "I have a whole $40,000 Ampex videotaping console, so I figured I might as well have the camera, too. It would be like having a tape recorder with no microphone."

"But why in the bedroom?"

"Well . . . ," Hefner smiles, his cheekbones coming out, his eyes turning on, "Who knows when something *very beautiful* might happen in this bedroom!"

What Wolfe didn't know, and what Hefner will explain if pushed further about the camera is that something "very beautiful" happens often: visual stimulation is one of his most passionate sexual pleasures. "I've got a kinky thing going, visually, while I'm having sex," he explains unself-consciously. Mirrors abound in his bedroom and he often watches himself and his partner making love, via his closed-circuit TV system.

He is insistent, however, that he is not a voyeur. He dismisses the analogy implied in the *roman à clef* by Henry Sutton called *The Voyeur*, published in 1969 (about a character called Irv Kane, who is described as "America's high priest of sex" and who publishes a magazine called *Tomcat*), as pure nonsense.

"Visual stimulation," says Hefner "in a nonparticipating way, holds no interest for me. But as an additional stimulus while having sex—sure, I'm all for it."

He also has, available as a pre- or intracoital stimulus, over 1,000 "blue" films—the largest private collection in the world—consisting of black-and-white, color, silent, and sound movies, which he projects directly from his bed, of virtually every conceivable sexual permutation and position possible among men, women, children, and animals. There is supposedly one very elaborately made feature-length "porno" movie in the collection, produced in color and sound, with highly professional camera work, judicious editing, attractive actresses, and, unlike most such motel-room-made films, even believable dialogue. The film's star is reported to be Hugh M. Hefner.

13

Off the bedroom there is a delightfully decadent, Roman-style bath which is large enough to hold over two dozen people simultaneously—and it has. Hefner had a special device installed in the bath in case he should ever—God forbid—want the sensation of being outside of the Mansion; all he need do is press a button and a gentle rain falls from above. In addition, colored lights play on the oiled and steaming, scented water. Soft music, with no discernible source, wafts mysteriously through the bath.

But Hefner is a man of many dimensions. Through a door on the north wall of the bedroom is his futuristic electronics room, looking not unlike a space-shot mission control center. The walls are crammed with every imaginable variety of electronic gadgetry, including eight separate TV monitors—one for each channel in Chicago—so that any TV program can be tape-recorded for playback at another time. A clock-control device activates the videotape recorder automatically at prescribed times, "so if I want to watch the eleven o'clock news at 2 in the morning or at 4 the next afternoon, I can do it," Hefner proclaims. A videotaped library of several hundred feature films has been recorded so that Hefner can watch them on his bedroom TV set. In his personal conference room adjoining his quarters, he has a videophone for visual and sound communication with the Playboy executive offices. "I'm in the center of the world," he told interviewer Oriana Fallaci.

And in another interview he explained: "The house is so ideally suited to my living habits that it's a world unto itself, and in most respects, far better than the world outside. The work and play rhythms of the house are in our control. Most creative people would like to work at their own natural rhythm. My day can begin at 7 A.M., noon, or midnight. It doesn't make any difference."

A. C. Spectorsky, *Playboy*'s late associate publisher and editorial director, believed that the operation of the house

on a twenty-four-hour basis was practically a psychic necessity for Hefner, pointing out that Hefner created a structure
that was almost symbiotically sensitive and enormously re-
sponsive to his eccentric personality and predilections. "He's
a man of no habits. He eats when he's hungry; goes to sleep
when exhausted; when he's rested, he wakes up." "Spec"
avoided the Mansion whenever he could, saying it looked
like an "impersonal hotel lobby decorated in early garish."
Not many of Hefner's guests agreed, however, and invitations
to spend an evening at the Mansion were highly coveted.

Hefner discovered that as he continued to add more
and more conveniences and gadgets to his house, it became
less and less necessary ever to leave. He could become
thoroughly involved, through electronic means, with his
far-flung enterprises while enjoying the sensuous pleasure
of his sumptious surroundings.

He has made some intriguing structural changes in the
house. "When I first bought the Mansion," Hefner recalls,
"it reminded me of one of those houses that were used in
horror films, my favorite kind of movie when I was a kid.
I was disappointed, though, not to find any secret passage-
ways, so I simply had some built in."

Today the mansion has secret doors, tunnels, passage-
ways, and whole walls that move by a press of a button; it
certainly would have delighted Peter Lorre or Bela Lugosi, or
an eight-year-old Hugh Hefner. "We really should rent Boris
Karloff to walk through the house on weekends," Hefner once
half-seriously suggested.

Whether because of its imposing appearance or because
of its imposing owner, Hefner's house has come to be spoken
of among the Playboy staff in semireverential terms. Never
merely "Hef's house," it was either The House or, more
formally, The Mansion. The speaker's tone supplied the
capitals. This elevation of Hefner's house to the level of
national shrine was so pervasive that one iconoclast in the

15

magazine's art department inscribed his private epigram, complete with gothic lettering and intertwined vines, and hung it above his desk:

OUR FATHER, WHO ART IN 1340.

As Hefner and his remarkable house grew in fame, colored by media-inspired legend, both nabob and celebrity found their way to his doors, to both hobnob with him and to see "how he lived" in what is probably the most famous private dwelling in the world. Few people outside of royalty have entertained, as visitors and houseguests in their homes, such a distinguished array of celebrities from all walks of fame. The following list, a classic study of name-dropping, is taken from his guest book and represents just a fraction of those who have come to visit—some for a few hours, some for a few months—with Hefner at his Chicago mansion: Dick Gregory, Lenny Bruce, John V. Lindsay, Charles Percy, Candice Bergen, Martin Luther King, Yevgeny Yevtushenko, Frank Sinatra, Anthony Quinn, Timothy Leary, Liza Minelli, Oleg Cassini, Tony Curtis, the Maharaja of Jaipur, Tony Bennett, Melvin Belli, Sidney Poitier, David Janssen, Mort Sahl, Steve Allen, William Saroyan, Saul Bellow, Alan Watts, Muhammad Ali, Kenneth Tynan, Studs Terkel, Paul Newman, Burgess Meredith, Carl Stokes, Warren Beatty, Gay Talese, David Niven, Robert Culp, Hugh O'Brian, Arthur Schlesinger, Jr., Danny Kaye, Otto Preminger, Roman Polanski, Alberto Moravia, Jane Fonda, Max Lerner, Nicholas Johnson, Jesse Jackson, John Kenneth Galbraith, George Plimpton, Jules Feiffer, Bruce Jay Friedman, Norman Mailer, James Baldwin, Joseph P. Kennedy, Jean-Pierre Aumont, Rudolf Nureyev, William F. Buckley, Jr., Tiny Tim, Masters and Johnson, Bernie Cornfeld, Bob Hope, Groucho Marx, Bill Cosby, Johnny Carson, Tom Jones, Dick Butkus, Budd Schulberg, Ray Bradbury, the Rolling Stones, F. Lee Bailey, Elizabeth Taylor, Ralph Nader, Linda Lovelace, Sammy Davis, Jr., George McGovern, and Ringo Starr.

16

The reason there is a preponderance of Hollywood names among those listed is because Hefner enthusiastically encourages relationships and friendships with movie people. He unabashedly admits to being star-struck. "But most of us are, no matter what degree of success we have achieved. I grew up in the thirties and forties and film stars were my idols as a kid, so the celebrities of show business have special meaning for me."

In addition to the now-abandoned Friday night soirées, one of Hefner's favorite ways of entertaining has always been by giving mammoth, Gatsbyesque parties. The bacchanalian intensity of the parties, however, has long been in contention. Some observers claim that they are dull, lifeless, and hopelessly middle-class, and that there is more sex at a teenage fraternity hop than at one of Hefner's gatherings; others, often those who have never been to a party at the Playboy Mansion, conjecture that an orgiastic revel is *de rigueur*, almost an automatic demand of all guests who attend.

As with many generalizations, the truth is somewhere in between, but after participating in and observing over a hundred Hefner parties of all sizes, shapes, and characters, from small, intimate, and almost delicate *tête-à-têtes* to hard-rock explosions of over 1,000 people, I can report that the former statement is, unfortunately, usually more accurate than the latter.

Though relatively sexless in an overt way (even though the Mansion is immense, there is difficulty finding privacy at a gathering of 1,000 people), the parties are hardly ever slow and never quiet. The food is superb: the three bars serve whatever and as much as you can imagine to drink, and for men there is the delightfully giddy experience of being outnumbered by women—and all of them beautiful— by approximately three to one. Columnist Art Buchwald, however, claims that the most exciting thing that ever happened to him during his visits to the Mansion was winning $33 in gin rummy—at a penny a point—from Hugh Hefner.

A writer by the name of Hal Higdon attended a Hefner party and described his experience this way: "The previous week I had attended one of Hugh Hefner's legendary parties. I had come away with the impression that if Pieter Breughel had been alive today he would have surely done a painting of one."

Joe Goldberg, in his book *Big Bunny*, describes the parties perceptively, but his conclusions are quite different:

Not *La Dolce Vita*, but another Italian film, *La Notte:* elegant strangers at a lavish party, wandering aimlessly, looking for someone to make contact with . . . when a party gets too aimless or disaffiliated, Hefner is likely to disappear into his own apartment for work or conversation. Later, when only those enjoying themselves are left, he will surface again.

Actually, Hefner sometimes boycotts his own parties entirely, even "important" ones with a large list of celebrities and superstars. He never offers an explanation of why he fails to attend any given affair. As the guests revel, Hefner, secure in his womb-room just a few feet away, mysteriously carries out and lives his subterranean secrets.

Novelist Nelson Algren, a frequent guest at Hefner's parties for a time, is categorically critical of them in his essay, "Chicago IV."

The great baronial hall was serving as a guest room for a gaggle of humans wearing all the clothes anyone could possibly need to break into society once they found a society to break into.

This plainly wasn't it. This was High Schlock house—employing the term in its Milwaukee Avenue sense to indicate a furniture store using colored lighting to lend an expensive glow to its sofas and chairs, and deducting the light bill from the markup later. . . .

I hadn't seen anything like it since Joan Crawford threw the lingerie party in *Dance, Fools, Dance.* . . .

18

If what was going on here was high society, Caroline Kennedy is President of the Veteran Boxers' Association. . . .

It's highly problematic whether to accept Algren's parody of the type of society that the Mansion scene represents, or even what went on, since a number of his evenings there were marked with a dark depression, ending in a crashing confusion in which he could be found talking to one of the medieval suits of armor that flank the entrance to the main room. ("They're the only ones at the party *worth* talking to," he once told me.) Algren was eventually "barred" from the Mansion because of his behavior and because of his unkind remarks, in print, concerning his host. Time mends, however, and as of late Algren is once again attending the Mansion frolics.

During parties at the Mansion, the guest rooms are usually locked (except to the guests who are staying in them), as are Hefner's quarters, so if a *liaison* is established and sex becomes an imperative, it is necessary to leave the house in order to consummate the act, which somehow seems preposterous in the home of Hugh Hefner. Occasionally a couple will attempt a "quickie" in the steam bath or in the underwater bar or in the cave behind the waterfall, or even in one of the powder rooms, but there is simply no wide-scale scene of wanton revelry at most Hefner parties, certainly not the large ones.

Hefner does, however, become annoyed at the press, and even at his guests, for stressing what they consider the *sterility* of his parties. "People come to a benefit party that I give for the American Civil Liberties Union and they expect an orgy. They have built up a fantasy that there is constant fucking on the floor around here. So when it doesn't happen, they think that there's *no* fucking at any time, and that Hefner's a queer."

The often-stated rumor that Hefner is possibly a practicing homosexual or, if not that, a "closet queen," is absurd. This is based on my own observations of him "in action"

19

over a number of years and in a variety of social and potentially sexual situations. He is thoroughly heterosexual and has intercourse—with a woman—virtually every evening of his life which, as he himself comments, "is pretty good for a forty-eight-year-old, and I am more potent, less jaded and enjoy it more than I ever have."

Vince Tajiri, Playboy's former photo editor, states unequivocally that over the years "Hefner has had a very high average in bedding down many of the Playmates." Another very close Hefner aide claims that Hefner has made love to "well over 2,000 women," since the magazine began.

Hefner has had a homosexual experience on at least one occasion, however, but a lone sparrow does hardly a spring make. He told me that before *Playboy* began he met a young man in a Near North Side bar—Hefner had been drinking—and decided to "experiment." He went through with the act at the other man's apartment, he said, but he offered no further details other than to say the deed was never repeated. It is reminiscent of Voltaire, who refused to accept a second invitation to a homosexual revel after distinguishing himself at his first encounter: "Once a philosopher, twice a pederast."

Actually, as Hefner will hint, there *is* a private side to his life that only a handful—or two—of people know about or participate in. It is centered in the Mansion and consists of abundant and ever-varied sexual experiences. Hefner enigmatically says that these continual, often experimental escapades "run the gamut of fantasy." He says no more, however.

Because Hefner is considered to be one of the high priests of sex in this country, rumors constantly abound concerning what goes on in the Mansion sexually. Though Hefner has told me that he "tried everything, including swinging scenes both organized and spontaneous," he is emphatic about stressing that his sexual preference is a one-to-one relationship with a woman. From what I know of Hefner as a man, I believe this to be true, but there have been stories about daisy chains the length of conga lines, serpenting from floor to floor; Hefner plugging his eight-inch penis into every variety of orifice; horses and other animals being delivered in trucks in the dark of night, as immense Bunny-studs; chains, whips, spurs; women loving women; men sleeping with children; in a sexual phantasmagoria, a Grand Hotel of the libido that takes place every night in scores of the one hundred rooms, all of which contain hidden closed-circuit television cameras. Even among people who work for Playboy and are somewhat close to Hefner, the speculation that the Mansion is a sexual nirvana is constant.

I once told Hefner that I had a humorous vision of him waiting for his last guest to depart after a long and crowded party, then tearing off his clothes and saying to a number of Bunnies, "O.K. girls, let's get down to some real business!" His reply was so rapid that maybe I was right: "Why do you think I never wear anything but pajamas?"

A Bunny who lived at the Mansion told me that Hefner once called her room late at night and invited her down to his private apartment. When she arrived, several other girls were already there. Eventually there were as many as ten, drinking and turning on. Hefner, nude on his round bed, was the only man. All the girls sat around him, one by one taking turns masturbating him.

"Is that all they did—masturbate him?" I asked.

"That's all he seemed to want," she replied. "But he was getting his kicks not from being masturbated but from the fact that we all were *watching* him being masturbated."

After several hours she left with the rest of the girls when Hefner indicated that he was going to sleep. He did, however, retain one girl for the remainder of the evening.

Another girl who was formerly a receptionist for Playboy once made a mysterious and suggestive remark to me about "the dogs." I had heard rumors about Hefner's dogs—he used to have an overly affectionate Saint Bernard named Humphrey, and now has two large sheep dogs—but I'd always failed to hear any "real" details. Her story, and the way she was telling it—drolly, as though it were a scene from *The Balcony*—made me believe that she had been directly involved. Occasionally, she said, there would be a private show in the Mansion in which a dog—or dogs—would have intercourse with one or more girls who had agreed in advance to let it be done.

She pointed out that most of the time the "dog acts," as she called them, were performed by girls other than those who lived in the Mansion. "They were far-out hookers and they were paid plenty for it," she said. "But you're not going to believe this: Humphrey somehow knew who was who and preferred fucking his favorites."

Whatever sexual pyrotechnics Hefner participates in in his 100-room mansion, it is undoubtedly an immense and frequent preoccupation on his part, with small, bona fide orgies organized at his pleasure.

However, I have never heard any woman who has been involved with Hefner sexually say anything to indicate that he ever *forced* anyone to do anything, or that he was unkind in any way. Some girls who have fallen in love with him have become depressed and disillusioned if he did not reciprocate their feelings. Others, the few who rejected his advances, report that though he acted the part of the unrequited lover, it did not greatly affect their relationship and it certainly had no bearing on the girls' jobs, whether they worked as a Bunny or for the magazine.

CHAPTER 2

"We were raised behind a wall of restrictions."

Moaning and gasping from pain, holding himself where the bullets had entered, Hugh Hefner staggered to his front door. Blood trickled and then almost spurt from his mouth; an ugly wound gaped the breadth of his forehead. Slowly, laboriously, he worked the door ajar, but at the top of the steps he dizzied, then reeled and plunged to the bottom. As he lay there on the cold pavement of that city street, his vision grew murky and then all went black. He feebly raised one hand a few inches as a signal for help or perhaps as a symbol of futility. He could neither talk nor move any other part of his body. Finally, his hand dropped. He was dead.

The skinny, sixteen-year-old Hefner was on his feet in an instant, as soon as he heard the camera cease grinding.

He eagerly questioned his cofilmmakers—his brother Keith, and a friend, Jim Brophy—about the effectiveness of the scene. The melted Hershey bar that he had used for blood had seemed a realistic makeup alternative, but he was now afraid it might have appeared too viscous. Jim and Keith assured him it had not. The film was completed after a week of writing, planning, and shooting; Hefner had produced his first cinematic effort. It was called *The Return From the Dead*, a 16-mm black-and-white home horror movie filmed mostly in his own basement, which had been converted into the laboratory of a mad Transylvanian. The Transylvanian's castle was located in the peaceful regions of northwest Chicago. Hefner's parents still live there.

His major achievement to date, the film was a rough, rather amateurish production, but Hefner had managed to bring it to fruition. It was, perhaps, a harbinger of his future, or at least an indication of the energy he was eventually capable of generating.

Hugh Marston Hefner was born on the ninth of April 1926 in Chicago, Illinois, where his parents had moved in 1920. His mother, the former Grace Swanson (who in her youth looked something like Gloria Swanson *sans* makeup), and his father, Glenn, had been childhood sweethearts in the farmlands of Nebraska, both living near the town of Holdredge in the south-central part of the state. Glenn was of German descent and had been born in a sod hut to very poor parents, a fact which Hefner the younger oftens likes to remember. Of Swedish extraction, Grace came from a relatively wealthy background; her family owned seven farms in the Holdredge area. The couple had attended high school together, and later both graduated from the same college. She had been the class valedictorian in high school and editor of the school newspaper; in college she also worked as an editor on the campus journal. Glenn, though a good student, was known more for his athletic prowess: he was both a track and basketball star. They were married shortly after graduation—a pattern that was to be repeated later by Hugh, though not with the same degree of success.

Hefner's childhood and adolescence were fairly typical of middle-class American family life in the thirties. His Dick-and-Jane neighborhood was a friendly section of private homes where people flew the American flag on Memorial Day, and children cheered after parades, hung on the backs of ice trucks, and bought Sugar Babies at the local candy store.

Throughout the Depression the Hefners managed better than most. They had enough money to buy a new Ford in 1936. "We never wanted for anything," recalled Hefner. "I guess you'd call us an 'upper middle-class' family. Money was never a thing I had to wonder or worry about." Glenn was an accountant for a large corporation, Advance Aluminum, and kept his job during the years when millions, including many of his friends and neighbors, were on welfare or working for the W.P.A. But to keep working and to maintain his relative prosperity, Glenn had to work long hours at the office, six and sometimes seven days a week, leaving each morning before the children were awake and often returning home after they were bedded down for the night. "I hardly ever saw my father as I was growing up," stated Hefner, and when his family did get together, Grace was invariably the discussion leader. Conversation was not one of Glenn's fortes.

Most of Hugh's care, therefore, devolved on Grace, and she exerted a great influence on him in many ways. "It didn't help that my mother was the strong parent, and that I was brought up almost entirely under her supervision," he once said. As a boy, Hefner keenly felt the lack of a strong male figure with whom he could identify, but on another occasion he offered this account of his development: "The absence of the father figure inadvertently affected me in terms of my turning inward and developing my own fantasies and in many ways was responsible for the beginnings of my becoming a person and enabling me to do the things I've done."

The older of two children (Keith is two years younger), "Hef," the sobriquet that was used by most people outside of his immediate family, was quiet and studious. Looking back at his childhood, he describes himself as "shy and introspective." All accounts seem to verify that judgment. Though Hefner's friends considered him somewhat "popular," they also felt he was an intrinsic loner.

This reserve was tempered with ingenuity and creativity, traits which showed themselves even when he was very young, so that Hefner was always, paradoxically, the leader of his social group. The Hefner basement was more than just a makeshift film studio; it was also used as a playroom, library, and party hall—the gathering place for all the children in the neighborhood. Forty years later Grace Hefner reminisced with Malcolm Boyd about her famous son:

When Hugh was young he was an early riser, but he needed a lot of sleep. He took naps even when he was going to kindergarten at four-and-a-half, which is one of the mistakes we made with him. You see, this meant that he went with the older children and he felt sort of inferior. I remember him coming home once and asking, "How do you skip?" The older children met in the morning and the younger ones in the afternoon. So we wanted him to go in the morning because of his nap. He didn't develop physically—skating, things of that sort—as quickly as his younger brother did.

When he was quite small, about two, he was very outgoing and at ease with anyone he met. Then we moved into a flat where the landlady said it would be all right to play in the backyard, but made him feel uncomfortable. He couldn't understand that she was very nervous, and from then on he met folks with a reserve. He wasn't sure how he would be treated.

We moved here when Hugh was just four. He really lived here most of his growing-up time. We bought this place because we felt the children would be less hampered. This area wasn't built up then; very few houses and back of us was mostly prairie.

There were meadowlarks and snakes. I'm sure he told you he liked to play with animals.

And he was fortunate with the youngsters he grew up with. None of them tried to dominate the others. There were two other families in particular, each had two boys, and the six of them usually played here on our back porch. We had an old table and they also used an old desk as a platform. They used to make clay figures and ships, and they'd act out stories which they made up.

Hugh never was particularly active in athletics because he wasn't very good at it. They played football on the prairie sometimes, but he didn't take much part in school athletics.

Grace and Glenn Hefner combined their hospitality and concern for their children's popularity with a strict Methodist morality. They had themselves been brought up under the weight of a puritanical ethic and attempted to instill this in their children. "We were raised behind a wall of restrictions," Hefner recalled. The boys were, of course, forbidden to smoke or drink in the house, even as young adults. On Sundays they stayed home or "out back." Movies were prohibited. Off-color conversation was unthinkable.

Hefner's reaction to these restraints was to withdraw into himself. His main outlet of expression began as elaborate doodling, labored over on lined looseleaf paper, paper bags, or whatever else was at hand. His drawing quickly developed into single-concept tableaus. Soon afterward his subject matter became even more sophisticated; he created actual characters whom he would use thematically again and again. "I don't know how old I was when I first began drawing," he has stated, but he was a doodler at four and by the time he was seven or eight he had begun to introduce into his artistic repertoire what became a stable of cartoon personalities. He wasn't a particularly *skilled* cartoonist, but he was prodigious in the amount of time he spent with pad and pencil, and in the amount of work he produced.

Hefner's early penchant for drawing led him into diffi-

27

culties at school, however, as the following note from his fourth-grade teacher indicates:

My Dear Mrs. Hefner:
I dislike complaining about Hugh but I feel I must let you know what he has been doing for the past week. I've had to speak to him two or three times. Every time he has a study period, he doesn't do his arithmetic, geography or spelling unless I stand right at his elbow. He *constantly* draws. I am enclosing a sample. I am about to reach the end of my patience with him and I told him just now that I would not take so much time from recitations in 3A to make him get to work. He has me at my wits end. I have tried persuasions, scoldings and appeal to his love for mother—all to no avail. Perhaps you can help. He will not pass if he doesn't do his work. I dislike writing notes as they never seem to convey just what I am trying to say. If you are over at school any time, please come in to see me.

Della A. Dawson

Mrs. Dawson secured the approval of Grace Hefner to send the errant Hugh to the school psychologist to see if a professional could offer some suggestions on how she could cope with him. The boy was found to have an I.Q. of 152, which is much above normal; those with a score of 150 or over are often said to be of the "genius" level. The determination of mental level is, of course, dependent upon the type of I.Q. test given. In this case, that information is unknown. Then again, it depends on whether one believes in the value of such testing. Whether or not Hugh Hefner was a genius is unimportant; he *was* a very intelligent child.

The psychologist reported to Mrs. Dawson that there was nothing wrong with the boy other than the fact that he was bored and added that Hugh Hefner was "the brightest child we have ever interviewed." School officials offered to arrange a scholarship at the Francis W. Parker school, a private institution for exceptional (and mostly rich) children, located on Chicago's posh Near North Side. The decision whether to enroll was left up to Hugh himself, but he decided that he wanted to stay with the friends he had known from first grade at the Sayre Grammar School rather than to risk a new situation. "I suppose it's a good thing I didn't go to Parker," Hefner recalled. "They might have straightened me out, and then I never would have had any fun."

Grace Hefner was a stern taskmistress toward her children, and reprimands from school authorities would not be tolerated without punishment or, at the very least, a verbal barrage. She was also sincerely interested in the boy's welfare. She had a love for learning and wanted her sons to share it. Hugh was commanded and cajoled to improve his attention at school. Having both teacher and mother prodding him in this way and receiving an added impetus from the ego reinforcement of the psychologist's report might have served as the needed catalyst for the marked improvement which occurred shortly after this incident. He began studying in earnest, but not before he himself made an amusing analysis of the problem, penned on January 26, 1936, when he was nine:

"Why I Waist Time"
by Hugh Hefner

I think I get to dreaming
Of something I might do
And I forget my studies
And what I'm supposed to do.

By the time he left for his summer vacation that year, Hugh had made such strides in his studies that he was given an "E" for "Excellent" on his report card in the subjects of English, spelling, arithmetic, and music.

Hefner had actually begun his life as a publisher shortly before he learned he was a gifted child. He began a neighborhood "newspaper" consisting of news and cartoons, all written and drawn by himself. Each issue was painstakingly typed out on an old Royal typewriter on single sheets of white paper, then stapled together and sold by Hefner, who knocked on doors in his neighborhood offering copies of his newspaper for a penny apiece. It was a remarkable enterprise for an eight-year-old, commanding the industry, creativity, and *chutzpah* that would become hallmarks of the adult Hefner.

His parents encouraged his first publishing venture, and starting at that point, there was no stopping the knickered entrepreneur. His next publication was *The 7B Star*, later renamed *The Pepper*; it is reportedly still being published today. Each issue consisted of seven or eight small stories and an occasional caricature. Hefner had begun to grow more sophisticated in his role as publisher; he secured the help of several of his classmates for this publication and got them to write stories—by-lined, of course. Then he went out and sold some advertising for it.

In January of 1939 he received an "E" in every subject—thirteen in all, during all four grading periods—plus a special commendation for "his fine and faithful work on the school paper." Graduated to Branch Junior High School, he started *The Hour Glass*, a paper apparently somewhat less successful than *The Pepper* since the paper ceased publication when Hefner left the school.

Hefner entered high school as something of a midwestern wallflower; he was an attractive kid, but his voice changed during this period of his adolescence, and he grew gangly. This probably accounted for some of his acute shyness. He was so bashful and inhibited that for a time stammering was his only means of communication with girls. Because of his upbringing, holding hands with a girl, even touching one, was in another libidinal universe which he was not yet capable of exploring. Speaking of his parents in an interview he gave to Bill Davidson of the *Saturday Evening Post* in the early 1960s, Hefner said: "Worst of all was their attitude toward sex, which they considered to be a horrid thing never to be mentioned. This led to serious conflicts when I entered high school. I remember the early

30

embarrassment of just putting my arm around a girl. I was very introverted, and this became one of the most difficult periods of my life." And in an interview he gave to the Rev. Malcolm Boyd, he said: "My parents gave me a lot, and yet there was a sense of suppression. Guilts were there, and a child is so sensitive to this, especially when their parents have sexual guilts. I'd have to say that my parents were extremely repressed, sexually, with all that this suggests. But of course, so was their entire generation." As a small boy, Keith recalls, he asked his mother why he had an erection and she reacted by becoming highly embarrassed.

But his mother's attitudes toward sex were not all embargo and avoidance. She revealed years later a fact that Hefner had conveniently forgotten: when both of her sons were entering adolescence, she thought it would be better if their curiosity about sex could be satisfied in some "healthier" way than street-corner hearsay. She purchased the most progressive sex education book she could find and made it available to them. Their cronies saw it too, of course, and word leaked back to one of the neighborhood mothers, who made an irate phone call to Mrs. Hefner, saying: "You keep that book about sex away from my son. As far as I'm concerned, that's something that God could have done differently."

It didn't take long for Hefner to begin to doubt his parents' values and to become skeptical of "the bullshit that they accepted," as he bluntly stated recently. "I began questioning a lot of that religious foolishness about man's spirit and body being in conflict, with God concerned primarily with the spirit of man and the Devil dwelling in the flesh. I was raised by parents who typified a generation that had passed. They really got that Horatio Alger kind of thing there, you know, and the Puritanism. I was given an intellectual awareness by my folks, but at the same time a certain tradition that my intellectual awareness told me didn't make sense. So I began asking questions very early and developed a kind of a—not a negative rebel attitude—I wouldn't have

31

taken candy from the stores or stuck them up or stolen hub-caps—but an upbeat kind of rebel thing. I just couldn't buy a lot of the old answers and I pulled away from my traditional religious training rather early and started looking for other answers."

When Hefner began to mature, then flourish in Steinmetz High School, he did so with the same force of purpose he had displayd in grammar school and throughout most of the rest of his life. He became inexorably involved in extra-curricular affairs, being elected as, among other things, president of the student council and vice-president of the acting and literary clubs. He acted in productions of the "Pink Curtain Players," wrote a jokes column called "Stuff in the Ruff" for the school newspaper, played the inevitable kazoo, and often dressed in the official Zouave uniform for teenagers of the thirties: a yellow fedora, a thin knit tie, a blue "fingertip" coat, and a white silk scarf. Hefner once referred to himself as dressing and acting like "a high school kid you'd see in a movie." When he was in high school, he told his friends that he hoped to "crack radio or movies someday." He did in fact do a few radio broadcasts for the Chicago Board of Education.

During the summers he worked at a variety of jobs including washing dishes at a soda fountain for $9 a week, a position he quickly relinquished because it was "too grubby," and as an usher at the Rockne Theater in the Austin section of Chicago for $10 a week. ("It was much better work and they ran triple features.") In his senior year he mixed paint in the chemical laboratory at the Glidden Paint Company.

Because of his work on his school paper, he was featured in a story in the *Chicago Herald*, which published his picture and called him a budding journalist. "I was so impressed, I decided to become one," he said.

His writing and cartooning continued almost incessantly, and he began a graphic diary/autobiography (rivaling the industry of a Samuel Pepys) which he continues to this day. He started it by drawing in vivid colors, six panels to the page, a comic-strip character, "Goo Heffer," a not-so-mythical version of Hugh Hefner. Hefner has long since abandoned actual cartooning of himself; his autobiographical diary, however, is kept *au courant* with photos, clippings, news releases, statements, and various memorabilia, by an archivist who has worked for Hefner for almost fifteen years.

During 1939 and 1940 Hefner produced what he called the "Photo Play," an original invention consisting of a series of captioned photographs, produced with a dramatic continuity using whatever talent, costuming, and props he could find among his classmates or neighborhood friends. He would figure out a simple plot and use pictures and a few words to tell a story, acting as director, photographer, playwright, and sometimes functioning as actor. His themes ranged from war stories to murder plots to tales of the supernatural.

From the age of thirteen to seventeen he wrote forty-two pieces: short stories, novelettes, radio scripts, and the fifteen-minute film, *The Return From the Dead*. He liked the weird, the macabre, the supernatural. His favorite authors were Poe, H. G. Wells, Sax Rohmer, and Arthur Conan Doyle. His interest in the cryptic and mysterious led him to start his most ambitious periodical yet: *Shudder Magazine* was issued in May of 1941. Hefner had just turned fifteen.

He wrote to Boris Karloff, Bela Lugosi, and Peter Lorre asking them to be honorary presidents of the "Shudder Club," and surprisingly he received acceptances from each of the actors. The magazine had at total circulation of one copy—the original—which contained sketches and comic strips of ghouls and goblins drawn by Hefner, stories of the macabre typed by him, and photographs of the "supernatural" which he made and selected. The single copy was passed around by hand for his "subscribers" to read.

The "Shudder Club" was an "international" membership society which readers could join for five cents. Members were entitled to a Shudder Club badge and special decoder.

In all, five issues were "published" before Hefner, the mogul of horror, turned to other less eerie ventures.

In addition to his writing and photographic talents, Hefner invented, along with his two closest friends, Jim Brophy and John Sereno, an ingenious 1,325-word language called *Muphbekian*, which included in its vocabularly the words *fusum* (girl), *muvum* (love), and *turjafum* (saphead). Devised for purposes of secret communication among the three of them, the crafty conspirators vowed to master twenty-five new words each week. They issued a dictionary of *Muphbekian* in a typewritten edition of three.

The paradox of Hefner's personality as a youngster was that his excruciating shyness forced him to engage in activities that would constantly bring him into contact with others, as his name became familiar through his publications.

Eldon Sellers, a friend who later became a Playboy executive, recently recalled his memories of the teenaged Hefner: "He was definitely a loner in that he was *removed,* often outside of the situation. But everyone—both boys and girls—took to him, as though he was somehow more mature and sympathetic than the rest of us. We would always go to him with our 'problems' and he would sagely 'give advice.'"

It is possible that this big-brother ambience, combined with his shyness, was partly responsible for Hefner's lack of any sexual contact while in high school. He has said that he had no sexual experience of any significant kind with others during his teenage years.

In 1942, at the relatively late age of sixteen, Hefner claims he "discovered the opposite sex and found out that girls were different from fellows." His new interest greatly reduced most of his inhibitions and gave him the confidence he was searching for. This manifested itself in his going steady, a pattern which he continued, though not necessarily with the same girl, until he left school.

He was a member of the track team (his father had been Nebraskan State High School Champion) but quit on the spot when the coach objected to the team's attendance at a Saturday-night dance. "I decided right there that there were other things more important than running."

By the time he graduated from Steinmetz (forty-fifth in a class of 212), his classmates voted him Class Humorist, One of the Best Orators, One of the Most Artistic, One of the Most Likely to Succeed, One of the Most Popular, and One of the Best Dancers. Though he hated to wear suits, he wore a tux for the first time at his class prom.

CHAPTER 3

"I knew I wanted to start a magazine of my own. The only thing wrong with that dream was the money: I didn't have any."

After leaving Steinmetz in February 1944, the seventeen-year-old, 113-lb. Hefner volunteered for the Army, since the draft at that time was inevitable. Though his military career was entirely undistinguished, he used the two years he spent as a clerk in various Army induction centers around the country to further his own career aims. He was beginning to solidify his feeling that publishing might be the career that he should follow, "but art, pure and simple, is not my goal," he wrote then. "Ideas are the mainstay of the cartoonist and I want to express them." And later: "I want to try my hand at professional cartooning. I want to write a novel and some short stories."

During the war he contributed cartoons to a succession of Army newspapers on a regular basis, and the by-line "Hef" began to gain recognition by military personnel. He even generated some news stories about himself, as a cartoonist, which later found their way into his scrapbooks. He had first been trained as an infantry rifleman in Texas and then was shipped to Fort Meade, Maryland, en route to an assignment overseas. A photograph of him wearing a helmet with white lettering, HEFNER, shows him holding an M-1 rifle which seems to be almost as long as he was tall. A typist was needed, and he landed the job and remained in the United States throughout his entire military career.

In one interview Hefner remembered his days in the Army as being "dreary." Actually he felt that he benefitted from them, that he had become more widely experienced and had met new people. Nonetheless, he was immensely relieved when he was eventually discharged. His first taste of an alcoholic beverage took place in the Army—a glass of wine, while on a date—and he considered that incident an indication that he was on the threshold of maturity.

Just two weeks prior to going into the Army, Hefner had begun talking to Mildred Williams, an attractive bobby-soxer who was in his class at Steinmetz. She was an intelligent girl and a talented violinist, coming from a family of amateur and semiprofessional musicians. Hefner and Millie had never socialized, and during the four years of high school they were hardly aware of each other. Now, however, after Hefner left home, they began corresponding. Hefner wrote virtually every day for two years. Since it was practically high treason *not* to write to servicemen during the war, reciprocal V-letters from Chicago reached him several times each week. Ultimately a paper romance developed through the mail.

Hefner spent his furloughs with Millie. They celebrated his eighteenth birthday by going to a Betty Grable movie on a rainy Wednesday afternoon. Gifts were eventually exchanged, families introduced, promises made, vows implied, and they became what is known among the great middle class as "unofficially engaged."

When Hefner was discharged in 1946, he fell victim to the ex-G.I. blues, joining the ranks of the disillusioned for awhile, becoming a member of the "52-50" club of unemployment-insurance collectors, and listening to his crew cut grow in. "I was hit by a kind of ennui experienced by a lot of guys who come out of the service," he said. "I didn't know what I wanted to do." He passed the time taking a course in figure drawing that summer at Chicago's Art Institute and picnicking at the Indiana Dunes at the southern tip of Lake Michigan with Millie. Later he enrolled through the G.I. Bill for fall classes at the University of Illinois in Urbana. He chose the school very carefully; its chief virtue was the fact that Millie was already a student there. Though journalism was his main interest, he elected to major in psychology and also took courses in creative writing, art, and sociology.

Hefner's college career was almost fictionally successful and idyllic. He began by starting a magazine, a campus humor publication called *The Shaft*, which was immediately successful. He was its managing editor for awhile, then he became its staff artist and cartoonist. In a very short while he became pledged to three scholastic fraternities: Psi Chi, Gamma Iota, and Phi Eta Sigma Chi.

Outside of his studies, he took flying lessons at Urbana airport in a Stearman trainer, a biplane of the type that Wiley Post loved. He secured a pilot's license and soon was successfully doing stunts such as stalls, pins, loops, and Immelmanns. He played almost countless games of Monopoly, hearts, gin rummy, pinochle, Lexicon, electric football, and bridge in his spare time.

According to his college roommate, Robert Preuss, Hefner had one thing in abundance that many of his schoolmates did not: energy. "No, we never talked about publishing, but Hef was a guy you knew was going to go somewhere. He was very sharp." As in childhood, Hef's room at college became the hangout for his group of friends. The housemother remembers him as being popular and cordial.

"He was the only one of the boys who made older visitors feel comfortable," she recalled. Hefner confided in Preuss that he had a vision of himself either succeeding greatly and "making a mark" in life at whatever he did or not succeeding at all. A middle-class vision of himself as being only moderately prosperous was unthinkable.

During his college years, Hefner says he became a "magazine nut," always studying newsstands and magazine racks for new periodicals and buying as many as he could afford.

Hefner contributed cartoons and articles to other student publications in addition to *The Shaft*, such as the campus newspaper, *The Daily Ilini*, where he worked with one of its editors, Gene Shalit, later to become a popular radio and TV personality. One of Hefner's submissions, his review of the just-published Kinsey Report, was amazingly prophetic of Hefner's later editorial crusades. In it he wrote, "Dr. Kinsey's book disturbs me. Not because I consider the American people overly immoral, but this study makes obvious the lack of understanding and realistic thinking gone into the formation of sex standards and laws. Our moral pretenses, our hyprocrisy on matters of sex have led to incalculable frustration, delinquency and unhappiness."

Hefner was not only expostulating as a critic of the social scene, but woven in between the lines is a comment on his own discomfort. When he graduated from college, he had been engaged to Millie for some time, and he had had almost a decade of contact, dating, and involvement with girls, especially during his Army years. Yet at the manly age of twenty-two Hugh Hefner had not yet slept with a woman. Since opportunities must have arisen, it's difficult to determine whether shyness, inhibition, or Grace Hefner's moral prescripts—or a combination of all three of those factors— were influencing him. In a short while Hefner would resoundingly indicate to the world how he intended to make up for the lost sexual time of his youth.

Aside from his sociological sophistication in the area of sex, Hefner had a solipsistic view of the world at large. In an almost pathetically self-revelatory description of his lack of social conscience, he wrote in the fall of 1947 that every Saturday afternoon was reserved for a football game, and that somehow campus spirit seemed higher than at any other time of the year: "Who cares if Communism is moving across Europe and Palestine is caught in the throes of civil war?! This is a world in itself," he declared.

But that image is now painful for Hefner to consider. He explains it away by calling it "irony." He then went on to say, "Only someone who is sensitive to the problems of the world could make such a statement. In other words, why bring up these other serious problems when you're talking about football," which was a noble attempt at justification that didn't quite succeed. Apparently he really *did* care more about football in college than about many other things. In the first season he was down there, Illinois lost the first game of the season—"a heartbreaker," Hefner recalls. They then went on to win all the rest of their games, the Big Ten Championship, and finally the Rose Bowl of 1947. Photos of the team's stars plastered Hefner's room and ultimately his scrapbook. He attended virtually every game.

In an interview in 1971, talking of his social consciousness and misremembering himself as a young man, he said, "It's been there since my early childhood. I was fighting what I felt were injustices in school and things from the time I was. . . ."

Hefner was intellectually progressive in matters of sex but had little interest, certainly none that would manifest itself overtly, in social questions concerning racial injustice, government and national and international politics. Yet such feelings did develop in time and ultimately manifested themselves in ways that were wholly his own. Certainly he considered himself an agnostic, if not an atheist. He wrote a play whose theme was a "scientific" discovery *proving* there was

40

no God. The final resolution of the play saw the suppression of the information because the people could not live with such knowledge.

On the fifteenth of June 1949, Hugh Hefner married Mildred Williams in the Saint John Bosco Rectory, not far from where they had both grown up. Millie was Catholic and Hefner nominally Protestant, though he had never been baptized and stopped going to church in his early teens when his parents allowed him to make the decision himself. He and Millie had many long and involved discussions about their religious differences and for a short while were not certain that they could be resolved. Hefner finally agreed to be married by a Catholic priest, even though he considered himself an agnostic. "That's the last I ever heard of the religion thing," Hefner confided in me. "Obviously, we did it just for the sake of her parents." Hefner borrowed his father's car and the newlyweds drove to Hazelhurst, Wisconsin, where they enjoyed a short, presumably bucolic honeymoon at Styza's Birchwood Lodge.

Since they had no money, they moved in with his parents, paid them a small amount of rent, and established a small but adequate apartment on the top floor of the house on North New England Avenue.

Hefner's first attempt at accumulating some cash to better operate his newly formed household was to try his hand at free-lance cartooning. He created a detective character, "Gene Fantas, Psycho-Investigator," and tried to sell a comic strip of Fantas' adventures to a national syndicate. When that didn't work he went directly to local newspapers, but he had no luck there either. Later, he produced some strips that chronicled the adventures of a collegiate character called "Freddie Frat," similar to "Archie," but was equally unsuccessful at selling it. Both comic strips were adequate in concept and execution, but they lacked a truly professional touch.

All through this time he was germinating an idea that

already had a strong grip on him. As he stated recently, by the time he graduated from college, "I knew that I wanted to start a magazine of my own. The only thing wrong with that dream was the money: I didn't have any." Nevertheless, his imagination kept working, and eventually he conceived the idea of a picture magazine—*Chi*—for and about the people of Chicago. He became "hot on the idea" and began making sketches for a format. Late in 1949 he approached a local newsstand distributor, told him what he planned to do, showed him a dummy issue, and was told that if the magazine was as good as the prototype indicated it might be and as Hefner said it was going to be, the dealer would handle it. Hefner then placed the following ad in the *Chicago Tribune:*

Wanted. Offset printing concern to join editorial staff for production for a new picture magazine for and about the people of Chicago. H. Hefner, 1922 North New England Avenue, Chicago.

Hefner's idea was to see if he could convince a printer to supply machinery, paper, ink, plates, and other production necessities as a basis for a partnership. Hefner planned to offer his services as editor, publisher, and advertising salesman, both parties to contribute their efforts gratis until the magazine had enough money to start paying salaries.

One adventurous printer responded to the ad. He was agreeable to investing his own time and machinery but wanted Hefner to pay for the paper and ink, a financial impossibility for the would-be publisher at that time. Hefner decided to shelve the venture temporarily, until "such time as a rich uncle" might leave him a few thousand dollars.

Since his free-lancing and entrepreneurial efforts had failed ("It soon became apparent that this was a good way to starve to death"), Hefner decided that the only way to get any money at all was to look for a steady job, and he began in the field he loved best: publishing. He systematically approached most of Chicago's magazine, newspaper, and book publishers with the request for editorial work, but with the implication that he would try anything they had to offer.

One of his first interviews was with *Esquire*, his favorite magazine at that time. He showed Catherine McBride, a copy editor there, some of his cartoons, but she was eminently unimpressed. She told him they had no openings and turned him down. He continued applying to other publishers, but postwar unemployment was high in those days. It was difficult for him to find a job despite his enthusiasm, his college diploma, and his status as a veteran. His lack of journalism credits from college hindered his chances. Also, it didn't help that most publishers of the kind he was looking for were located in New York.

Eventually he accepted a job at a carton printing and manufacturing company on Chicago's South Side. "It was the closest thing to journalism I could find," Hefner said. The job, his first as an adult, paid $45 a week, and he worked in the company's personnel department. In screening prospective applicants for jobs, he was told to ignore all "blacks, Jews and men with long, foreign-sounding names. . . . I hated it." When his conscience became too immersed in indignity and disgust, he quit. His first real confrontation with racial prejudice revolted Hefner and left a lasting mark upon his social attitudes. Years later, Hefner's own personnel department was, by his orders, emphatically color-blind, this much before fair-employment practices were in vogue or in spirit in most companies.

Hefner then returned to making halfhearted attempts at cartooning. He tried to sell his efforts but had only intermittent success, although the *Saturday Evening Post* and *True* magazine did buy some of his submissions. Hefner, in appraising his work of that time, now says that the writing of the cartoons was good but the art lacked maturity. One of his friends recently said: "Most people go on work binges when they first get married. Hefner did just the opposite and sat around the house for almost a year trying to tune in to his inner directives." He was determined not to go back to a regular job; the carton company experience was too distasteful and regimented.

Millie became edgy. She was teaching at a grammar school and providing the entire income for both of them and couldn't see why her husband wasn't at least *looking* for a job. After many long soul-searching conversations Millie finally convinced Hef that if nothing else he ought to go back to school and do some graduate work. Hef in turn convinced himself that with some graduate degrees he would be able to teach and continue to pursue his free-lance cartoon career on the side. In January of 1950 he enrolled in Northwestern University as a master's candidate in sociology. He bought his first car—a used 1941 Chevy club coupe—to travel back and forth each day to Evanston.

Hefner's career at Northwestern was brief. Perhaps the following incident had something to do with his leaving the school after one semester. In a term paper, he examined U.S. sex laws in light of the findings of the Kinsey Institute's research into human sexual behavior, concluding that a drastic revision of legal statutes regarding sexual behavior was badly needed. He made specific recommendations about the laws. His professor gave him a double grade: an "A" for research and a "B+" for his conclusions, because, the professor reasoned, Hefner's recommendations were "abhorrent." It is interesting that only a few years later the American Law Institute published its now-famous *Model Penal Code*, incorporating sex-law recommendations that were almost identical to Hefner's, and the Wolfenden Report, published in Britain, made similar recommendations.

Shortly after submitting his paper on sex, Hefner glumly left Northwestern and began looking for a job again, still hoping to crack the publishing industry. And again he had no luck securing an editorial job. He wrote at the time that prospects in his life were "grim."

In June of 1950, however, an ad in the *Chicago Tribune* advertising for a writer attracted his attention, and he applied. Carson, Pirie, Scott and Co., a large, venerable department store located in Chicago's Loop needed a copywriter for men's fashion. Hefner got the job and started at $40 a week.

Hefner states that he "learned plenty" from promotional copywriting and that he really enjoyed it. Though the salary was small, he was happy to be working. After a few weeks, with his savings from the job, he made his first purchase: a television set. Millie had left her teaching post and was working as a bookkeeper for Mars, the candy bar company.

At night Hefner continued his cartooning, trying to perfect his technique. He also wrote some film reviews for a small, unimpressive publication called *Dale Harrison's Chicago* and started work on a book of cartoons satirizing the city of Chicago which he called *That Toddlin' Town,* a rowdy burlesque of the city's morals and manners, a humorous poke at its culture, its institutions, and its sex life. Millie, Hefner's brother Keith, and Leroy Neiman, a free-lance men's fashion illustrator for Carson, Pirie, Scott, helped him make the final selection of the cartoons that he included in it. He approached a number of publishers with it and though he received some favorable comments, he couldn't get anyone to agree to publish it. As a result, he "dug, scraped and swiped enough money to put it out independently." The book was dedicated to "Millie, my soul mate and sole support." Hef published the book himself, selling it directly to bookstores and also by mail order from his house. He convinced Werner's, a bookstore on South Michigan Avenue, to feature a small display in their window consisting of some of his original artwork from the book, and the result was a sale of approximately fifty books a week from that source alone. The book enjoyed a moderate success with a respectable sale of around 5,000 copies.

Hefner was beginning to experience what he considered

to be some meaningful momentum. Though an amateurish production by today's standards of sophisticated cartoons with pungent and risqué punch lines, *That Toddlin' Town* was a "total package" that once again indicated Hefner's ability to complete a job he had begun. Perhaps the book lacked excellence or even style, but he had nevertheless executed it. He had made a conscious decision to produce "something different" and had roughed out over 350 cartoons, working for months on the project.

Chicago's media began to notice Hefner and his book; invitations to radio and television interview shows began to come his way. Mike Wallace, among others, interviewed him. Hefner supplemented these unsolicited invitations with promotions of his own, and though not experiencing anything like celebrity status, a small amount of fame did come his way as a result of the publicity he received from the publication of the book. In its review, the *Chicago Tribune* called it "an irreverent satire of Chicago," one which put "the emphasis on the honky tonks with a collection of drawings that look like the kind *Esquire* might judge too racy for their readers."

Newly confident, in January of 1951 Hefner left Carson, Pirie, Scott and went to work briefly as a copywriter for the Leo P. Bott Advertising Agency, a job he kept for just five weeks; he was fired for not giving the two-man agency the devotion and expertise they demanded. He then applied to *Esquire* again, and this time he was hired—as a $60-a-week promotional copywriter. *Esquire's* offices were located on East South Water Street, with an attractive view overlooking Lake Michigan. Hefner was twenty-four years old.

Inspired by his minor success with *That Toddlin' Town*, Hefner spent nights at his desk at *Esquire* working on his own material, doing a series of cartoon roughs for a book on the 1920s.

He soon discovered that *Esquire* (pronounced Es-QUIRE, accent placed pretentiously on the last syllable by sophisticates on the inside) was not all that he dreamed it would be. The editorial and art staff had been moved to Manhattan before he even started, and his fellow employees were not particularly urbane; Petty girls did not really exist. His job was to write direct-mail subscription solicitations. That was far enough removed from editorial work as it was, but he was also forced to write them mainly for *Coronet*, a poorly edited sister publication of *Esquire*, which was sort of a *Reader's Digest* with pictures and owned by the same parent company. Years later Hefner recalled his experience at his "dream" job. "Esquire had from the outside a great deal of meaning to me; it was however, a disappointment when I got there. I discovered, for one thing, that it was just another job and working there was just a nine-to-five routine. I had the feeling that it would be an extremely stimulating and exciting atmosphere in which to work; that it would be markedly different from another office job. But it lacked the glitter and glamour from inside that I had anticipated when I was younger; also the magazine itself was editorially changing."

Though he was bored, Hefner remained with *Esquire* for all of 1951. Losing most of his reverence for it week by week, his final judgment was that it was no better than "a limited interest *Harper's* with graphics."

By the end of 1951, a major turning point in Hefner's life occurred: *Esquire* announced that it was moving all but its accounting offices to New York City, and Hefner was invited to go along—with a cost-of-living increase of $20 a week in his salary. He was perplexed. Though his disillusionment with *Esquire* was real enough, he was beginning to experience at least a taste of what the publishing world had to offer. At company parties he had met such authors as James Jones and Willard Motley, and many artists, illustrators, and photographers; and though *Esquire* had no live models, he was very self-impressed at being able to hobnob with the great and near-great. Also, he could and often

47

would say that he worked for *Esquire,* and that fact had a certain amount of social prestige attached to it. If he remained with the magazine for a while, there was also the credit he would have toward future publishing employment.

There were factors militating *against* his going East, however, not the least of which was Millie. She thought the idea not only preposterous, but she displayed the typical Midwesterner's distrust of New York, a feeling shared by Hefner and which he still has today. Millie also had no intention of being separated from either her own or Hefner's family. Then, too, the idea of *Chi* magazine was still very much alive in Hefner's imagination, and he liked the publicity he had received from the publication of his book. He was a much bigger fish in Chicago than he could be in Manhattan. "The thing I really want is here in the Windy City," he noted then.

When the time came for Hefner to render his decision on whether or not he was going to New York, he asked for a weekly raise of $5, simply as a stalling ploy. But not only did the stall fail—he was immediately refused the raise—but he was forced to suffer an hour-long lecture by the head of the promotion department who tried to convince Hefner that he was less than a steadfast "company man." The failure to get the raise gave him the way out that he really wanted: he quit on the spot.

Esquire left for New York, blissfully unaware that in not entertaining the modest requirements of one of their junior assistant copywriters, they were virtually signing, if not a death warrant, at least a declaration of publishing warfare.

48

*"I was so uncertain about the magazine's
chances, I figured, well, if it doesn't sell
out in the first month, we'll leave it on the
stands another month."*

By the beginning of 1952 the idea of starting some sort
of a magazine of his own had almost become an
obsession for Hefner. In addition to *Chi,* he briefly considered publishing a much less ambitious trade magazine for
cartoonists. But with no money and little experience—no
professional editorial experience at all—he lacked the confidence to make a total commitment. He wasn't even quite
sure how it could all be done without money.

Hefner took an $80-a-week job for the Publisher's De-
velopment Corporation in Skokie, a nondescript northern
Chicago suburb. The company published twelve trade pub-
lications and "nude" magazines including, *Guns, Guns
Quarterly, Shooting Goods Retailer, Modern Sunbathing,
Sunbathing Review,* and *Modern Man.* Most of the maga-

zines were poorly conceived and unimaginatively edited; nevertheless, all were money-makers because they were published with a minimum of overhead and had strong distribution on newsstands. Hefner became PDC's sales promotion manager and set himself the task of learning everything that he could possibly absorb about how to sell magazines. Some of this learning was a highly calculated exercise, but much of it was spontaneous; he learned simply by doing the job, shelving away in his mind information that he would later need and use.

It's interesting to note that despite his liberal sexual attitudes, Hefner had qualms concerning the editorial content of these magazines. He characterized his new employer as "an outfit that specialized in nude photo magazines and other questionable enterprises." His uncertainty as to what should or should not be published in a magazine, however, did not affect his long-standing resolve to start a new publication of his own. This was the only career he could conceive of for himself.

He made a conscious effort to ingratiate himself with the newsstand dealers who handled PDC's titles and to get to know them personally. He also made sure that they knew him, through friendly phone calls, visits, and letters. Publisher's Development Corporation proved to be one of Hefner's most valuable training experiences, for each day's work became a study lesson in publishing.

While Hefner was at *Esquire* he had become very friendly with Burt Zollo, a free-lance magazine writer who had been newsstand promotion manager for both *Coronet* and *Esquire* and who had helped him promote *That Toddlin' Town*. Zollo also elected to stay behind when *Esquire* moved East and was almost as eager as Hefner to launch a new publication. He thought Hefner's idea of a magazine about Chicago had merit, and together they created a formal presentation, a projected budget and editorial statement, renaming the future periodical *Pulse*—the picture magazine for and about Chicago—and soliciting the potential help of other *Esquire* staffers who had also remained in the midwest. Zollo's father was willing to invest $10,000 in the venture, but their budget called for an initial minimum of $100,000. (In reality, they were looking for as much as $176,000, the amount they felt was necessary to begin publishing.)

Attempts were made to secure other backers, and though people did show interest in the magazine, no money was forthcoming and no printer could be convinced to join the project as a partner. Hefner shelved the project once again.

On Memorial Day, 1952, the Hugh Hefners moved into a large, rambling, five-room apartment on the first floor of 6052 South Harper Avenue in the Hyde Park section of Chicago. The rent was cheap, the rooms were "dreary and dirty" according to Hefner, but the neighborhood was a stimulating and pleasant one: practically on the University of Chicago campus, very close to the lake, it was one block from the *Plaisance*, the long stretch of green that was the site of the famous Columbian Exposition of 1893. Also, just one block away was Jackson Park.

Millie and Hef had been forced to make the move to a larger apartment when it was discovered that she was pregnant. They were expecting their first child that November. They immediately set out to brighten up their home; both worked for months on it, plastering, painting, decorating, and generally getting it into shape for the baby's arrival. Hefner spent evenings constructing a handsome record cabinet of which he was very proud.

Hefner's great love for cartooning was reflected in the decor of his apartment. Enlarged photostats of abstract drawings and cartoons from William Steig's book, *Lonely Ones*, lined the halls; Pogo comic strips, in full color, were used as wallpaper in the baby's room, and various of Hefner's original cartoons could be found in every room of the apartment. He wanted to hang a professional photograph of both

51

himself and Millie but couldn't afford the cost. His compromise solution proved more interesting than the original plan. He mounted and framed their chest X-rays, labeled them "Millie" and "Hef," and hung them instead. He borrowed over $1,000 from his parents to buy some very modern furniture, designed mostly by Eames, Knoll, and Herman Miller, and by the end of the summer he and Millie had settled in to what they and their friends considered a showplace apartment. One friend remembered it as an apartment of excellent taste even though "Hef and Millie hadn't spent *that* much money on it." Hefner worked on the place with a perfectionist's attention to every detail.

The *Chicago Daily News* thought the decoration of the apartment unique enough to do a two-page picture spread on it in their Sunday supplement entitled "How a Cartoonist Lives," adding to Hefner's now growing status as a minor Chicago celebrity.

In the early part of 1952, the publicity concerning the phenomena of flying saucers sparked the imagination of a large segment of the population, including that of Hugh M. Hefner. He was quite fascinated by the concept, especially after *Life* suggested that the objects reported to have been seen might actually be power-driven craft from another planet. Hefner immediately set about cashing in on this new interest by creating a comic strip about flying saucers, and once again he paid a visit to the syndicates and newspapers to try to peddle it; but he was refused publication for no specified reason other than an implied disinterest in his technique.

Hefner was an avid reader of *Life* magazine, and in an issue that appeared during September of 1952, the magazine published the pictorial story of another phenomenon that caught his interest. He was, true to form, American enough to make a note of it in writing: "A young lady named Marilyn Monroe skyrocketed to movie stardom this summer with a couple of run-of-the-mill pictures, a nude calendar showing off a very un-run-of-the-mill body and some high-powered publicity."

All throughout 1952 Hefner continued making contacts among newsstand dealers, printers, and other people who would become germane to his eventual career as a publisher. He also befriended Jerry Rosenfield, another employee of PDC, who would eventually play a significant role in Hefner's life, first as his principal newsstand distributor and later as a large investor. While at PDC, Hefner learned that their most successful titles were the girlie magazines, noting that the feature that sold the magazine was not the sham editorial content, which was poor in quality, but the pictures of the scantily clad young ladies talking on the telephone, taking bubble baths, and walking their dogs.

In an informal survey made by PDC at that time, it was learned that a large percentage of the men who bought one of their magazines also bought another, so that a new girlie magazine on the market might have an opportunity of succeeding if readers could be counted on to buy virtually all such magazines.

By December of 1952 Hefner was working as circulation promotion director of *Children's Activities* magazine, a popular children's periodical with a prosperous circulation of 250,000. He was hired specifically to develop a direct-mail campaign to enlist new subscribers at the fairly respectable weekly salary—for a twenty-six-year-old in that year—of $120, a figure considerably above his $80-a-week job at PDC. He created an entire direct-mail campaign to go out to subscribers before their subscriptions expired, using cartoons of talking animals with plastic tears pasted on them. And in his first attempt to solicit new subscribers, he elicited a successful response.

In his spare time he experimented with the possibilities of publishing what are known as "eight-pagers" or "slam books," which are small, pornographic comic books. Hefner did the cartooning himself using the heads of the comic characters of Dagwood, Blondie, and their dog, Daisy, and cartooning their three nude bodies in various stages and convolutions of foreplay and intercourse. Though he completed a number of the books, he never published them, dismissing the project as too frivolous. On November eighth, the day after he had vacillated about voting for Eisenhower and had finally cast his vote for Illinois' favorite son, Adlai Stevenson, Hefner became the proud father of his first child, a daughter, who was named Christie Ann.

The move from PDC to *Children's Activities* had been undertaken mostly for financial reasons, but Hefner also hoped that he would continue learning and add to his growing knowledge of the publishing business.

Hefner claims that it is difficult to trace precisely when the idea of publishing a specifically men's magazine began to grip him; he was however certain by 1953 "that I was never going to be happy until I was doing a magazine of my own."

And what were his alternatives? There were virtually none. He had tutored himself toward one goal and one goal alone: to own and publish his own magazine. Although he would probably have been qualified to work as a full-time cartoonist, his image of himself was unswervingly more ambitious.

If he had remained with *Children's Activities* or considered riding the executive merry-go-round in publishing, he could foresee an unspectacular future of nine-to-five jobs for the rest of his life; Hefner had already convinced himself that no such fate was acceptable. "I was twenty-seven years old and I was afraid that if I didn't try it on my own soon, I might have to learn to be a good company man after all."

His experience at PDC kept haunting him: girlie magazines sell. He visited some old bookstores in Chicago's Loop and ferreted out early issues of *Life*, *Look*, and *Esquire* and pored over them. It was comparatively easy to determine how they had become successful. Almost from their inception they had produced articles that bordered on the sensational.

54

In March 1937, *Look,* one of America's original girlie magazines, had run the famous *Ecstasy* water scene and front shots of the nude Hedy Lamarr. In this same issue they featured a bath shot of Myrna Loy from *The Barbarian,* and in May of the same year came back with seminude photos of Carole Lombard. *Life* increased its circulation markedly by running the first publicity photo of a rising young starlet—nude from the waist up—Lucille Le Sueur, who later changed her name to Joan Crawford. That was followed by a half-nude Claudette Colbert taking a milk bath in *Sign of the Cross.* Hefner knew that his new magazine must start, from the very first issue, with a feature that could be promoted and ballyhooed, something that would be talked about and give the magazine an instant identity.

He even went so far as setting up a photographic session with a nude model which was shot in 3-D, a craze that was then appearing in movies and comic books with accompanying paper-framed glasses. Hefner conjectured that a magazine feature which displayed a woman's breasts in three dimensions, zooming off the page at the reader and practically close enough to touch, would have to gain widespread attention; a pair of green and red 3-D glasses would be bound into each issue. For a while he even considered starting a girlie magazine that had all or most of the photos done in the 3-D process. He abandoned the idea, however, when he learned of the prohibitively high expense of such a venture, and also because he calculated, correctly as it developed, that the craze would quickly abate.

Hefner paints an almost poetically melodramatic picture of himself walking through the nighttime streets of Chicago's Near North Side and pondering the high-rise apartments facing Lake Michigan, wanting to become a part of the "good life" that he imagined was being led in those apartments. "I wanted to be where it was happening—whatever 'it' was," he has said. The transition from being part of the "good" or "beautiful" life to publishing a magazine about

55

that way of life evolved naturally and was thoroughly consistent with Hefner's style. Researching, writing, and editing amounted to a learning, maturing process for him.

One of his methods of coping, playing the role—real or imagined—of the "outsider," had always been to start a magazine or periodical. Other people withdrew from their feelings of inadequacy by reading or dreaming or walking or a thousand other methods of escape. Hefner published.

He wrote at that time:

I'd like to produce an entertainment magazine for the city-bred guy—breezy, sophisticated. The girlie features would guarantee the initial sale, but the magazine would have quality too. Later, with some money in the bank, we'll begin increasing the quality— reducing the girlie features, going after advertisers—and really making it an *Esquire*-type magazine.

Many men's magazines thrived following World War II. Hefner correctly believed the most successful to be the outdoor-adventure types, with articles on hunting, fishing, shooting, and searching for Adolf Hitler in the Brazilian jungles: magazines such as *True* and *Argosy*. *True* enjoyed the largest circulation of them all and possessed an editorial format widely imitated. Hefner felt that his tastes reflected more urban interests than could be found in those magazines, something closer to the sophistication of *The New Yorker* or a more liberal, lighter *Esquire*. He said in an interview that appeared in *Playboy*:

I'm an indoor guy and an incurable romantic, so I decided to put together a men's magazine devoted to the subjects I was more interested in—the contemporary equivalent of wine, women and song, though not necessarily in that order. *Esquire* had changed its editorial emphasis, eliminating most of the lighter material— the girls, cartoons and humor. So the field was wide open for the sort of magazine I had in mind.

It is worth noting that *Esquire*'s circulation had begun to dip. They had become frightened about losing their second-class mailing permit. A crackdown—possibly a result of the McCarthy-era conservatism that affected many areas of American life—had led to a rash of arrests of publishers of other magazines for obscenity. Indeed, *Esquire* had suffered through a lengthy trial themselves and had won. They had even taken the step of putting clothes back on the harem girls that would normally appear nude month after month in their cartoons. It is equally true that *Esquire* was consciously attempting to change their image; they were thoroughly engaged in, as publisher Arnold Gingrich stated, "the process of ridding *Esquire* of any last vestigial traces of the girly flavor that had become the dominant side of its personality with the war years."

Hefner's life at that time was a busy one. By April of 1953 he started making specific plans for his magazine, including notes, sketches, rough layouts, and finished data on what he thought he would need to produce the first issue.

He did all of this while keeping his demanding full-time position with *Children's Activities*. He had conceived and executed a direct-mail campaign for them which had proven quite successful in attracting new subscriptions. At the same time, a subscription renewal series, also designed and written by Hefner, was resulting in an increase over previous years. The publishers were happy with his performance but began to grow suspicious when he had to take more and more time off for "personal business," sometimes starting his work day for them as late as 6 or 7 at night. Nevertheless, he did accomplish all that he set out to do, and because of his subscription successes, his eccentric hours were tolerated.

There was a crucial question to be answered before Hefner could consider starting his own magazine: where was the money to come from? Hefner was worse than penniless. "I really had no money at all—*no money.*" He was in debt. His bank account was nonexistent, and he still owed his parents several hundred dollars. The furniture that he owned and the 1941 Chevy, which by now was plagued by a hanging fender and questionable brakes, were his only assets.

Hefner applied at Lake Shore National Bank for a household loan. Since he did have a steady job, his application was accepted, but as his employment record was unstable, he was given only $200. This was hardly enough to start a publishing enterprise. So Hefner walked out of the bank and went down the street to the Local Loan Company and put up his furniture—which was new and in good condition—as collateral for another loan. This time he was luckier; they gave him $400.

With that $600 Hefner started out to create his magazine, unaware, of course, that he was embarking on the establishment of a virtual publishing empire. His sole *raison d'être* was now centered on the publication of this first issue of his new magazine, devoted to the urbane interests of the sophisticated man; in effect, to take up where *Esquire* left off: "to produce a magazine of the type that *Esquire could* have become if they had not gotten off the track along the way."

Hefner tried to spend as little money as possible in getting his venture under way. A corporation was formed, using his initials as its name: HMH Publishing Company, Incorporated. He realized that $600 was hardly enough to pay for a letterhead and envelopes and start buying artwork and stories, let alone cover all the expenses that would be incurred in publishing a national magazine. Until he had something more substantial to show, other than just sketches and a very rough dummy, he knew that it was a nearly impossible task, and yet he had no way of obtaining additional capital. Still, there was no question of calling off the project and going back to the prospect of just working at his job. He simply went ahead, with determination and no money.

Recalling the magazine's beginning, with the aid of hindsight, Hefner now says, "it was a nutty idea, right from the start. The only reason I tried it was because I had no conception of the almost insurmountable difficulties and the odds against my success. If I had known then what I know now, I doubt if I would have even tried. But once I had made up my mind, I worked on the idea with everything I had, and for the first time in my life I felt truly free. It was like a mission—to publish a magazine that would thumb its nose at all the phony puritan values of the world in which I had grown up."

Once Hefner actually started working on the magazine, he claims he got "lucky, with a capital L." He spotted a news story in the Chicago-based *Advertising Age* about the famous Marilyn Monroe calendar, which had been written about in *Life* in conjunction with its cover story on her. She had posed for the calendar "with nothing on but the radio," as she explained in her own inimitable way. Millions of Americans had hung the calendar in their homes, offices, and wherever else people hang calendars of lovely, undraped women. It was quite notorious. Coincidentally, the story made reference to the fact that the John Baumgarth Company, located in suburban Melrose Park, had printed the calendar. Hefner had hardly finished his breakfast when he happened across that fact, and in a matter of minutes he was in his car and heading north on Lake Shore Drive, then west to Melrose Park.

Hefner walked in "cold," without an appointment, met the head of the company, John Baumgarth, and walked out with "the gimmick of the decade"—the right to reproduce a color photograph of Marilyn Monroe in the nude in his yet-to-be published magazine.

Monroe, lying seductively against a backdrop of red velvet, was lusciously beautiful, and she displayed a lack of inhibition, combined with a sense of her own sensuality, that practically burst from the page. "We'll probably never know how much money that one picture really meant to us," Hefner said years later.

Marilyn Monroe had posed for photographer Tom Kelly in Los Angeles in 1949 for three nude pictures and a series of seminude photographs to be used specifically for calendar and pinup art. Kelly sold the photos to Baumgarth, who held them for future publication. After Monroe made her first movie, *The Asphalt Jungle*, Baumgarth decided there was a market for the pictures, so he produced what became one of the most famous pinup calendars in history.

Baumgarth had a wide variety of photographs—girl pictures, baby pictures, pastoral scenes. Monroe was just one of many. He knew that the Monroe nudes had a certain amount of fame attached to them, but since he had paid the photographer $500 for the entire lot and then paid $600 for the plates, he welcomed any opportunity to get some return on his investment; hence, he agreed to sell Hefner the rights to publish one of the nude studies.

No magazine, however, with the exception of *Life's* postage-stamp reproduction in two colors, had bothered to publish the Monroe nude photos, perhaps out of fear of an obscenity arrest or perhaps simply because of a lack of imagination. The calendars themselves were not mailed or sold publicly on the newsstands; they were used as giveaway premiums by gas stations, grocery stores, and trucking firms. Baumgarth had produced a special edition of the calendar, however, which he would sell to firms who wanted to send it through the mail; it consisted of the same Marilyn Monroe photo, but a black negligee was printed over her nude body so as to remove any possibility of Post Office harassment on grounds of obscenity.

Hefner asked for and secured permission to use the nude shot that had *not* been used on the calendar, which he felt was the "sexiest" of the three and which also had the advantage of not having been seen before. It was entitled "Golden Dreams." He paid a total of $500 to Baumgarth: $400 for the right to use the subject, $25 for duplicate 8x10 negatives made from the original plates, and $75 for the use of the plates themselves. Baumgarth showed Hefner the model's release, giving Baumgarth—and hence Hefner—full permission to use or publish any of the photos in any way they pleased. The release was signed, sadly, "Mona Monroe" and dated May 27, 1949.

With $100 remaining in the HMH bank account, Hefner left Baumgarth with the "sensational" idea he had been searching for. With his remaining money, he had stationery printed for the Nationwide News Company, which wasn't really a "company" at all but simply a title that Hefner felt would lend his new magazine prestige, especially if newsstand dealers felt the magazine was backed by a reliable company.

He then set out to name his forthcoming magazine. After much vacillation he came up with *Stag Party;* because of its kinship to "stag movie," the implication was that it would portray the happenings at a wild party. Hef felt that "stag" was a decidedly masculine term; to make certain that his potential readers had no doubt, he added the subheading, "The New Magazine for Men." In a letter (dated July 9, 1953) to a potential contributor who didn't like the title, he wrote:

You may very well dislike *Stag Party*—though I'm certain on different grounds. I've had several kicks on the title—too sexy, sounds too much like a girlie book, etc.—and the critics include some of our own staffers. My feelings run to something like this: our magazine is to be a general entertainment book for men, with a certain emphasis on the racy—and *Stag Party* hits that right on the button. And if the name seems to run a little too heavily to the "girlie" end—then we've got to face some hard facts, in the first issues—with a small budget and the need for prompt acceptance by Mr. Buying Public, sex is surefire and the early issues will include more than their share.

His friend Eldon Sellers remembers that Hefner was toying with the idea of using the name *Stag Party* as early as September of 1952; appropriately, they had discussed it on the night they watched television together and saw Rocky Marciano floor Jersey Joe Walcott with one punch in the thirteenth round to win the heavyweight title.

From a card table in his living room, Hefner composed a letter which, together with a postpaid business reply card, he mailed to the twenty-five largest newsstand wholesalers throughout the United States, some of whom he knew personally through his position at National Periodical Distributors.

Reading it now, the letter, though adequate, could be described as innocuous by today's high-powered promotional standards. Hefner felt that at the time it was "exciting," and he might be right; there is a personal charm attached to it which undoubtedly had an effect on the newsstand dealers. "They couldn't see a guy sitting at a card table—all they could see was a magazine being described as something like *Esquire* used to be," said Hefner. "Everything I had was put into that letter." Because it documents the most crucial step in his rise to success, it becomes the most important letter Hefner ever wrote.

Dear Friend:

We haven't even printed our letterhead yet, but I wanted you to be one of the very first to hear the news.

I've been a very busy guy since I left NATIONAL PERIODICAL DISTRIBUTORS the first of the year—busy cooking up a deal that should make some money for both of us.

STAG PARTY—a brand new magazine for men—will be out this fall—and it will be one of the best sellers you've ever handled.

It's being put together by a group of people from ESQUIRE who stayed here in Chicago when that magazine moved east last year—so you can imagine how good it's going to be. And it will include male-pleasing figure studies, making it a sure hit from the very start.

But here's the really BIG news! The first issue of STAG PARTY will include the famous calendar picture of Marilyn Monroe—in *full*

color! In fact—every issue of STAG PARTY will have a beautiful, full page, male-pleasing nude study—in full, natural color!
Now you know what I mean when I say this is going to be one of the best sellers you've ever handled.

STAG PARTY will sell for 50¢ and you'll receive your copies at a profitable 38¢. It will be supplied to you on a *fully returnable* basis and, of course, we will pay all shipping costs.
Fill out the postage-paid AIR MAIL reply card enclosed and get it back to me as quickly as possible. With 4 color printing on the inside pages, we've got to confirm our distribution quantities right away.

It will be nice doing business with you again—especially with a title as good as this one.

Cordially,
Hugh M. Hefner
General Manger

At first, the orders began to trickle in; then they came full force: 1,000 for Norfolk, Virginia; 2,000 for Newark, New Jersey; 3,000 for Philadelphia; 8,000 for New York City. Only two of the twenty-five wholesalers—Boston and New Orleans—wanted to wait and see the first issue before committing themselves to an order. Hefner then began approaching, by mail, the other 800 independent wholesale distributors around the country.

Hefner had figured that if he could eventually get orders totaling 20,000 copies, he'd be in business.

Based on the *minimum* sales percentage of two comparable publications that had started just a few years before (*Modern Man* and *Art Photography*), Hefner figured that with a sale of 30,000 copies he could break even with the first issue. He knew from working with PDC that neither of those magazines had ever fallen below a 65 percent sale and that the addition of the second title through the same outlets actually increased, rather than impaired, the sale of the first. Therefore, he concluded correctly, the market was nowhere near being saturated.

Before waiting for all the returns to come in from the wholesalers, however, he set about raising the cash he now desperately needed to fulfill the orders.

One of his first approaches was to the man who printed *That Toddlin' Town,* Herbert Stamats, of the Stamats Publishing Company, located in Cedar Rapids, Iowa. Hefner and Eldon Sellers flew to Cedar Rapids to talk with Stamats but could not convince him to either print the magazine on credit (for a piece of the corporation) or to invest any money in the operation. He did give Hefner one piece of advice: sell shares of stock in his corporation. Hefner was both impressed and influenced by the advice.

He did issue stock in his new corporation. With a $180 loan he had managed to raise, he bought 18,000 shares at a penny a share, giving him a half-interest in the company; he issued another 18,000 shares at a dollar a share, which he and Sellers (who had moved across the courtyard from Hefner and who assisted him) sold to whomever they could get to buy. "I went to friends, relatives, friends of friends—anyone who'd listen—and managed to raise another $3,000," Hefner recalled. "I took whatever I could get; a hundred dollars here; $50 there."

Some of Hefner's biggest investments came from his own family. His parents, who were not thoroughly aware of what the editorial content of the magazine was going to be (if they had, they might not have invested anything since they had been shocked by the content of *That Toddlin' Town*), came up with $1,000 to help their son. His brother Keith produced an investment of $500 (which he paid in installments of $300, $100, and $100) for some "preferred" stock which Hefner promised to buy back at twice par value in one year's time. Keith had hoped to be able to invest $1,000 but could not raise that much cash so, as he ironically related in a letter to Hef that August, he would have to "settle for a $250,000 return instead of $500,000." A man who lived

64

across the courtyard from Hefner withdrew his life savings from the bank and invested $500.

It's difficult, however, to determine exactly how much cash Hefner actually raised by selling HMH stock. In a 1974 interview, he stated that he raised $3,000, although one of his biographical press releases puts the figure at $10,000. In a 1962 interview he stated that, including his $600, the figure was "something between $6,000 and $7,000—that was it, that was the total investment."

Though it's hardly an important point, since Hefner's *personal* investment was indeed just $600, his confusion about the other moneys probably stems from the number of different deals that he had instigated in attempting to finance the publication of the magazine. Burt Zollo, for instance, writing under the name of Bob Norman, contributed an article for the first issue for $400 and took his payment in stock (which has made him a millionaire), and other people did artistic work for shares in the corporation. An engraving company agreed to do all the plate work for the magazine for one year, taking stock in the corporation in lieu of cash payment.

As Hefner watched the newsstand orders come in, passing even the 35,000 goal he had dreamt of reaching, he knew he'd be successful in getting out at least the first issue of *Stag Party*. By May of 1953, he had received 50,129 orders. In addition to his relentless pursuit of financial backing, he began to work even more diligently on the editorial and artistic format of the magazine, trying for a quality product with flair. That the first issue would be published he had no fear; whether the magazine would be read and talked about was another question altogether. For the first time, Hefner allowed himself to speculate on the possibility of future issues, of a regular, monthly magazine. But he was concerned that unless issue number one excelled in many areas, there would be no demand for any further issues.

Hefner had confidence in his editorial judgment in selecting material for his magazine. He spent much time going through old books and magazines looking for the sort of article that might be suitable. When he found something he liked, due either to its style or its subject matter, he made a note of the writer, the title of the piece, and the publisher. For the most part, however, he searched carefully for material that was in the public domain, which at that time meant anything published before 1900 (copyrights expire after fifty-six years); in addition he hunted for stories that had been published in books, ones for which he felt he could secure the magazine rights at a reasonable rate. He also had numerous discussions with friends concerning what kinds of articles they'd like to see published in a "sophisticated men's magazine." In the end, however, he relied most heavily on his own opinions.

Though he began making progress in contacting writers and receiving permission to reprint their stories, Hefner was not as successful in securing the art direction he felt the magazine needed. He first worked with an illustrator-designer who did some layouts for the stories Hefner was considering for the first issue. They were close to what he wanted, but they weren't perfect, somehow failing to capture that elusive quality of sophistication that Hefner was seeking. He continued to shop around Chicago for an art director, one with imagination, talent, and the foresight to work, like himself, for potential rather than immediate returns. Through a friend he knew at *Esquire*, Norman Sklarawitz, Hefner was given the name of Art Paul, a gifted young designer who was already making a name for himself as a free-lancer for some prestige accounts, though none of them were magazines. Paul's style as an artist was "linear": clean, uncluttered, futuristic, almost Oriental in its simplicity.

Hefner went to see him at his studio in the Loop, located at the noisy intersection of Van Buren and State Streets. Amused, Paul recalled that first meeting: "You have to imagine what this guy looked like at that time," he said. "His coat was frayed, he had a two- or three-day growth of stubble on his chin, and on the day that I first met him he had a stiff neck, which made him look a little like Igor, Frankenstein's helper."

Though Art Paul was hardly impressed with Hefner, Hefner gained instant respect for Paul. "Are those advertisements on your walls samples of your own art work or are they just advertisements that you admire?" asked Hefner. "They're all mine," Paul replied proudly. Hefner sensed immediately that this was the man he was looking for.

"It took us several sessions of discussion before I agreed to work with Hefner," recounted Paul. "I don't do things lightly and I didn't then. Hefner seemed to have energy and he seemed to have a vision. I agreed with his notions that *Esquire* had lost its vitality and I had to agree with him that there was, indeed, room for a good men's magazine."

After taking a few weeks to think it over, Paul agreed, though somewhat gingerly, to art-direct the first issue on a free-lance basis. Because of prior assignments, however, he insisted that Hefner do the "leg work" in supplying the photographs, picking up the illustrations from the various artists, and getting them to Paul's studio—in other words, all of the minutiae that Paul himself had not the time to handle. Hefner did this gladly, and the two men began a relationship that has lasted for two decades.

With a brilliant art director working for him and the sensational Marilyn Monroe nude feature to grace his first issue, Hefner became progressively more confident. If the editorial and artistic prospects were bright, the financial possibilities seemed even greater: the mailing to newsstand dealers had netted over 70,000 orders, over twice the amount that Hefner felt he needed to break even.

Whether or not to begin mailings soliciting subscriptions was considered by Hefner and then rejected. Though he felt that the magazine would be acceptable enough in terms of postal law, he didn't want to risk *any* chance of censorship problems. He explained his view of the situation to a prospective investor in a letter dated April 23, 1953:

. . .There's nothing illegal about printing and distributing nudes. Calendar, magazine, and book publishers all do a big business in the undressed female form.

Most of the big, general interest magazines print nudes from time to time. *Life* printed a miniature of the Marilyn Monroe calendar a few months back; all the photography magazines run full-color and black-and-white nudes every month or so to keep up the newsstand sale; every photography annual carries more than a sprinkling; and it was a full-color nude plus three or four black-and-whites that kept *Coronet* in business in the early forties.

The problem revolves around the Post Office, primarily. Despite the U.S. Supreme Court's '45 ruling (unanimous) in favor of *Esquire* in which they pointedly indicated that the Post Office could not use the 2nd class mailing privilege as a censoring device, most publishers are afraid to step on the postal authorities' toes, because of the expense and time of taking each case through the entire court system (the P.O. fights them all—all the way up to the top—with taxpayers' loot).

As I mentioned on the phone, they were let off with a warning, but it's important to note that even in that case the only outfits threatened with a severance in postal service were the magazines (*Modern Sunbathing*) and the distributing corporation (Transamerican). The other corporations using the same address (Jones, Publishers Development Corporation, et al.) were not involved at all even though they all are part of one outfit owned by one guy.

With the sort of book we'll be producing, I wouldn't be surprised that we could actually get a 2nd class permit—but I personally feel it's better to stick to newsstand sale and stay away from the whole silly business. There's more than enough to be made in that end of it.

The only other problem we will ever run into is local censorship boards. Those never affect the publisher and distributor, but are a pain in the neck because they bring pressures on various local distributors so that they sometimes have to cancel the books for a while (Georgia is now undergoing a situation like that). Both of our competitors, Transamerican and Empire, are anxious to have local dealers bring such cases to court and supply cash for that purpose, but the dealers usually prefer to let the things ride—so that's usually what happens.

In June, with orders for 70,000 copies secured, Hefner approached the Rochelle Printing Company, located in a small suburb about ninety miles northwest of Chicago. He had dealt with them when he was at PDC. The company generously agreed to print the black-and-white letterpress sections of the magazine for half-payment upon shipment with the remaining half of the bill to be paid ninety days thereafter. Hefner later calculated that this credit alone was worth over $10,000 to him in his immediate financing, and if considered against the history of his entire operation, the gesture was worth millions. Dick Sax, owner of Rochelle, was willing to undertake this arrangement since he had just purchased a new printing press and needed work for it. To prevent "down time"—that is, to avoid shutting down the presses and having his crew stand idle—he was willing to take what he considered to be a reasonable gamble.

Hefner also appealed for credit to Owl Printing, a company that had done business with *Children's Activities*, and was lucky enough to secure sixty days of deferred payment on the costly color section of the magazine.

Empire News, a new national newsstand distributor owned by Jerry Rosenfield, Hefner's friend from PDC, took over the entire distribution for the magazine, and since Hefner had proof of at least 70,000 orders, he demanded and received a better deal than most magazines, especially new ones, can command from distributors. Not only did he get a higher percentage per copy, but Empire also advanced money to him—without seeing even a page of the prospective first issue.

While engaged in the nonstop activity of putting together a magazine, establishing a working company, and floating 18,000 shares of stock, Hefner successfully continued to hold down his job at *Children's Activities*. On September 11, 1953, he announced to his direct supervisor, Clifford Schabile, the general manager, that he was starting a magazine of his own. "Don't worry," said Hefner, "the kind of magazine I'm starting is very different from *Children's Activities*." Schabile asked him to remain until the fall subscription mailing was completed and the results tallied. Hefner agreed and stayed for a few more weeks. Hefner recalls that "Schabile told me in a somewhat friendly, though really threatening tone, "If this fails, Hefner, you won't have even a shoestring left!' "

By then, the final editorial decision of what was to go into the first issue was fairly well established. He had been refused the rights for various articles but still had enough material to go ahead. Random House asked $1,000 for John O'Hara's story, "Days," which Hefner felt he couldn't afford and therefore turned down himself. James Thurber forwarded Hefner's request for reprint rights to his story "The Greatest Man in the World" to *The New Yorker* editorial offices; they rejected the request on the grounds that only magazines of "established reputation" could be considered as possible reprint vehicles. And Charles Scribner's Sons refused permission to reprint Ernest Hemingway's story "Up in Michigan," due to its special "literary status" and because Hefner's magazine had not as yet "demonstrated its character."

Probably one of the most amazing aspects of Hefner's engineering of his new magazine was the economy with which he put together the entire editorial, art, and photographic package of the first issue.

Most of the nonby-lined text was written by Hefner. Virtually no original or assigned photos were taken, though a photo of Eldon Sellers appears on page seven as a model for a story on alimony. Like the photo of Marilyn Monroe, most of the illustrations were secured by bargaining with photo-

70

graph agencies. About ten of the photos in the first issue were bought from Graphic House in New York City, for the grand total of $75. Some of the nude and seminude studies were run with captions underneath them (written by Hefner, of course), forming a photo-cartoon which was not particularly effective but which filled a page with a pretty girl and an attempt at humor.

The estate of Sir Arthur Conan Doyle received a check for $25 from HMH for the use of a Sherlock Holmes story, even though the story was in the public domain. Hefner wanted to establish a reputation for fairness. An original Hefner cartoon, of course, cost nothing but his time. An Ambrose Bierce story was also in the public domain and cost nothing to use.

Photos illustrating a football article, "The Return of the All Purpose Back," were supplied free of charge by the University of Illinois, and an entire article on desk design for the modern executive was provided gratis. The manufacturer of the desks also threw in the photographs to illustrate the two-page feature.

In addition to the Monroe photo for which he received the color separations for virtually nothing, enabling him to produce a four-color page in his magazine for a fraction of the normal cost, Hefner also came up with another ploy that furnished him an additional page of color. He had discovered a new color separation process, called the Bourges System, which enabled the artist, rather than the printer or engraver, to make the color separations himself by an ingenious method of overlaying red, yellow, and blue tissues on the artwork. Finding the Bourges System was fortuitous for Hefner since color separation is usually one of the most expensive aspects of producing a magazine. The method could not be applied to photos, but Hefner had a full-page cartoon done by the Bourges System in his first issue, thereby giving a full-color appearance to the magazine while saving over $500 per page.

When he culled all of his articles, photos, and illustrations and totaled the costs, the first issue cost Hefner less than $2,000. Printing, paper, and engraving costs came to an additional $6,000. While the magazine could hardly be considered a paragon of publishing expertise and artistic merit, it was an impressive package which indicated ingenuity and shrewdness on Hefner's part, for he had produced a magazine of adequate editorial content on the shoestring he was warned he might not have. Though he wasn't ecstatic over it, Hef was pleased with his first attempt at a "real" national magazine.

By early November 1953, *Stag Party* was just a few weeks away from being published. Hefner had contacted the magazine *American Cartoonist* and initiated publicity to stimulate cartoonists to submit their work to him. They proceeded to run a fairly large story outlining *Stag Party*'s editorial format and requirements. Hefner began to receive submissions from all over North America. The story also produced some unexpected and unwanted mail. Only days before the presses were scheduled to print his first issue, a registered letter from a Manhattan law firm which had seen the story in the *American Cartoonist* arrived at his apartment.

The attorneys represented the publishers of *Stag* magazine; when their clients had learned of Hefner's venture, they decided that *Stag Party* was too close to the name of their own magazine. They wrote Hefner a strongly worded cease-and-desist letter threatening a law suit if he didn't change the name of his magazine immediately. Hefner now admits the crisis was a disguised blessing.

Hefner had had reservations for weeks about the title *Stag Party*, feeling that it was perhaps *too* earthy and didn't reflect the image he was attempting to create. He believed that another title, perhaps a superior one, could be found if he just took the time to think about it. The letter from *Stag* was the catalyst he needed to come up with a different and perhaps more appealing title.

He, Millie, and Eldon Sellers devoted an entire weekend in the apartment at 6052 South Harper, brainstorming new titles, trying to come up with something more imaginative and meaningful. *Gent* was suggested and rejected. So were *Gentry* and *Gentlemen*. Someone hit upon *Sir*, but that was immediately voted down since Hefner recalled that there was a magazine with that name already in existence. The group felt that *Pan* could be identified with *Peter Pan*, and people might think it to be a children's magazine. *Satyr* was considered a very strong possibility, but Hefner, thinking the word was not in common enough usage, finally rejected it himself as being "too highbrow"—which was paradoxically inconsistent with his concept of producing a *sophisticated* publication.

Sellers remembered that an attractive automobile—long obsolete—that his mother once owned was called *Playboy*, and he offered that as his suggestion. Hefner immediately pounced on the name as focusing on the image that he wanted to project; it had an instantly positive effect on him. Millie, however, thought the word was too obsolete. "It makes you think of the 20s," she said. That bothered Hefner not at all, as he explained that a title that was somewhat different or special was a shrewd idea. "That way," he said enthusiastically, "we can make it suggest whatever the magazine becomes." He felt the connection with the twenties was exactly what he wanted: it suggested high living, wild parties, wine, women, and song, the very ambience he hoped to create in his magazine.

That night he called Art Paul and asked him to begin working on another symbol to replace the jaunty stag that was to have adorned the front cover of the first issue. He wanted a nonhuman image so as not to appear imitative of *Esquire's* pop-eyed *boulevardier* in evening clothes, "Esky," or *The New Yorker*'s conservative sophisticate, "Eustace Tilley." Hefner thought a rabbit in a tuxedo presented a debonair and suggestive image. "Rabbits are the playboys of the animal world and they have a sexy reputation," he said. And of course a new logo for the magazine would also have to be designed. Paul spent exactly one half hour in designing the rabbithead, totally unaware, of course, that it would eventually become one of the most recognizable symbols in the world. The magazine would be called *Playboy*.

The first issue of *Playboy* was printed in October of 1953. Hefner, Art Paul, and Eldon Sellers drove to Rochelle and waited in a coffee shop across the street from the printer for the first of 70,000 copies to come off the press. Like a group of young actors who had just finished their first play, they felt tired but important. Years later Art Paul stated that he had not "been particularly proud of it," because some of the artwork had not been initiated and approved by him. Hefner has indicated that he wasn't really satisfied with the general appearance of the issue either, but that he had hopes for the future of *Playboy*—if, indeed, there was a future.

Though the first issue bore the legend, "Volume 1, Number 1," Hefner decided at the last minute not to include the date anywhere on it. "I was so uncertain about the magazine's chances, I figured, well, if it doesn't sell out in the first month, we'll leave it on the stands a second month."

Hefner was unsure what the public's reaction toward his magazine would be. He may also have wondered how the law might react to a nationally distributed periodical with full-page photos of nudes. *Playboy* was hardly the first or only magazine that published pictures of naked women, but since *Esquire* had relinquished its position as the leader of the "class" magazines that took a delight in the undraped female form, *Playboy* immediately assumed that role.

In any event, whatever the reason, nowhere in the first issue of *Playboy* can Hefner's name be found. Despite his anonymity (or perhaps because of it), Hefner provided the first issue with a strong, explicit, straightforward editorial, declaring precisely what kind of a magazine he intended to publish. It is an amazingly prophetic indicator of the editorial content of the once and future *Playboy*:

If you're a man between 18 and 80, PLAYBOY is meant for you. If you like entertainment served up with humor, sophistication and spice, PLAYBOY will become a very special favorite.

We want to make clear from the very start, we aren't a "family magazine." If you're somebody's sister, wife or mother-in-law and picked us up by mistake, please pass us along to the man in your life and get back to *Ladies Home Companion.*

Within the pages of PLAYBOY you will find articles, fiction, picture stories, cartoons, humor and special features culled from many sources, past and present, to form a pleasure-primer styled to the masculine taste.

Most of today's "magazines for men" spend all their time out-of-doors—thrashing through thorny thickets or splashing about in fast flowing streams. We'll be out there too, occasionally, but we don't mind telling you in advance—we plan spending most of our time inside.

We like our apartment. We enjoy mixing up cocktails and an *hors d'oeuvre* or two, putting a little mood music on the phonograph and inviting in a female acquaintance for a quiet discussion on Picasso, Nietzsche, jazz, sex.

We believe, too, that we are filling a publishing need only slightly less important than the one just taken care of by the Kinsey Report. The magazines now being produced for the city-bred male (there are 2—count 'em—2) have, of late, placed so much emphasis on fashion, travel, and "how-to-do-it" features on everything from avoiding a hernia to building your own steam bath, that entertainment has been all but pushed from their pages. PLAYBOY will emphasize entertainment.

Affairs of state will be out of our province. We don't expect to solve any world problems or prove any great moral truths. If we are able to give the American male a few extra laughs and a little diversion from the anxieties of the Atomic Age, we'll feel we've justified our existence."

Hefner's whole future, his life, seemed at that time to

hinge on the success or failure of that first issue. Since his company had no cash reserve, he knew he would be out of business in a matter of weeks if it failed to ignite the imagination of the public.

He had also taken a calculated gamble in setting the price of *Playboy* at fifty cents at a time when most magazines were selling for twenty-five or thirty cents.

The crisis entailed more than just losing a business, however; Hefner's own finances were in disastrous shape. Though it's not generally known, he had personally guaranteed to pay back most of the money he had borrowed in behalf of his corporation. He had received investments in the thousands, perhaps as much as $10,000. If the magazine failed, he envisioned himself paying off the debt for many years.

By the beginning of November, *Playboy* was fairly well distributed nationally; it was sitting on the newsstands of America, waiting to be bought. Hefner spent an inordinate amount of time driving all over the South Side of Chicago, checking the newsstands almost daily to see if the magazine was selling. Often, when the newsstand dealer wasn't looking, Hefner would straighten up the copies of *Playboy* and perhaps move them to what he considered a better position, a spot that would command more attention and one that would catch a buyer's eye. Sometimes he would sandwich copies of *Playboy* in between two tested sellers, like *Esquire* and *The New Yorker*, in the hopes of getting it more attention.

Hefner noticed that in a compartively short time the small stacks of *Playboy* were getting smaller, at least on those stands that he could check in Chicago. Only two weeks had passed from the first day the magazine went on sale when he received a telephone call from Jerry Rosenfield of Empire News: preliminary checks made at key newsstands in major cities across the country indicated that *Playboy* was selling strongly. "It's the hottest title we've ever handled," said Rosenfield excitedly, and he wasn't talking about the content. An article in *Saturday Review* referred to "a new magazine called *Playboy* which makes old issues of *Esquire*, in its most uninhibited days, look like trade bulletins from the W.C.T.U." And *Time* called it "slick and sassy . . . the latest phenomenon in U.S. magazine publishing" while *Newsweek* observed: "For twenty years the late Daniel A. Smart's *Esquire* has dominated the men's indoor field. Last week, Smart men probably were peering uneasily over their shoulders. A rival, younger by a generation, bolder by several inches of neckline, was fighting its way into the old gentlemen's hunting grounds." Exactly *how* successful the magazine was going to be would have to be calculated by the eventual returns. The magazine wholesalers had agreed to handle *Playboy* on consignment, and they could return whatever copies remained unsold at no cost to them—and no profit to Hefner. It sometimes takes months to receive all the unsold issues of a magazine, so that an exact sales figure is impossible to predict, but indications pointed to a substantial success. Hefner then had to make the decision whether or not to go ahead with the second issue.

The response as gauged by Empire convinced him that he should take the gamble. If the projections on what he thought he would sell materialized, then he'd have enough money to pay off the cost of the first issue and perhaps even enough to pay for a second. He immediately began creating and editing a second issue of *Playboy*.

Almost symbolically, Hefner's old Chevy totally collapsed just as the magazine was going on sale and had to be towed away to the junkyard. When he discovered that he would have some money to spend, he bought himself an automobile that was more in keeping for a publisher of a magazine: a spanking new 1953 red Studebaker convertible —the car everyone said looked the same whether going forward or in reverse—complete with whitewall tires and a gleaming white top.

Unlike most magazines that make their incomes from advertising, *Playboy* carried no ads in the first issues, with the exception of "The Men's Shop," a page of "house" advertisements placed by Hefner himself, touting such items for the "sophisticated" man as a fur-covered ice busket and a "silent" valet chair. Hefner had made arrangements with a merchandising firm to supply the photos of the items, maintain an inventory of the products, and ultimately fulfill the orders—the process is called "drop-shipping"—all without Hefner becoming directly involved. He merely included a small markup on each item for himself.

"The Men's Shop," though a clever idea, brought very little money to the operation. For the same pessimistic reason that he had not put a date on the first issue—his uncertainty as to the fate of the magazine—there were no subscription rates offered and *Playboy* was, therefore, forced to prove it could survive by newsstand income alone.

Actually, because the newsstand business at that time was not particularly strong, news dealers were always looking for something new and were willing to give a little push to a beginning magazine to see whether it would develop as a steady seller. *Playboy* received a fair share of attention from the news dealers because of this. When the final returns on the first issue were tallied, even Hefner's wildest expectations were bested: 53,991 copies of the forty-eight-page issue were sold, making *Playboy* an unprecedented instant success. Hefner then had enough confidence to date the second issue, January 1954, and he even included a subscription blank, which indicated to Hefner—and, he hoped, to his readers—that *Playboy* was going to be in business for some time to come.

CHAPTER 5

"We were rolling in dough."

THE first three issues of *Playboy* were laid out and edited from Hefner's Hyde Park apartment; he would work either in the kitchen or on a small card table that he set up in his living room. Despite Millie's admonitions to be quiet lest he wake the sleeping baby, he managed to complete his editing and correspondence without too much disturbance to his household.

In the first few months after the initial publication of *Playboy*, Hefner's life became almost hopelessly hectic. Eldon Sellers served as a general assistant, though his publishing and editorial skills were nil (he had been variously an Air Force pilot, a violinist with the Indianapolis Symphony Orchestra, and a credit investigator for Dun and Bradstreet). Art Paul became more and more involved with the artwork and made a gigantic contribution to the magazine at every stage, but the delicate balance of attempting to improve the magazine creatively while promoting it and establishing its style was mainly Hefner's albatross.

He assumed an enormous work burden, and his schedule kept him going for fourteen to sixteen hours a day, seven days a week, doing everything from rewriting articles to selecting photos to cartooning. Functioning as editor, publisher, business manager, and personnel director, he also proofread, edited, and handled the production of the magazine. Fortunately, his father helped him with setting up bookkeeping procedures and acted as the company's freelance accountant.

After the first few issues, Hefner's taste as an editor outgrew his talent as a cartoonist, and he began rejecting his own work. As a result, his cartoons have not appeared in *Playboy* in over twenty years.

It could be argued that Hefner's lack of professional assistance might have been a fortunate circumstance for him, since experienced publishing people might have insisted that it was close to insanity, or at least hopelessly naive, to start a magazine on such an insignificant amount of money. Time, Inc. launched *Sports Illustrated* at about the same time that *Playboy* began and went through more than $30,000,000 before the new magazine finally began to show a profit. *Playboy*, despite or because of Hefner's sublime and magnificent ignorance, realized a profit from its very first issue.

The circulation figures for the second issue of *Playboy* were greater than for the first, and the third proved to be even larger. "We were rolling in dough," Hefner proudly recalled.

Why was *Playboy* so immensely popular from its very beginning? There is no question that publishing full-color photos of beautiful, bare-breasted women was one of the major factors. Until then, with the exception of the nudist and photo magazines, an occasional nude in *Esquire,* and a monthly miniature in *Coronet,* only *National Geographic* possessed the academic temerity to publish photographs of nude women (aborigines) on a regular basis. When *Playboy* appeared, the young men of America were struck senseless with admiration, awe, and near disbelief over *Playboy's* centerfold—"The Playmate of the Month." Perhaps for the first time in their lives they were seeing photos of nude women in color. Thousands of males were buying *Playboy* each month and the centerfold was pasted upon the walls of locker rooms, gas stations, Army barracks, and the bedrooms of America's youth, instantly elevating Hefner's status to catalyst of more masturbatory orgasms than probably any other man in history.

But pictures of girls with pneumatic breasts were just one factor in the soaring circulation. To understand the real reason why *Playboy* succeeded with such force is to understand something crucial about American society in the mid-1950s.

In many ways, *Playboy* was the inevitable result of the conformity of the Eisenhower-McCarthy era. America and the silent generation finally rebelled, but the rebellion was two-directional. The Beat Generation strode in with a stamp of its sandaled feet. Beards, beads, and all the other accoutrements—or intentional lack of them—indicated revolutionary status for a rapidly growing group of young people. Another segment of American society, a fairly large one, was equally restive under the Puritan ethic. For them, however, the solution was not a sleeping bag on a bare floor. They sought the "good life," and *Playboy* became their handbook just as surely as Kerouac's *On the Road* was required reading for the nihilist beatniks.

Hefner had instinctively realized what sociologists had been proclaiming for years: the Puritan ethic was dying, and pleasure—more specifically, a respect for both hedonism *and* the luxuries that money can buy—was the new way of the world. Uninhibited enjoyment of sex and all the other pursuits of the "good life" became the great American imperative, and Hefner established himself, through *Playboy*, as the pop prophet of a new ethic, guru of the upbeat generation.

From its very first issue, there was an intense level of rapport between *Playboy* and its readers. Hefner explains this by pointing out that his attitudes toward sex hit a sympathetic note with a variety of young people who grew up at the same time as he: "I am very typical of my generation," he says. "I was trying to put out a magazine for myself, one that I would enjoy reading. It described an urban world and the play and pleasure parts of life. If you had to sum up the idea of *Playboy*, it is anti-Puritanism. Not just in regard to sex, but the whole range of play and pleasure—you know, Puritanism outlawed the theater and many sporting events; it couldn't stand the idea that somewhere someone was having a good time."

Playboy's success was immediate; Hefner describes it this way: "I think it was the right idea in the right place at the right time. A great many of the traditional social and moral values of our society were changing, and *Playboy* was the first publication to reflect those changes. We offered an alternate life-style with more permissive, more play-and-pleasure orientation. People get less sense of identity out of their jobs now than ever before, and with increasing affluence, how one spends one's leisure time and finds value in it is more important than ever. An article in a university quarterly a few years ago offered an interesting comparison of *Playboy* and *Poor Richard's Almanac*. Ben Franklin was writing a guidebook for coping with life when a more frugal, work-oriented Puritan ethic was essential to survival in a frontier society; *Playboy* came along and offered a new set of ethical values for the urban society. The editorial message in *Playboy* came through loud and clear: enjoy yourself. Paul Gebhard, director of the Institute for Sex Research, once said that the genius of *Playboy* was that it linked sex with upward mobility, and that's a sociologist's way of expressing what I'm talking about."

Hefner's newly found affluence and the rapidly expanding circulation of the magazine, and hence the need for a larger staff, prompted him to seek office space and move out of his kitchen. Starting with the fourth issue, *Playboy* was edited in a four-room apartment located in a gray, Dickensian building at 11 East Superior Street on Chicago's Near North Side. It was close to the nightclub section known as Rush Street and in the midst of the city's advertising and commercial-art section. "Very Bohemian, very nice" is how Hefner described it to a friend. "Communications were simple. We just shouted down the hall." The building was directly across the street from Holy Name Cathedral, a Chicago landmark since it was still possible to see the holes in the wall caused by the bullets which killed mobster Bugsy Moran one Sunday morning in the 1930s. By setting up an office with a staff of five, Hefner felt he was moving out of "the rat-race class," to which he felt his operations belonged while working out of his apartment. The Near North Side represented a wonder world to Hefner. It had the same ambience for him as New York, Paris, or San Francisco, and he could hardly believe that he actually had an office there.

Hefner persuaded Art Paul to give up his free-lance work and become full-time art director for *Playboy;* it was the first time Paul, who cherished his independence, had ever worked "for" someone, and both he and Hefner were excited and concerned about how it would work out. On his first day in the office, Hefner casually asked Paul whether he would mind dumping the wastebaskets on his way out at five o'clock. Paul refused; "I wasn't *hired* to dump *wastebaskets,*" he glowered. Hefner is now quick to point out that that incident was "atypical" of his relationship with Art Paul—they have managed to work together successfully for over twenty years with scarcely an unpleasant incident of any kind.

Hefner began hiring other people, including a secretary-receptionist and an assistant for Art Paul. At first the magazine occupied only one floor of the building (another tenant made kneeling pads for Catholic churches), but as the magazine continued to expand, more space was leased until the fledgling corporation enveloped the building like a strapping young octopus.

As soon as Hefner moved into his new offices, he began a routine of working twenty-four or even thirty-six hours without a pause, finally falling onto a cot in his office in total exhaustion and sleeping for a few hours, only to awaken and instantly resume his nonstop editorial and promotional activities.

This monomaniacal devotion to *Playboy* was undoubtedly a crucial factor in building the magazine to the heights it finally attained, but it also caused havoc in his personal life. From the day he moved his operation into the building at 11 East Superior Street, he almost totally abandoned his role of husband and father, a fact which Hefner does not readily enjoy recalling. "In spirit," he claims, "the marriage had ended years *before* I ever started the magazine."

Hefner knew that working at the magazine while neglecting everything else was causing problems. Just a month after the magazine began, he wrote: "Though I've never been happier, working at the job I prefer over any other in the world, it has put a real strain on my marriage."

He made an arrangement with Millie: he would go home on weekends and spend the work week at the office. But according to one of his coworkers at the time, he rarely ever made it home at all. "There's the assumption in some quarters that Hefner got married, started the magazine, was surrounded by beautiful girls, and ended the marriage." He goes on to state that "in fact, it ended because two people were immature and unprepared for marriage."

Hefner still describes Millie as "a great lady," but apparently she was not quite great enough to remain his wife. From 1954 to 1959 they were separated more often than not, though on occasion unenthusiastic attempts were made at reconciliation.

Another child—a boy, David—was born in August of 1955, and for a short while they both thought that that was a signal for them to get back together again, but the rift was too deep. In the summer of 1957 they were legally separated.

One friend theorized that the reason the marriage failed was because Millie had not "grown" along with her husband; that seems unlikely, however, since she was, and still is, attractive, vivacious, and well-educated.

A more realistic rationale for their breakup is Hefner's own: a dread of being fettered coupled with his inexperience. "I went from a controlled home situation, to a controlled situation in the Army, to a controlled situation in college, to a controlled situation in marriage. I was married without ever having a free moment in my life."

There was another problem, which the young Hefner was unable to accept. Millie was Hefner's first woman—in every sense of the word—but she had had a meaningful relationship with a young man before her courtship with Hefner. When Hefner discovered that fact a few years after they were married, he was aghast. Despite his libertarianism, he went into a genuine rage, then became disillusioned and, finally, quietly depressed. This personal trauma weighed heavily upon a marriage already encumbered with other problems, among them Hefner's relentless quest for a romantic *dolce vita* and an overpowering sense of freedom, something he felt he needed and his relationship with Millie lacked.

In 1956 Hefner met Victor Lownes III; a scion of a well-to-do family, he was a dapper and sophisticated man-about-Chicago, who, it was said, discovered Brooks Brothers when he was still in diapers. Lownes, who is two years younger than Hefner, had the bearing and tastes of the landed gentry. For Hefner he embodied the essence of the true playboy image. In his love of the rich, the bad, and the beautiful, he was like a Porfirio Rubirosa or an Aly Khan, but without quite all of their money or power. Hefner longed to be considered a playboy of Lownes' stature. He hired Lownes, first as a photographic model for a story on business executives and eventually as promotion director for the magazine, a job which Lownes took to with a flair, almost a genius, in sensing how to promote both *Playboy* and Hefner. The two men became almost inseparable, and a true friendship developed which has lasted, though not without its permutations, until this day.

Many of Hefner's friends and associates now claim that Lownes' influence on Hefner was enormous both in a positive and negative way; the words "Mephistophelian" or "Machiavellian" are often applied to Lownes' name when referring to his relationship with Hefner. "Wherever Lownes sat became the head of the table," recalled one of Hefner's top executives, "and though they were never locked into a power struggle—Hef always remained the boss—Victor constantly influenced Hef to try out far-out and off-color things, like drugs, group sex, other exotica."

At one point Hefner even gave up his pair of traditional penny loafers and Bix Beiderbeckean white socks and under Lownes' tutelage began to dress the part of a successful publisher, instantly ridding himself of all his broad-shouldered, wide-lapeled 1950s zoot suits.

The two men were night owls, and they would usually work until 3 or 4 A.M.—sometimes later—often to be joined by Lownes' then-current girl friend, a dancer in the Empire Room's chorus at Chicago's Palmer House. She would often bring a friend or a coperformer along for Hef's pleasure. As these predawn dating sessions continued, they added to the continuing decline of Hefner's marriage.

Working slavishly at *Playboy* became the real cause *and*

effect of Hefner's marital decline; the longer he stayed away from home and evaded his emotional responsibilities, the more difficult the situation became, making it increasingly more difficult for him to go home. As he stayed away week after week, it became easier to stay away even longer. The more time he spent in the Near North Side, living the life of a bachelor, the more opportunities arose to establish other liaisons. His relationship with Millie dive-bombed.

In one attempt at relieving the tension and establishing a closer connection between his working and married lives, Hefner moved with Millie and the children into a luxury apartment at 5801 North Sheridan Road, overlooking Lake Michigan. It was a large, cheerful, and well-appointed home, just ten minutes by car to his office. The gesture proved to be too little too late, however. He hardly spent an evening there. Emotionally, the marriage was over; only "appearances" kept them together as long as they were. They were divorced in 1959, Millie receiving a settlement of $1,417 a month for child support and alimony. Hefner wrote: "The reasons for the failure of our marriage are multiple and it is hard to place the blame, but in the end, she has suffered the most from it, for I have the magazine to keep me going." Though he was relieved to be removed from his relationship with Millie, he was unhappy to be separated from his children, whom he felt he really didn't know since he had spent so little time with them. Paradoxically, he also felt a deep affection for Millie. Years later he wrote to her stating that he wouldn't want the "rapport" between them to entirely disappear, since he was sure there still existed "some feeling for one another as human beings. I would never want the warmth, the interest and concern I feel for you to disappear or die away. You have been too important a part of my life for me to forget you." In recent years they have maintained a true friendship and see each other frequently.

Immersing himself even more in his work, Hefner watched his magazine grow in giant leaps, the newsstand circulation sometimes doubling from one month to the next. After the first few issues, however, the subscription rolls were still small, amounting to just a few hundred copies; Hefner and Eldon Sellers would affix the postage and post them themselves each month at the mailbox on Michigan Avenue. But by the end of the first year, *Playboy* was selling 150,000 copies each issue on the newsstands and had 4,000 subscribers.

Hefner began hiring a few other staff members, though most, like himself, had little professional editorial experience. Ray Russell, a small, vital, and globular 28-year-old who looked like a miniature Orson Welles, was named executive editor mainly because he had written a few stories for *Playboy*, edited a house organ for Walgreen drugstores, and was willing to work for the magazine at a starting salary of $100 a week. He was brilliant, irreverent, and zany and added a flair to the editorial approach of the magazine that can still be sensed today. He would do anything to get attention. Sometimes he would wear a sign affixed to the fly of his pants proclaiming, "We think you'll know the difference" or "We try harder." Often he would sit cross-legged on the top of his desk dictating memos to his secretary. Russell recalled his first meeting with Hefner: "When Hefner and I first talked on the phone about my possibly working for *Playboy*—before we met face to face—he sounded like a man of about 50. He was very glib and self-assured and I was impressed. His voice was deep. I expected to meet someone who looked like a cross between Henry Luce and General Douglas MacArthur. When we met in a bar in the Loop, I immediately became deimpressed: Hefner looked like a scrawny kid with a crew cut who might have difficulty editing a school paper. But once he started talking I became impressed again. I realized that he had the conviction and brilliance to sustain a magazine. He persuaded me to quit my job and go to work for him."

At *Playboy*'s first anniversary party, held inconspicuously in a booth at Charmet's Coffee Shop on the corner of Michigan and Chicago Avenues, the staff of seven celebrated with sandwiches and coffee. Hefner, when reminiscing about that party, stresses that "the *total* staff was seven, not just the editorial people." He knew he was in business to stay, he says unabashedly, "so I picked up the check. I still had no idea, of course, that *Playboy* would become the most successful magazine of its kind."

If Hefner had any doubts about his financial future, they were totally dispelled shortly after that. In March of 1955, he was approached by a representative of a financial syndicate who invited him to lunch, the acceptance of which was somewhat of an effort for Hefner since he didn't usually wake until 1 or 2 P.M. and then always went directly to the office.

When Hefner appeared for the lunch, he was greeted by three businessmen who offered to buy him out. They owned a defunct publishing company with a $700,000 deficit, and they were attempting to acquire other publishing ventures against which they could apply tax-free profits over a period of five years. Hefner listened quietly and studied the three men and himself as though he were watching a movie. The offer was real but almost unbelievable: for 100 percent ownership of *Playboy*, they were willing to pay him ten annual payments of $100,000 each, or a total of $1,000,-000. In addition, they agreed to retain him and the entire staff on salary, to continue editing and publishing the magazine as they had been doing.

Hefner told the group that he would give them an answer within twenty-four hours, but as he walked back to his office, he had already made his decision. Though he had been a virtual pauper only fifteen months earlier, he sensed —he *knew*—that the magazine would continue to grow and that eventually $1 million would seem to be almost an infinitesimal amount of money to him. Years later, talking about that offer, he said, "just being rich wasn't as important to me as realizing my ambition to publish the best men's magazine in the country." Combined with this inner confidence and direction was the unavoidable fact that hundreds of thousands of young American males were going to the newsstands each month and paying a half-dollar to read *Playboy*, and that the HMH bank account was already in excess of $250,000.

When Hefner arrived back at the office, he told Art Paul of the offer and his decision to refuse it. "I wouldn't know what to do with a million dollars, anyway," he quipped.

Hefner's disdain of the million-dollar offer and his low priority concerning immediate monetary self-enrichment are not indicative of a noninterest in money or the things that it could buy. He enjoyed his new affluence and began to collect many of the trappings that he trumpeted in his magazine. Soon after starting *Playboy*, Hefner, wearing a white shirt open at the neck and looking quite unprosperous, walked into a Cadillac showroom and approached the first salesman he saw. The salesman, leaning against a counter, didn't stir.

"Do you have any brochures?" Hef asked.

"No" said the salesman, disinterestedly. "I think we're all out of them."

"Well how much does an Eldorado cost?"

"About $6,500."

"How long would it take to get a bronze-colored one?"

"Oh, I suppose a couple of weeks."

"Okay, here's a check for $1,000 as a down payment" said Hefner. "When you deliver the car, I'll give you another check for the rest."

Hefner walked out of the showroom with a certain sense of triumph, while the salesman stared at the check, shaking his head in amazement.

Though his life was inexorably intertwined with *Playboy*, Hefner attempted to find himself socially outside of work. He spent a great deal of time, after hours, at the East Inn, an attractive, wood-paneled bistro on Superior Street inhabited mainly by students and airline stewardesses, which had, at that time, a reputation as a "singles" bar. Hefner would play Ping-Pong with Sellers and Lownes, have an occasional Jim Beam tempered with Pepsi-Cola, and often pick up girls. He was becoming a social fixture on Chicago's Near North Side and began attending parties and hosting a number of them himself.

Most of Hefner's parties in those days were given at the *Playboy* offices or at a coach house located on Dearborn Street that he rented with Sellers and Lownes. This quaint but large house served as a bachelor "pad," party hall, and place of assignation, and when he wasn't staying at the office, with Millie, or with someone else, Hefner slept there.

The male *Playboy* staffers, for the most part, were divorced or unmarried, and they used the magazine as an entry to meet the women they photographed and wrote about. Anson "Smoky" Mount, who had been a taxicab driver working on a Master's degree when he wrote a story for *Playboy* and was consequently hired by Hefner, recalled that "nearly all staff members could be found at work at midnight. In various combinations, the staffers shared apartments or lived in the same buildings, conducted wild parties and had a wonderful time."

Ski parties, costume parties, wine tastings, and just parties-for-the-sake-of-having-a-party were held almost weekly by Hefner and his cronies. Lownes would always show up with a few celebrities. Lenny Bruce and Jonathan Winters came on occasions. Most often the gatherings were large, loud, blustery affairs, but occasionally Hefner would entertain a small group, and they would play anything from strip poker to charades or an encounter-type game called "Buzz," which was played to the beat of Hefner's own bongo drums. Many of the parties had the ambience of a fraternity smoker, and the group seemed more typical of high school or college students than men in or entering their thirties.

91

But aside from this dalliance, Hefner the businessman continued to improve and build the magazine. By the end of the first year of publication, he had bought back almost half of all of his stock, and he was slowly amassing a fortune. By December of 1955, the magazine had reached a newsstand circulation of 800,000, and subscriptions were coming in at the rate of about 1,000 a day, forcing Hefner to take more space in a building across the street from his editorial offices.

Most periodicals realize their profits from advertising; often newsstand and subscription revenue simply does not pay for the actual cost of printing and publishing an issue of a magazine. After newsstand dealers and wholesalers get their cut and overhead and postage costs have been deducted, there is usually little—sometimes nothing—left for the publisher. But from its first issue, *Playboy* operated under a different financial structure.

Hefner knew that until his circulation was high enough, the question of securing advertising was academic, but aside from the numbers of readers he might or might not have, he assumed—and correctly so—that the editorial and photographic content of *Playboy* would intimidate a great number of potential advertisers. Advertising agencies and advertisers of "blue-chip" companies are a group known for their timorousness in approaching new media, so that even when Hefner's circulation had risen to a competitive level, he knew he would have difficulties in selling advertising space in *Playboy*. Therefore, for its first two years of existence, the magazine carried virtually no advertising and Hefner made no attempts to solicit it. Reading *Playboy's* first rate card produces a feeling similar to what one gets when looking at a turn-of-the-century Sears catalog: circulation guarantee was 110,000; a full black-and-white page cost $650; a four-color page was $1,075; and the back cover went for $1,300. Today the rate-base circulation is 6,000,000—the black-and-white-page rate is $30,800; the four-color page is $42,950; and the back cover costs $53,685.

In order to overcome what he projected to be his major financial obstacle, Hefner proceeded to make his money entirely from reader revenue. By charging fifty cents for a single copy, coincidentally making *Playboy* one of the highest priced magazines in the country at that time, and by keeping his editorial, production, and overhead costs as low as he could possibly make them, he accomplished what few other magazines in contemporary American publishing were able to do: enjoy a profit without carrying a line of advertising.

As it developed, the absence of any advertiser pressure greatly affected the editorial tone of *Playboy*. Without having to cater to or worry about gain or loss of revenues because a major advertiser might object to some of Hefner's increasingly outspoken editorial policies, he was as bold and as irreverent as the law would allow, while he sharpened the editorial edge of the magazine and made it a virtual demand item on newsstands across the country.

When circulation mounted and the magazine was beginning to be noised about in news stories and profile pieces of Hefner himself, advertisers took notice and expressed fervid interest. They approached *Playboy* on their own. But Hefner reacted cautiously: he established an advertising acceptability policy that made even *The New Yorker* seem a trifle frivolous, rejecting any type of advertising that he felt was not consistent with the *Playboy* image. Advertisements in "poor taste" for products such as elastic bandages or skin creams were unequivocally rejected. "Sometimes this hurt us financially," explained Hefner, "since there were times when we could have used some advertising revenue when our projections weren't going exactly as we thought they would on the newsstands. But I just wouldn't compromise the appearance of the magazine to bring in the dollars." He wanted *Playboy* to reflect the good life, and as a result nothing was admitted which might make his readers aware that life was anything less than beautiful.

There was another very real, and as it turned out, astute reason why Hefner declined what he considered objectionable advertising: when the time came, as he knew or hoped it would, when he would start to approach advertisers, he wanted to offer them a magazine unblemished in advertising image: to give them, as he stated, "the 'Schweppes Commander Whitehead' or 'Man in the Hathaway Shirt with Eyepatch' kind of snob appeal."

Hefner, together with Art Paul, started developing *Playboy* into a magazine of unmistakable style, consisting of sophisticated artwork in glowing lithographs (*Playboy* won an award for an illustration in its first issue and has won more prizes for graphics than any other magazine in history), stories by some of the best writers in the country, and a mélange of well-written and well-researched articles. A typical issue contained a thought-provoking article by billionaire J. Paul Getty, "The Vanishing American"; an examination of "The Love Cult" by distinguished literary critic Alfred Kazin; an intriguing memoir by Ben Hecht; a remembrance of Ernest Hemingway written by his brother; and a polemic on the shortsightedness of men of science in the last half-century, "The Hazards of Prophecy," by Arthur C. Clarke. *Playboy* editors also answered questions about everything from the proprieties of courtship in business to the correct length for a tie; from how to select a diamond to how much sex is physically "safe"; from which wines should be chilled and/or aged to whether or not mentholated cigarettes suppress the sex drive (they don't); and from where to find a formal gambling school to which living creature has the largest penis in relationship to its body size (the flea).

Playboy readers wrote in to ask about an astonishing variety of subjects. At first, as with many magazines, *Playboy* handled these letters through its Reader Service Department, which mailed personal answers back to each questioner.

As the volume of daily letters increased, however, it soon became apparent that they could profitably form the nucleus for a monthly editorial feature which developed into a sociosexual column for the lovelorn and a cultural guidepost for the *innocentia*.

In September of 1960, *Playboy* inaugurated a new editorial feature, "The Playboy Advisor." Its purpose was to answer, via a monthly column, "all reasonable questions" submitted by readers which would be of interest to the urban male—*Playboy*'s avowed audience. The subjects, as indicated in the notice that follows each column, may range from "fashion, food and drink, hi-fi and sports cars to dating dilemmas, taste and etiquette. . . ." Personal answers were still made to each query accompanied by a stamped, self-addressed envelope, but the most interesting letters sent to either "The Playboy Advisor" or *Playboy*'s Reader Service were thereafter examined for possible inclusion in the "Advisor" column. Hefner insisted that all the letters used in the "Advisor" column be real, from genuine readers with genuine questions. Occasionally, the editors would edit a letter, shorten it, or rewrite it, but they were scrupulous when it came to publishing only legitimate queries. The most common question out of the thousands that arrive each week documents the reader's concern over the length of his penis.

The questions selected to be answered in the column were given careful thought and consideration. Where necessary, varying degrees of research would be done to provide the best possible answer. The result was a feature that gained readers with each issue and which did a good deal to further the reputation of the magazine as a whole.

While many of the queries dealt with such lighthearted topics as dating etiquette or purchasing a car, some letters revealed serious problems, which the growing staff of the "Advisor" took care to answer with support and reassurance:

An Army wife, lonely for her absent husband, confesses

her great distress and guilt whenever she dreams—with no conscious desire for fulfillment—of having sexual relations with other men. She mentions that, according to her religious training, the thought is virtually as bad as the act.

The Advisor informs the young woman that her thoughts are quite natural, normal, and in no way cause for any feelings of guilt. It quotes a psychoanalyst who says in part, "A thought of infidelity a day (without guilt) keeps the psychoanalyst away," and ends with Clarence Darrow's comment: "I've never killed a man, but I've read many an obituary with a great deal of pleasure."

A newly married man writes in to say that, while he had always considered himself "normal in every respect," his bride has several times questioned him about the curved shape of his erect penis. While the man professes to have normal, satisfactory intercourse, he wonders if his penis is abnormally shaped.

The Advisor states, quite definitively, that curved penises are not only normal but quite common and then goes on to explain the physiological reason such bending occurs. After this reassurance, though, the Advisor does insert a word of caution: "It seldom interferes with sexual functioning, as you have observed, and the worst thing you can do is worry about it."

A recently divorced man sadly seeks a way to reestablish contact with his former wife. He was the cause of the divorce, he explains, and when their marriage ended, his wife made him promise never to see or contact her. Now he wants her back and is afraid that she will laugh at or reject his efforts to meet with her to apologize for his mistakes and try to work out a new relationship.

The Advisor tells the man to ask his former wife out for a casual lunch, at which he can acknowledge his mistakes and express his willingness to correct them. Cautioning the man not to "eat crow," the Advisor does offer the hopeful note that his ex-wife's request that they never see each other again indicates that she still retained some emotion for him at the time of their divorce, even if the emotion was only anger. As the column suggests optimistically, "Indifference would be far more difficult to overcome."

This was all topped off each month with a color photograph, printed on a three-page foldout (suitable for pinning up), of a nude, beautiful, and large-breasted young lady. The magazine was true to its slogan, supplying its readers with monthly "Entertainment for Men." *Playboy* at its beginnings seemed to be the voice of an organization; those who bought it almost had the feeling that they belonged to a club which the magazine was representing. "What is a playboy?" the magazine asked rhetorically.

Is he simply a wastrel, a ne'er-do-well, a fashionable bum? Far from it: he can be a sharp-minded young business executive, a worker in the arts, a university professor, an architect or engineer. He can be many things, provided he possesses a certain *point of view.* He must see life not as a vale of tears, but as a happy time; he must take joy in his work, without regarding it as the end all of living; he must be an alert man, an aware man, a man of taste, a man sensitive to pleasure, a man who—without acquiring the stigma of the voluptuary or dilettante—can live life to the hilt. This is the sort of man we mean when we use the word playboy.

By publishing this editorial statement, Hefner gave *Playboy* an instant, self-awarded imprimatur which rationalized and made respectable its contents to a large segment of young males. They identified with the description of how they saw or would like to see themselves.

Reverend Roy Larsen, in an article published in *Motive* entitled "The Lowdown on the Upbeats" explained the effect *Playboy* had on its readers in this way:

My own personal explanation for its popularity goes like this: *Playboy* has a strong, almost irresistible appeal for the self-conscious young man who is struggling to establish his own identity, to define his own personality, to work out his style of life.

Caught up in a reaction against "Blah," he does not want to be just another person, but wants to show, by his manners, his personal taste in music, food, drink, and apparel, that he is someone who is distinctive.

But he is unsure of himself. He doesn't know his "way around." He is deathly afraid of being ludicrous. He doesn't want to goof. He doesn't want to do anything which would indicate that he's a hick, a square, or a clod. And so he needs impersonal guidance and direction and help.

Where does he get it? From *Playboy* of course.

And Hefner sounded like he was giving a political campaign speech, elevating *Playboy* to party platform status when, in an interview, he stated:

Playboy is dedicated to the enjoyment of "the good life" that is every American's heritage, if he's willing to display a little of the initiative and derring-do that made the country great in the first place, instead of settling for job security, conformity, togetherness, anonymity and slow death.

And just incidentally, while trying earnestly to climb that ladder of success, through creativity, thought, initiative and daring to be different. Americans supply the only chance this country has of moving back into a position of world leadership.

This isn't the negativistic kind of snob appeal that says, "I'm better than you are because my father's name was So-and-so," or "I'm descended from the Revolution," or "I'm white," or Protestant or what have you. It's tied closely, instead, to the prestige of accomplishment and the rewards for same. We say life is wonderful—enjoy it—make the most of it.

In the area of clothing, *Playboy* has been, paradoxically, more avant-garde in women's fashion than in men's. In 1954 Hefner ran a cover with a girl in a bikini bathing suit, and in the mid-1960s miniskirts quickly found their way into the pages of *Playboy*. In both instances, *Playboy* was the first American magazine to take serious notice of this new risqué clothing long popular in Europe.

Though Hefner's magazine was being accepted by a

growing and enthusiastic group of men, he was having trouble with another, larger coterie: the government.

According to the U.S. Postal Act of March 31, 1879, periodicals that are published on a frequent basis, have paid-up subscription rolls (as opposed to giveaways), and have more editorial than advertising pages in their overall content have the right to apply for and receive second-class mailing privileges. This allows publishers to mail their periodicals at a much-reduced rate of postage. Without a second-class permit, most publishers would probably not be able to stay in business. If a publisher doesn't qualify for a second-class permit, for example, it is three times as expensive for him to mail his magazines, and he is given much poorer postal service besides. Second-class mail is afforded near first-class status in being sped from publisher to post office to reader. Third-class mail is delivered when the post office has time to deliver it and can sometimes take weeks longer to arrive.

Hefner applied for a second-class permit on October 14, 1954, almost a year after the publication of his first issue. He had been mailing issues of *Playboy* at the third-class rate and paying the extra cost during his first year of publication since he had few subscribers and could bear the expense. But as the subscriptions began to pour in, he knew that he would have to secure second-class privileges. The Post Office accepted his application and, as a normal procedure, sent an inspector to his office to check over the subscription rolls and determine if everything was in order. Hefner waited to have the application approved. He heard nothing. Often, due to governmental bureaucracy and in order for the Post Office to determine that the publication is going to be issued on a regular basis, the issuance of a permit can take a month or so.

In *Playboy's* case, almost six months went by without any official word from the Post Office, though Hefner kept checking with them periodically. "Sorry, the application has not come through from Washington yet," he was told. Hefner became suspicious—or at least concerned.

By the spring of 1955, he was printing 350,000 copies of *Playboy*, where two months earlier the circulation had been only 175,000; everyone from the receptionist to the editors was working nights, and they hadn't been able to keep up with the demand. His explosive success almost plunged the magazine out of control; he simply didn't have the personnel to handle all of the business and editorial tasks that needed attention, nor was the operation properly organized to handle such an influx of business. In addition, he had just accepted his first four-color, full-page ad—for Springmaid sheets—and he was in the midst of establishing a burgeoning advertising department. The net result of this hyperactivity was that he personally fell so behind in his editorial duties that *Playboy* was forced to skip an issue—March 1955—because Hefner and his staff couldn't get it out on time. An editorial assured readers that they would get one extra issue at the end of the year and that the jump from February to April was to enable *Playboy* to match its sales periods to its competitors'.

That inadvertent lapse was all the Post Office needed. A clause in the Act states that permits are only granted to periodicals that are issued on a *regular* basis. A monthly magazine must publish twelve issues a year, dated *consecutively*, in order to qualify. Hefner's application was immediately returned, rejected.

He doggedly applied again, on April 27, 1955, and this time he was kept waiting over three months without receiving any official reply. When the determination finally arrived from Washington, it was negative again, but now the Post Office was more outspoken: *Playboy's* application was refused because of the editorial content (indicating that this was the real reason that the original application had been rejected.)

Hefner was determined not to allow a mere governmental agency to interfere with his vision of himself as potentially one of the country's most successful publishers. He immediately took legal action to have the ruling overturned. In addition to the fact that magazines much "worse" than *Playboy* were enjoying second-class privileges and had been doing so for years, he also had proof, through readers and other sources, that certain post offices had simply not been delivering the magazine for arbitrary reasons, clear only to the postmaster and the carriers of those particular stations. Officials from the Post Office insidiously indicated that if the contents were altered to suit the department, *Playboy* would be afforded second-class privileges. "We don't think Postmaster General Summerfield has any business editing magazines," blasted Hefner. "We think he should stick to delivering the mail." Hefner went to court, expecting a major obscenity battle. He vowed to take the case to the Supreme Court, if necessary. It wasn't. In November of 1955, in a federal district court, he secured a successful injunction against the Post Office Department of Chicago restraining them from further interference with the mailing of the magazine. Judge Luther W. Youngdahl intervened to prevent the Post Office from holding up delivery of *Playboy*. In a direct challenge to procedures that had been used for decades, the judge ordered the department to give temporary second-class privileges to *Playboy*. Hefner sat back to see whether they would go to a higher court or try some other tactic in their attempt to tamper with the delivery of the magazine.

Playboy continued to publish with its second-class permit "pending" and in May of 1956, Hefner was informed that his permit was finally approved; starting with the June issue he could "officially" begin mailing at the second-class rate. To sweeten the victory, he was awarded a refund of over $100,000.00 as the difference between the postage rates he had been paying and those that he should have paid if his application had been accepted the previous August.

"Henceforth, *Playboy* will be edited in Chicago, not Washington," avowed Hefner victoriously.

It's not difficult to ascertain the reasons why the Post Office felt so critical toward *Playboy*. Though the pictorial selections were certainly risqué by conventional standards at that time, they were certainly less explicit than many of the photos that were being published by *Modern Man* and *Modern Sunbathing*, for example. Therefore, the major objection promoted by the Post Office, and it might very well have been almost an unconscious one on the part of their censors, was that unlike other magazines, *Playboy* was proclaiming in not so cold print that the publication of its nudes was healthy and natural and part of the natural scheme of things on this planet and because, as Hefner explained it, "That's the way men prefer their women."

Talking about the reasons why he thought *Playboy* had been under the scrutiny of censors, Hefner said, "We try to edit the magazine with honesty, insight, taste and integrity, for we very much believe in what we are doing and enjoy it. Now if you set out to edit, with honesty, any magazine for adult males, you aren't going to come up with *McCall's* or the *Reader's Digest*.

"*Playboy*, of course, is not a very sexy or shocking magazine and the fact that some few people consider it so is a sad commentary on the sexual mores of a portion of our population. Of course, it is the nature of the beast to find the prude and the bigot most anxious to *force* his or her opinion of what is right on the rest of us. What the would-be censors have neglected to notice is that, in addition to the lightly clad beauty in the center of the magazine—our 'Playmate of the Month'—*Playboy* regularly publishes some of the finest fiction, articles, art and photography appearing in America today."

CHAPTER 6

"Can you imagine what the readers would say if they could see me now; if they knew that this is the way that Hugh Hefner really spends his time?"

Critics of *Playboy* are among the first to point to the Playmate as being Hefner's most prominent vehicle to success, and Hefner himself acknowledges his debt to the centerfold but claims that it is only partly responsible for the magazine's prosperity.

"Without question, the Playmate is an important part—I'm not denying it in the least. Sex is an important part and I think that probably *Playboy* is a combination of sex in the Freudian sense and status. These are probably its two major appeals. Well, they happen to be the two major appeals in life, fortunately. I think we are mining a pretty solid ore here, because when you put both sex and status together you can't miss. A guy works for his romantic image of himself for the women and the status thing for men.

"Now the sex thing depends on how psychoanalytical you want to get about it. The sex actually includes not only the Playmate and the cartoons and jokes which describe boy-girl situations, but go right down in all the service features. Why do you want to drive that smart Bugatti? Why are you interested in a Mercedes-Benz? Why do you wear the latest kind of suit? Why are you interested in the hi-fi rig and the new stereo sounds and the new jazz records, etc.? Why are you interested in good food and drink? Just to sit in the corner and contemplate these things? I think not. To sit in a corner with a fellow? I rather doubt it. With some other magazines you may wonder.

"There's no such confusion with *Playboy*. It is devoted to the boy-girl relationship, to a heterosexual activity in modern society. And in the best sense *Playboy* is sexual like a sports car can be sexy. We don't suggest all the components in the hi-fi as a replacement for the boy-girl relationship. We don't suggest sports-car racing as a replacement. We suggest these things in a context of boys and girls together."

But aside from the philosophical rationale, Hefner's Playmates were different from all the nudes that had ever been published in a magazine before. At first, he had started off with calendar photos (like the Marilyn Monroe nude) and stock shots from photo houses: many of his photos consisted of pictures of pretty, though often slutty-looking girls in bored, obviously staged-for-the-camera poses that had been seen a hundred times before in other magazines. Some of the girls looked simply like tired hookers. M. J. Sobran, Jr. in the *National Review* offered the following description of the initial Playmates:

Despite the girl-next-door aura that helped make the Playmates famous, many of them, in those early days, had a rather self-conscious fallen-woman look about them; rather like the girls in other girlie mags, like *Rogue* and *Dude*. You know the pose: breasts thrust forth, tummy sucked in, legs coyly crossed—and the face, oh the face! What it lacked in beauty, it made up in ardor and mascara. Come hither, reader, it said—chin up, mouth open, tongue between bared teeth, eyes half open but gazing right at you, mister, and yes it said yes—though she looked like a girl who, off camera, chewed gum and said yeah, that Playmate of yore.

In 1955, though, Hefner's cameramen began photographing the centerfold model themselves; Hefner and Art Paul would get involved in the shooting, aiding the photographer in his concept and sometimes suggesting ways they could improve their technique. They searched for models who had a younger, fresher, more innocent, child-woman look, and they found some of the most beautiful girls in America willing to pose. Most of the girls were teenagers. Very few were older than twenty-one. Lenny Bruce, from the stage of Chicago's Gate of Horn, once described a Playmate as "a winner chick, a real kissy-looking chick"; and holding up the then-current gatefold for the audience to see, he asked, "You find this lady indecent? She's the most decent goddamn chick I've seen for a long time. A tramp? This sweet, pink-nippled, blue-eyed chicken? A tramp? This is a lovely lady, boy. I sure dig her." In February of that year, a young, full-breasted girl by the name of Jayne Mansfield was the centerfold Playmate. She caused quite a stir among readers and helped to push *Playboy*'s circulation ahead a few notches, even though *Playboy* didn't use her name.

Some months later, Hefner accidently stumbled upon a formula for Playmates which has not varied to this day. *Playboy*'s subscription fulfillment manager was a woman named Charlaine Karalus, a twenty-year-old slender but statuesque platinum blonde who was the heartthrob of every man who worked at the magazine, and who, boasted *Playboy*, measured "36-24-36 from top to bottom or vice versa."

Charlaine needed a new Addressograph machine for her department and, like a dutiful employee, had complained to Hefner on several occasions that *Playboy* should invest the money in a new piece of equipment. When she approached him in July, it was at a time when he was trying to decide how to fill the centerfold pages for the upcoming issue; he had had no luck in securing a Playmate for that month through his regular sources. "I'll tell you what," he said to her, half-jokingly, "if you'll become our Playmate for July, I'll get you that new Addressograph for your department." Charlaine at first refused—she had never done any professional modeling, certainly none in the nude—but then agreed after some additional coaxing. She not only solved Hefner's immediate editorial problem but enabled him to articulate the centerfold concept for which he had been searching: publishing photos of girls who were not models. It resulted in making the name "Playmate" a household word.

Hefner selected a new name for Charlaine—Janet Pilgrim —as a protection against crank calls at her home, as is sometimes the case when a beautiful girl has her name and picture in a newspaper or magazine; he also chose the name because it had a show-business lilt to it.

Most of the *Playboy* editorial and art staff doubted whether Hefner should mention in print, as he told everyone he planned to, that Janet Pilgrim actually worked for the magazine. The editors felt that opening the doors and, in effect, showing what went on behind the scenes might diffuse the mystery and hence destroy the romance between the reader and the alluring, mysterious, and unknown Playmate. Hefner adamantly disagreed: "There is relatively little appeal in a nude that has no name and is often posed in a salon-photography way that is stylized (olive oil rubbed all over)— as far from nature as a statue, as interesting as a beautiful chair is, but as a human being, no." Hefner felt that the Playmate was the "discovery of the All-American beauty, based upon the concept of the girl next door." Hefner's position is ironic when one considers that his Playmates have over the years become the most stylized pinups in the history of the art. The not-so-subtle airbrush retouches almost all of the Playmate photos to remove blemishes where body makeup could not effectively do the job. The result is a sanitized, hairless, and plastic look, more like the mannequin-next-door. One Playmate described her immediate reaction to the centerfold photo for which she had posed. ". . . That girl standing there in the wherewithal, gripping a striped shower curtain with pink soap in the background just wasn't me. I just didn't know that girl." The Playmates were often shot in highly air-conditioned rooms to prevent even a hint of perspiration and to make their nipples stand out in what Hefner thought to be an erotic profile. If that failed, ice cubes were pressed gently against the nipples to harden them just a second before the photographer activated his shutter. In addition, to provide the rosy glow of health, the nipples were often tinted with a stylish shade of rouge.

In the issue in which Janet Pilgrim appeared, an editorial stated:

We suppose that it's natural to think of the pulchritudinous Playmates as existing in a world apart. Actually, potential Playmates are all around you: the new secretary at your office, the doe-eyed beauty who sat opposite you at lunch yesterday, the girl who sells you shirts and ties at your favorite store. We found Miss July in our own circulation department, processing subscriptions, renewals and back-copy orders. Her name is Janet Pilgrim and she's as efficient as she is good looking. Janet has never modeled professionally before, but we think she holds her own with the best of the Playmates of the past.

Coupled with this purification of the centerfold Playmate, little by little Hefner introduced a picture story around her which was almost a study in sexual foreplay, building from clothed to semiclothed poses. The Playmate would first be seen fully clothed—window-shopping, horseback riding, dancing with a friend. Then the camera would discover her alone in her apartment, perhaps reading or preparing dinner. The excitement would mount as the Playmate, now in bra and panties or sheer negligee, revealed tantalizing glimpses of her obvious charms. And finally, quite literally bursting forth with its foldout format, the climax: the centerfold, showing as much of her body as was possible. Pubic hair and genitalia, however, were always airbrushed out of existence; as late as 1961, Hefner believed that the *Playboy* audience would be "shocked" by photos of nudes with pubic hair. Suggestive poses and the accoutrements of any kind of fetishism were *verboten,* and though the girl never looked as though she had just indulged in sex—or was about to—a necktie or cigarette case, often suggestively introduced by the photographer, hinted that there was a man in her life. In the July 1955 photo of Janet Pilgrim, a shadowy outline of Hefner himself can be seen in the background. After her first Playmate appearance, "Miss Pilgrim" became one of Hefner's steady companions and remained so for a time.

It wasn't until January of 1971 that *Playboy* risked running its first centerfold Playmate (Liv Lindeland) sans airbrush, with her light brown pubic hair highly visible. Hefner made the decision with trepidation, knowing that he was chancing a mammoth obscenity battle should a local censorship group become offended by the picture. Perhaps to temper the erotic effects of the hair, Miss Lindeland's amply proportioned nipples appear powdered, as if to minimize them.

Anthony Haden-Guest, in an article in *Rolling Stone*, described Hefner's pubic-hair decision: "The picture was set up in Chicago, where it found Hefner in a receptive mood. 'It wasn't a decisive thing, immediately,' says Vince Tajiri, the photo editor. 'It was left in a kind of ambivalency until the last moment, when Hefner said: "Lets' run this one, and we'll see. *Let's do it.*"

" 'I happened to see the proofs in the production manager's office. The pubic hair was definitely there. The photograph was lit with sidelights and everything, so that the hair itself was highlighted and obvious. And I said, "I think we're gonna have to knock down the highlights on the hair." The production manager, John Mastro, said "O.K. We're gonna do that." '

"Mastro took the proofs over to the Hefner Mansion. Hefner pored over them on his light box. Considered. Came to the final decision, alone. 'Leave the highlights as they are,' he said."

Since that time the display of pubic hair has become virtually *de rigeur* on all *Playboy*'s Playmates, and it is now shown on both men and women as a matter of course. Occasionally even a lonely, flaccid penis will appear in a pictorial feature, as will a hint of a vaginal slit. In what was perhaps even a more daring gesture, Hefner extended his new pictorial liberation to the sensitive, all-important cover. The miss who graced the June 1974 issue showed more of her body than had ever been seen on a cover of *Playboy* or virtually any other nationally distributed magazine: with Hefner's approval, one of her nipples was showing. In a general directive to some of his key staffers, Hefner indicated that a discreet amount of pubic hair would henceforth be welcome on *Playboy*'s pages, but organs penetrating organs were still to be considered taboo. Erect or semitumescent penises were strictly *verboten*.

Despite a retrospective criticism over the years of exploitation of the women he has photographed, Hefner knew exactly what he was doing in terms of building his circulation. "There's something wrong," he said, "either psychologically or glandularly, with some guy who isn't interested in pictures of pretty girls. If the pictures replace the girls themselves, the guy may have problems." Many American males proved they had no difficulties, however, generating interest in such pictures, and as Hefner continued to find more and more "girls next door" who were willing to shed all of their clothes and appear in a national magazine *déshabillé*, *Playboy* quickly became one of the most popular men's magazines in the United States with readers multiplying with the prolificacy of rabbits. Said Hefner, "We've played a decontaminating role in changing attitudes toward nudity. The feminists who criticize us don't realize how *Playboy*, far more than the women's magazines, is responsible for the nongirdle look, the bikini, the miniskirt, the openness to nudity.

"You'd think that female emancipators would separate their friends from their enemies. We've helped their movement in several ways. And after all, woman has the vote; she can hold property; she gets more than a square deal in divorce laws; and she's taken great strides forward economically. The major strides ahead are of a sexual nature, like abortion, and undermining the surviving social attitudes that there are only virgins and nonvirgins, good girls and bad girls. But we can't ignore the fact that there also exist a large number of competitive females who are trying to castrate the guys they come in contact with because they're unhappy with the whole male-female relationship. They're out to show how impotent the male is, in conversation, in bed, or a thousand other ways. Instead of a love relationship, it becomes a hostile war of the sexes."

By January of 1957, after three years of publication, *Playboy*'s circulation was 687,593 as compared with its chief competitor, ironically the twenty-three-year-old *Esquire* with 778,190.

Hefner kept a keen eye on maintaining the editorial balance of the magazine and attempted to manipulate its contents so that *Playboy* would not be known merely as a classic study in mammoth mammaries. This urge to publish quality fiction and articles by key writers and Hefner's success in securing them were undoubtedly significant in the growth of *Playboy*. But Hefner recognized that he could not edit the magazine all by himself, even though he would have liked to. He was also aware that he had few strong contacts in the literary world. Consequently, he hired three top editors who would ultimately affect *Playboy*'s entire tone and editorial policy and therefore become extremely crucial elements in Hefner's story of success. An astute judge of character, Hefner has the ability to spot those who may prove useful to him. Many Hefner-observers have long felt this to be one of his most remarkable business attributes. Hefner once looked at me in what seemed to be an overly intense fashion and said, "Sometimes I can almost see through people." Sorcery notwithstanding, he does have the amazing ability to appraise not only people, but what they are saying; his perception of what people really mean, not what they're mouthing, is astonishing. He is a ravenous listener and soaks up much of what he hears.

In 1955 Hefner met Jack Kessie, a tall, acerbic, nattily dressed ex-trumpeter who had been advertising manager for Coronet Instructional Films. Kessie had submitted a well-written free-lance article entitled, "The Well-Dressed Play-boy—Playboy's Position on Proper Attire." After contributing a few more pieces—all on fashion—he was hired in June of 1955 as *Playboy's* first associate editor. While being responsible for assigning and editing articles, he continued to write about fashion under the pseudonym of Blake Rutherford. In 1960, he became managing editor.

The second important addition to the staff was a soft-spoken photographer from Los Angeles named Vincent Tajiri who joined *Playboy* as photo editor in 1956. A former editor of *Art Photography*, his work had appeared in *Look, Life,* and *Time*. During his fifteen-year tenure as *Playboy's* photo editor, he gathered together a staff of professional photographers—both free-lance and salaried—stylists, photo researchers, and librarians. He also has to his credit the construction of a mammoth photo studio and laboratory for *Playboy* which does on-the-spot color and black-and-white processing.

Perhaps the most important addition to Hefner's staff during the early years of *Playboy*, however, was Auguste Comte Spectorsky; a Parisian-born sophisticate, author of three best-sellers (of which the best known is *The Exurban-ites*), former editor of *Park East*, and onetime literary editor of the *Chicago Sun*, Spectorsky founded the first book supplement published outside of Manhattan.

With the approach of spring 1956, the editorial tasks were becoming too numerous for Hefner to handle by himself, and though Russell and Kessie were excellent front-line editors, Hefner wanted someone who had solid publishing experience and could run the magazine in all its aspects. He decided to create a new position, that of editorial director, and inquired of a few agents and publishers whom he knew personally if they had any suggestions on who might fill the spot. The potential editorial director would have to have contacts among well-known authors and writers and be capable of making more. Spectorsky's name kept surfacing as a possibility. Hefner telephoned him in New York, where he was a senior editor with WNBC-TV. Spectorsky was at home, having a drink, when the phone rang.

"My name is Hugh Hefner," said the voice at the other end. "Have you ever heard of me?"

"No," said Spectorsky.

"Have you ever heard of *Playboy* magazine?" asked Hefner.

"No."

"Well, may I ask you another question? Are you irrevocably wedded to television?"

"I'm not irrevocably wedded to anything," replied Spectorsky, perhaps thinking of his three previous marriages.

"Good," said Hefner. "I'll be in New York tomorrow to see you."

Though Spectorsky had no intention of leaving New York, he soon found himself agreeing to Hefner's offer of a starting salary of $750 a week, stock options, a generous expense account, and a lavish hotel suite until he found a place of his own. He moved to Chicago, eventually leasing a town house in the Near North Side, and began immediately trying to improve *Playboy*'s image.

Spectorsky's first formal suggestion to Hefner posed something of a problem: he felt that the magazine's name should be changed to *Smart Set*. Hefner had just gone through an exchange of memos on a similar theme; Victor Lownes felt that the subtitle, "Entertainment for Men," should be deleted from the cover of the magazine as limiting its appeal. Hefner had quickly vetoed Lownes' idea, but he had to give Spec's suggestion greater consideration. *Playboy*, argued Spectorsky, sounded too much like a girlie magazine title. If Hefner, he advanced, was sincere in wanting the image of the magazine upgraded, if he truly wanted to attract the top writers in the magazine field, he would have to come up with a name more sophisticated and with a more legitimate tone than *Playboy*. Hefner assumed a posture that he would maintain in making many of his editorial and business decisions over the years: why change something that is known to be succeeding just on the hope of making it better? "Why cook the golden goose?" he asked Spectorsky. "We know *Playboy* is a title that is working phenomenally. If we change it, it may do better. On the other hand, we could also wreck the magazine. Let's try to change the image with evolution, rather than revolution."

Spectorsky was compelled to obey his young employer (Hefner was almost twenty years his junior), and he consequently attempted to secure name writers by other means: patience, intelligence, and a special charm that was almost second nature to him. Possessed of the manner of an aristocrat, he was a classically perfect dinner companion, an asset he used to win new advocates for *Playboy*. Always low key, he was *au courant*, impeccably courteous, and cynically humorous. Within the first year of Spectorsky's relationship with *Playboy*, the public domain reprints began to fade away, slowly, then more rapidly replaced by contributions from such super- or near-celestial *novae* as Alberto Moravia, Philip Wylie, Budd Schulberg, Nelson Algren, John Steinbeck, and Lawrence Durrell.

Though Spectorsky must be credited for all his polished, publisher-luncheon, New York–intellectual persuasiveness in lining up these original literary guns, it was Hefner's money—

roughly $2,000 for a solid piece of lead fiction as compared to the $400 paid by *Esquire*—that finally convinced them to "allow" *Playboy* to publish their work. And Hefner is quite clear on the subject of Spectorsky's contribution to *Playboy*; to some it will undoubtedly sound unappreciative. "Spectorsky added to the literary excellence of the magazine but if it wasn't him, it would have been someone else. It was more than my money that added to the improvements, however; it was *my* insight."

Hefner's relationship with Spectorsky was a curious one. Though they worked closely together for over sixteen years, they never socialized—even for an occasional lunch—and most of the editors who knew them both described their relationship as very much a love-hate, master-slave situation. Hefner once said that he found it interesting to watch as Spectorsky became "hooked" on *Playboy*. "One by one, he began to divest himself of most of his free-lance activities: the articles he would write here and there, the book reviews for the *Saturday Review* or *The New York Times Book Review*. Now his major interest is *Playboy*. This is it. I don't think he'll ever leave."

I once indicated to Hefner that Spectorsky was hurt that he never socialized with him. When I said I guessed that he was trying to "keep Spec on his toes," Hefner seemed genuinely aghast at my presumptuousness. "I don't manipulate people in that way. I can't even do that with girl friends where it would really be to my advantage! You see, my personal life is an *island* to which I escape, where I leave behind me the things that I devote the rest of my life to. Christ, I've never even been to Preuss' home! But don't you think it would be sticky if I surrounded myself all the time with my executives? It would be like a King and his court!" He has, however, on several occasions referred to his own ménage as a "magic kingdom."

"Some people think you already have a court now, complete with jesters," I responded.

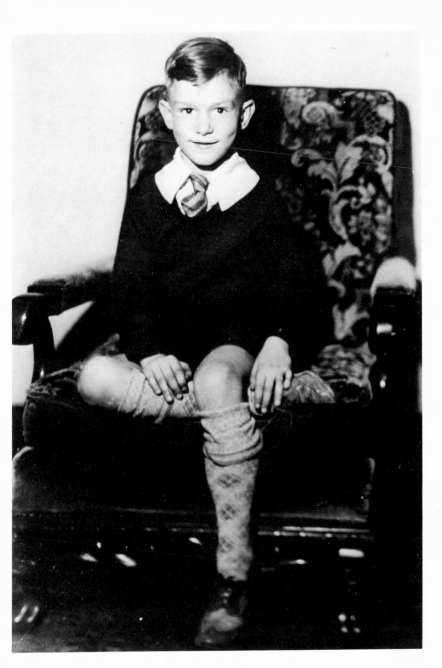

*At about the time this picture was taken, when
Hefner was eight, he was already typing out copies
of his own newspaper on an old Royal and selling
them door to door for a penny each.*

Hefner enlisted in the Army during World War II, when he was seventeen, first serving as an infantryman and finally as a company clerk. Home on leave in his native Chicago, he poses with his father, his younger brother Keith, and his mother.

Hefner married his high school and college sweetheart, Millie Williams, in 1949. A difficult marriage almost from the start, it lasted ten years. This snapshot is from Hefner's scrapbook, with his own annotations.

MILLIE AND HEF AT COLONIAL MANOR'S FORMAL THIS SNAP HAS BEEN TITLED "BEAUTY AND THE BEAST." MILLIE IS WEARING (FOR THE FIRST TIME) THE FORMAL HEF GAVE HER FOR HER 21st BIRTHDAY.

While at the University of Illinois, Hefner tried on the role of amateur stunt pilot at nearby Urbana Airport and became highly proficient at tailspins, stalls, and loops.

At the age of twenty-seven, without one day's professional editorial experience, Hefner started Playboy with a personal investment of $600, all of it borrowed. For the first three issues his office was his living room and kitchen, where he put the magazine together on a card table.

The first issue of Playboy, with Marilyn Monroe on its cover, was an instant success; Hefner was in the publishing business to stay.

*Inside the first issue was Playboy's first Playmate,
the nude Marilyn Monroe, who posed, as she put it,
"with nothing on but the radio." The photo helped
to sell out the issue on the newsstand.*

Hefner's eccentric life-style as a publisher quickly gained the attention of the press: he worked thirty-six to forty-eight hours at a time, sleeping only when exhausted, often working in his pajamas from his office bed, and consuming twenty-four to thirty-six bottles of Pepsi each day.

Hefner with the late A. C. Spectorsky, Playboy's top editorial executive. Though they worked closely together for seventeen years, they never socialized.

Hefner scrutinizes a transparency while working with Art Paul, Playboy's first and only art director. By taking shares of stock instead of salary in the early days of Playboy, Paul, like Hefner, became a multimillionaire.

In what has become a monthly ritual, Hefner, with his production manager John Mastro, examines proof sheets of the centerfold playmate. Hefner often requests corrections or changes in color; the reproductions must be "perfect" before he will give his final approval.

During the early and mid-1960s Hefner was a virtual hermit. Remaining in his mansion for months on end, he would rarely venture outside. One of his major preoccupations was the "Playboy Philosophy," to which he dedicated a great deal of time. It appeared in Playboy in twenty-six installments totaling a quarter of a million words.

During his reclusive period Hefner worked by himself for days and weeks in the quiet of his windowless private apartment located deep within his mansion. Even some of the forty-eight servants who worked in the house round the clock would not see him for months at a time.

In the early days of Playboy impromptu staff meetings were held whenever several of the editors found themselves together in the same room. Here, discussing a forthcoming article are (clockwise from left) Art Paul, Joe Paczek (an art assistant), Hefner, and editors Ray Russell and Jack Kessie.

Hefner's 100-room, one-million-dollar mansion at 1340 North State Parkway in Chicago has been his home since 1960. It is here that he gives his frequent Gatsbyesque parties, often with over 1,000 guests present in one evening.

Most of Hefner's work is done in his immense circular, vibrating, and rotating bed. Built in are telephone, television, hi-fi, and refrigerator.

Actor Tony Curtis was to play the role of Hugh Hefner in a movie called Mr. Playboy, to be produced by Columbia Pictures in the early 1960s. Hefner would not give script approval, however, and the project was abandoned.

Hefner's infrequent, high-level executive meetings
often assume marathon proportions. Some have been
known to last as long as twenty-six hours.

Hefner often hosts a Sunday evening dinner party
for fifty carefully selected guests and celebrities when
he is in Chicago. After dinner a first-run movie is
shown in the mammoth living room.

Lenny Bruce was one of Hefner's first television guests on "Playboy's Penthouse." A strong rapport developed between them and Hefner later published—first in the magazine, then as a book—Bruce's autobiography, How to Talk Dirty and Influence People.

Frequent guests Jerry Lewis and Sammy Davis, Jr., together with a bevy of beautiful girls, clown it up on a segment of Hefner's television show.

At a fund-raising party at Hefner's mansion for Illinois Senator Charles Percy, Hef chats with the Senator and singer Diahann Carroll. At the end of the party Percy and Hefner engaged in a ping-pong contest that lasted several hours.

Millionaire Hefner receives an autographed copy of How to Be Rich by billionaire author J. Paul Getty. For years Getty has served as Playboy's financial editor.

Mick Jagger, a week-long houseguest of Hefner's during the Rolling Stones' 1972 American tour, enjoys a glass of wine as he chats with his host.

Surrounded by bodyguards who are constantly with him, Hefner attends one of his own parties in his living room in Chicago, accompanied by his then–girl friend, Playmate Karen Christy.

Before entering his five-and-a-half-million-dollar DC-9 jet for a transcontinental trip, Hefner pauses for a publicity shot with three of his Jet Bunnies, specially trained as stewardesses.

Hefner poses in front of his multimillion-dollar castle, located near Hollywood. Since moving there in 1970 he has transformed it, through his lavish parties and entertaining, into a virtual salon for celebrities.

At a dinner given on behalf of the BBC, Hefner enjoys the company of Karen Christy.

On the grounds of his Los Angeles mansion, Hefner relaxes with Barbi Benton in his own private redwood forest, the largest in southern California. Many friends and Hefner observers predict the couple will eventually marry.

"I do and there's no way of avoiding it, nor would I want to avoid it. They're a mixed bag and they're here for a variety of reasons. Some of my friendships have been made just because I enjoy backgammon and they are some of the best backgammon players in the world. My relationship with Shel Silverstein just grew out of knowing him in college and then working with him from the beginning of the magazine. But I never consciously avoided Spectorsky. Our life-styles were completely different. Spec enjoyed having a few martinis and then sitting down to a long dinner. I hate that! My idea of having a good time is hanging out with friends at the house, rapping, playing games, running a movie, making love."

Shortly after joining *Playboy*, Spectorsky began to assume more and more of the responsibility for the editorial direction of the magazine, and at first, he even gave the advertising department a key push in securing some favored accounts. Both Art Paul and Ray Russell felt somewhat threatened, or unloved, and initially remained aloof. "I thought Hef should have given me the job as editorial director," said Russell years later. "It was the beginning of my disillusionment with *Playboy*." Art Paul felt less personally in danger than Russell, but he was afraid that the integrity of the artistic values of the magazine might be in jeopardy. "One of the first things I did after Spectorsky was brought in," Paul said, "was to visit his office to see how it was decorated and what kind of art he had on his walls. I was suspicious!" This prompted Spectorsky to issue a memo in which he stated, in part, "The executives of this company behave like college fraternity men who feel that every man has to be ridiculed, hazed, criticized, treated like a social outcast, and generally made miserable—and presumed guilty of incompetence until he proves himself innocent—before being accepted into the inner sanctum of the palace guards."

Hefner did nothing to ease the situation among his top executives, and though a relatively smooth working arrangement developed, it was not without some serious problems.

Spectorsky and Art Paul were at odds for years about whether the art or editorial department should have the upper hand. Spec continually bombarded Paul with patronizingly soft-shoe memos: "the editors," he said, "and the editors alone, can ascertain whether or not we are contemplating a pictorial presentation which contradicts the text material." He went on to say that it was "the role of the Art Department to 'work for' the Editorial Department. . . . We are always interested in the Art Department's opinions and feelings, but the Art Department should not be in a position of determining policy or directing action."

Paul didn't necessarily go along with the idea that his illustrators and designers were without interpretive ability, but he eventually had to give way to Spec's growing power. Spectorsky convinced Hefner to name him senior vice-president of the corporation and a member of the board of directors. Paul was neither. As an added display of dominion, Spectorsky insisted that his name appear in the magazine's masthead on a separate line just under Hefner's and above Art Paul's. When he first arrived at *Playboy*, their names were given equal billing.

Hefner delighted in the fact that Spectorsky seemed to be capable of running the corporation—at least creatively—though he did, however, lament the fact that Spectorsky was never a functioning associate publisher as he should have been. Hefner told me that . . . "he did act as an excellent editorial director. He was weak as an executive but he was very good on paper. Basically, though, I felt very let down by Spec because he wasn't strong enough. He had the responsibility of giving us a Book Division and a Book Club for *years* and never did anything. And, incidentally, he's the reason why we never had any other magazines. It was obvious that eventually I would have to start them myself."

Spectorsky's increased involvement in the creative aspects of the magazine, however, gave Hefner more time to concentrate on the many details he judged important and also to indulge himself in other areas simply because he enjoyed confronting them. An inordinate amount of Hefner's time, for example, was spent on editing the "Party Jokes" page that appeared in each issue. Though only ten or twelve jokes were published each month, Hefner insisted that his editors submit hundreds of jokes to him as a selection, which he would then read carefully, rewrite, and reedit; he sometimes composed long, involved memos to the Jokes editor on how a particular quip could be improved with judicious editing. Hefner developed a "policy" covering what kind of jokes were acceptable to him (e.g., no military, animal, or salesman–farmer's daughter jokes), and this regimen had to be followed slavishly, under threat of dismissal for the editor responsible for compiling the selection each month.

Also, the choice of the final photographs used for the centerfold Playmate was a task that Hefner approached each issue with what seemed to be near-religious devotion, or at least genuine love. Thousands of photographs would be shot before the final three-page foldout would be selected, and this checking involved days of Hefner's time as he scrutinized each tiny transparency, searching for the one photo he felt captured both the image of the girl and the image of *Playboy* he was attempting to project. Occasionally he would find that none of the photographs pleased him, and in a state of irritation and frustration he would order a new shooting.

Several proof copies of the first few issues off the press each month were always brought to Hefner for his inspection, and one of the first sections he would examine, always with a magnifying glass, was the Playmate, more often than not requesting that more of the evocative color red—one of his favorites—be introduced into the inking. These initial copies had to be approved by Hefner before the presses were allowed to roll, and he would often delay the final printing until the quality met his approval. If for any reason Hefner was not available to approve the copies, it would and did cost him tens of thousands of dollars in overtime or waiting

117

charges because the huge printing presses and printers had been standing by, scheduled to run at an earlier time.

Hefner never seemed to care about expense if it would improve the quality of his magazine. He claimed that his perfectionism not only refined the specific layout he might be working on, but also set the tone for a pursuit of quality that would permeate every level of the magazine, hopefully becoming *de rigueur* among most of his staffers. A *corrigendum* was prepared by Hefner almost every month, and immediately upon that issue's publication, those responsible were memoed to take precautions against a future recurrence. Spectorsky believed that Hefner's preoccupation with minor details ("There's too much yellow in the reflection in that girl's eye," Hefner once angrily complained), next to Spectorsky's negotiations for editorial purchases that amounted to tens of thousands of dollars, was a waste of good editorial talent on Hefner's part. But publicly, Spec always perpetuated the myth of Hefner as boy genius and would offer what seemed to be cogent and perceptive insights about Hefner; this, however, was merely a pose Spectorsky assumed with Hefner for the entire duration of his career at *Playboy* (he died in 1971). "You can compare him somewhat to Harold Ross of *The New Yorker*," Spec once said of him.

They are alike in several ways: dynamism, unwillingness to accept the word of experts—in quotes—above their own intuitive feelings. Ross was constantly and childishly delighted with evidence of big-city sophistication. Hef is somewhat the same. His delight with being Mr. Playboy has the same unjaded quality.

Privately, however, Spectorsky would always talk both patronizingly and pejoratively about Hefner and subtly attempt to implant in the listener's imagination the idea that it was *his* judgment and taste that prevailed in the company and *his* brilliance and wisdom that made *Playboy* the success it was. "Hefner's starting *Playboy*," he once said confidentially, "is a classic case of overcompensation. The fellow simply had no talent and couldn't get a decent job in publishing so he had to start a magazine of his own."

Spectorsky was offered a "small fortune" to write the inside book on Hefner and the Playboy universe but declined, knowing that it would have meant leaving his job, something he was not prepared to relinquish.

Occasionally Spec would combine his love-hate feelings toward Hefner in a single statement. He told Malcolm Boyd, "To me, Hef is unique, a brilliant walking paradox. He's always been a man of utter extremes. He can be bone-hard selfish, egocentric, anally retentive, suspicious, almost paranoid; he can also pour out love, humanity, act out all the beautiful clichés that cynics no longer believe possible. But he's not a bleeding heart. When he goes out on a limb, he's perfectly aware of the dangers to himself; he just does it as a matter of principle, without hesitation.

"Another paradox: his genuine intellect, and yet the degree to which his responses are mostly visceral. He's sometimes agonizingly patient with people he has little regard for, and brutally impatient with those he cares for. I've heard him say, 'You can finish that sentence if you want to, but I know the end of it, so let's get on.'

"Of course, I have an intensely personal feeling about him. It's been the most significant relationship in my adult life."

After his death, Spectorsky's wife, Theo Frederick, told Hefner that despite the disparity in their ages, Spec always looked to Hefner as a father figure. Hefner states that this curious reversed role was one of the keys to his relationship with Spec.

Spectorsky was also jealous of the amount of personal publicity Hefner received, bitterly resenting it. He would often advise, by way of memo or informal discussion, that offers of interviews be rejected, suggesting that Hefner was too busy or that the publication that wanted to conduct the interview was not "good image" or that the timing of it was not "quite right."

Spec tried to give the impression that he humored Hefner, whom he sarcastically referred to as the "boy wonder" or the "owner," but in actual fact he was thoroughly dominated by Hefner, almost pitifully so. In addition to the social snubbing that Hefner perpetrated, for whatever reason, he would often keep Spectorsky waiting for hours beyond a scheduled meeting and on many occasions would simply not appear at all, even though a formal confirmation had been made. This breech of etiquette, a pointed display of power on Hefner's part, at first would send Spectorsky into a quiet rage and finally reduced him to despair. Pasted on the pull-out writing panel of his desk (presumably so that it could remain hidden from eyes other than his own), Spec had this uncredited aphorism:

The American executive seems especially enslaved by his attitudes toward time, so much so that the amount of time he allots to a subordinate and the point in the day when the time is allotted tells the subordinate something about his status and the urgency, to his superior, of the issue under consideration.

When a meeting is scheduled, who waits for whom and for how long says important things about relationships. Most organizations or cultures develop informal tolerance ranges for lateness; to keep a person waiting beyond the tolerance limit is a subtle way of insulting him.

When the meetings did take place, Spectorsky acted like a schoolboy sitting in the principal's office: he would agree with almost anything Hefner proposed, whether it was right or wrong. Avoiding even the hint of confrontation, he would cower and back down at the least sign of kingly displeasure, refusing to stand up for the very points he had made to his associates just five minutes before the meeting began. "Hefner can be brutal in a meeting," he once complained. Nonetheless, he did nothing to stop it.

Spectorsky's cowardice was a result of his thorough dread of losing his job. When he died in 1971, he was making $186,606 a year, plus options, owned a large yacht, was constructing a magnificent house on St. Croix in the Virgin Islands, and was living in one of Chicago's most lavish apartments. He had also established a comfortable and stimulating little fiefdom which encompassed lunches with a William Saroyan or an Arthur Schlesinger, dinners with a Bennett Cerf or a Norman Mailer, and the enjoyment of the status and power of being one of the country's leading literary entrepreneurs.

Even though Spectorsky could be hardhearted, unfair, and sometimes ruthless with his subordinates, he was submissive to Hefner's every wish. The reasoning behind Hefner's retention of a pantywaist as his chief editorial executive becomes clear when one understands that Hefner has had a lifelong obsession about not relinquishing authority. Those strong-willed men who take pride and pleasure in making decisions on their own almost always found themselves in trouble with Hefner, and many such "fighters" who have ever worked for *Playboy*, with some exceptions, have either been dismissed or have walked out in disgust.

It's true that Hefner has always loved his work, but it's equally accurate to say that from the first layout of the first page of the first issue of *Playboy*, he has trusted no one's judgment but his own on even the most minute detail. For example, he could and would spend hours reworking a sentence so that it would read exactly the way he wanted it to read, shifting commas, playing with syntax, cogitating laboriously about the most esoteric and, to others, most trivial aspects.

Once, a meeting at which I was present began at 5 P.M.; I was still sitting at the conference table with Hefner ten hours later as he rewrote an answer to a letter to the editor that was scheduled to be published. He kept talking about the letter (concerning some ludicrously trivial matter) until

I was ready to scream or walk out. After a period of long silence, he looked up at me, finally realizing the absurdity of the situation; he smiled and said, "Can you imagine what the readers would say if they could see me now; if they knew that this is the way that Hugh Hefner really spends his time?"

As late as 1967, Spectorsky, who was then commanding a much higher salary than the President of the United States and was second in command over Playboy's entire publishing machine, controlling hundreds of employees and millions of dollars, had to secure Hefner's approval to order an engraved letterhead for one of *Playboy*'s new editors.

Hefner's perfectionism always manifested itself to those around him as a monumental display of distrust; it was responsible for the air of insecurity which affected even his most trusted and valuable coworkers and lieutenants. Perhaps Art Paul best described this insecurity when he said, in a somewhat diffident tone, "I've had my bags packed for twenty years."

Despite the internecine uncertainty, *Playboy*'s circulation continued to climb. *Esquire*'s publisher, Arnold Gingrich, relates in his book, *Nothing But People,* that in the mid-1950s he filled his briefcase with a batch of *Playboy* imitators—there were then over a dozen on the market—to study at home over a long Fourth of July weekend. He wanted to determine how he might keep *Esquire* separate and distinct from them and from *Playboy*. He decided to do away with *Esquire*'s pretty-girl gatefold and replace it with a sports star. John Smart, a principal owner of *Esquire*, said in an article in *The Wall Street Journal* at that time that they didn't "even want to be mentioned in the same article as *Playboy. Playboy* wants to be compared with us, but we don't feel we're in the same league."

Indeed, for nearly a decade *Esquire* pretended its chief competition did not exist by omitting *Playboy* from competitive advertising statistics. Ignorance refused to father bliss, however, as *Playboy*, with its soaring circulation, its constantly improving editorial content—made possible partly by paying the highest rates for writers in the industry—and its maturing photographic treatment of women, was burgeoning. Soon it became simply a better edited and more successful magazine than *Esquire*, and droves of readers responded by buying it. By January of 1959, after barely five years of publishing, *Playboy*'s circulation had reached 858,656, compared, ironically, to *Esquire*'s twenty-fifth-anniversary figure of 812,531. *Playboy* was also capturing a younger audience: 25 percent of all copies were sold on college campuses.

"*Playboy* is aimed editorially at a healthy, nonembarrassed approach to heterosexuality," Hefner proclaimed, rightly implying that *Esquire* had relinquished its position as patron of the art of sensuality. Hefner went on to say, "I'm not really certain what *Esquire* is today, but of one thing I'm reasonably sure—it isn't a men's magazine any longer, urban of otherwise, even though it still says "The Magazine For Men" on the cover and includes men's fashions on the inside. The *Esquire* Girls are gone—full pages, spreads and gatefolds —photographs, in black and white and color and the paintings by Vargas and Petty; the sophisticated cartoons are gone, too, that used to fill every issue; and so are most of the male-interest service features on various aspects of urban living. In their place is a wide range of literary stuff—much of it very good, but of equal interest to both sexes. And I'm quite certain that *Esquire*'s editors planned it that way—the pattern is too well established at this point for it not to have been."

As for *Playboy*'s competitors, Hefner felt they were barely competition at all and always referred to them as "imitators," pointing out that "they look like we did in our first year."

Hefner continued a strict and paradoxically puritanical policy of advertising acceptability, and as more and more advertisers wanted to purchase space, he turned down four or five ads for every one he accepted. Frederick's of Hollywood, for instance, a mail-order firm specializing in see-through lingerie and other exotica for women, was categorically refused acceptance time and again by Hefner because their advertising was what he considered inconsistent with the elitist image he was attempting to project. Hefner explained his policy this way:

"What makes an ad unacceptable in our eyes? Well, a wide variety of things—a viewpoint that seems in conflict with the concept of the magazine, ads of questionable taste, ads of questionable value, ads that sell too hard, or are unattractive or that do not compliment the *Playboy* reader—his intelligence, education, income level, taste, etc. . . . For example, we will not accept any ads for weight-reducing aids, earn money in your spare time, or the like. . . ."

The advertising picture for *Playboy* was hardly gloomy, however. In the beginning months of 1959, the magazine was charging $3,850 for a full black-and-white page, almost half of *Esquire*'s $6,150 rate, and for a higher circulation to boot. One of the most essential considerations in the purchase of advertising space is the cost per thousand readers, and *Playboy* was ahead of *Esquire* in that category also. A thousand *Playboy* readers could be reached for $4.48. It cost $7.57 to display a message to 1,000 readers of *Esquire*. All of this meant that *Playboy* had made a financial success of their desire to fill the editorial gap left by *Esquire*, and in a mere five years.

CHAPTER 7

"Where we're unique is that we're directly related to what many people see as part of their own identity."

Because of his rapidly increasing staff, in 1959 Hefner moved his offices from 11 East Superior Street to another location on the Near North Side: a red-brick, factory-like building at 232 East Ohio. Though small, *Playboy's* new quarters were substantially larger than those they were leaving. Hefner signed a long-term lease, allowing him to continue his love affair with Chicago, and put in over $500,000 in decorations and improvements. Several of Hefner's executives suggested that he should have moved the operation to New York to be in the midst of the publishing scene, with presumably more access to potential advertisers and available writers, artists, and photographers. He thought the idea preposterous, pointing out that *Playboy* was already beginning to enjoy top status as the most sucessful magazine in the Second City, whereas in New York it would just be "another" publication and, perhaps, hardly noticed. Spectorsky agreed with him and offered this further rationale: "I don't think *Playboy* could have succeeded in New York. We've been able to maintain our youthful, almost wide-eyed view of the world which would have probably ended the moment we packed ourselves East. Playboy would have become jaded, very quickly, by the nihilism of the Manhattan publishing scene."

For Hefner, moving into the new building marked the inception of a distinctive life-style that he had been maneuvering toward ever since he founded the magazine: elusiveness, constant variegation with women, eccentric work patterns, the obsession to enlarge upon what was becoming a small empire, and an intensity of work and play, supported by drugs, that would sometimes keep him going for as much as seventy-two hours on a frantic, nonstop merry-go-round.

Hefner once stated that he approached his work with a "bright flame," and one might demand, with reason, if he were not burning his candle at both ends. "I hate sleep," he told *Look* magazine. "I never have enough hours to do everything I want to do anyway. Sleep just makes me fall further behind." In addition to the twenty-four to thirty-six bottles of Pepsi-Cola that he chain-drank each day (containing enough caffeine to keep the most lethargic awake for days), he was introduced to amphetamines ("speed") by one of the other Playboy executives. To keep pace with his runaway world, he began taking Desoxyin and Dexedrine so that his mind and body would be better able to defeat the sleep he so bitterly resented. At first, Hefner only took the pills when something of supreme urgency required he forgo the rest he needed. As his corporation continued to expand, however, the one or two pills every night were replaced with several every night and finally with two or three each hour, even shortly after waking. His secretary became his pharmacist *pro tem-*

pore, handing him tablets as if they were letters for him to sign. He'd buzz his intercom for her to come in: "Hit me," he'd say, and she would provide him with a small paper cup of water and one or two pills. For a period of about two years he took the incredible and potentially destructive amount of thirty-five pills a day. There has been relatively little written about Hefner's use of drugs, mainly because he prefers not to talk about it.

Perhaps because of his well-known Homeric consumption of Pepsi-Cola, it is assumed, erroneously as it happens, that Hefner rarely if ever drinks anything stronger. Though he was never what could be called a problem drinker, in the days before the magazine began he was a fairly constant tippler, spending a good deal of time in a variety of Chicago bars, such as the Black Orchid, the Cloisters, and Trade-winds. He still consumes a fair amount of bourbon, to this day laced with the inevitable Pepsi. I've seen him drink as many as a half-dozen bourbons in one two-hour sitting. When I once commented on his ability to hold his liquor, he said, "When I'm drunk—bombed out of my head—people don't know it, because my personality doesn't markedly change—only really repressed people go through personality changes when they drink." Of course, the opposite can also be true: those who are so inhibited that they are fearful of exposure may repress the effects of alcohol in order to always appear sober.

Even those on *Playboy's* staff closest to Hefner believe that he is a near-teetotaler. One executive who was with the magazine for over fifteen years believed that Hefner "only took a drink when he had a cold," unaware that the Pepsi façade disguised the harder drink. The Playboy corporation, perhaps because of the fallacious belief that its top editor is motivated by temperance, is basically a nonalcoholic society: two drinks at lunch by *Playboy* editors is considered almost decadent. At the same time, an unbelievable amount of Pepsi-Cola is dutifully consumed by sycophants in the office and at the parties, a silent sacrifice and homage, albeit misdirected, to the Big Bunny himself. Only Kessie and Spectorsky, of Hefner's closest aides, openly regaled the pleasures and virtues of drink, both traditionally diving into a tank of martinis at any opportunity.

Hefner has avoided the psychedelics, even though he had eminent opportunities to partake of them when the high priests of the LSD culture, Leary and Alpert, were his house-guests on several occasions. Paul Krassner, known for his satirical—and often untrue—stories in *The Realist*, talked about a mammoth LSD trip that he went on with Hefner which simply never occurred. One of his closest friends once gave Hefner two acid tablets, which Hef stored in his bedroom refrigerator. A year later he asked Hef how he had enjoyed the experience. "I could never find the twelve hours necessary to go on the trip," he responded, returning the tablets. "Perhaps that's an indication of the psychological reservation that I have about taking it." Since virtually every American adult in the communications business below the age of fifty has tried marijuana, I leave it up to the imagination of the reader to determine Hefner's possible experience with that drug.

During the time of Hefner's most pronounced celerity—the late 1950s and early 1960s—his career as publisher-entrepreneur flourished perhaps more greatly that at any other period in his life. The more time he put into his businesses, the more they continued to grow, which in turn called for even more involvement. One project dovetailed into the other until Hefner had become so busy with his operations and with deals of every imaginable sort that, as he humbly said, he was more difficult to reach by phone than the President of the United States.

In the year ending June 30, 1960, newsstand sales of *Playboy* amounted to $3,006,268, while subscriptions generated $1,097,631. Products sold directly by the magazine to the deeply involved reader, most with the rabbithead emblem affixed, such as cuff links and cigarette lighters, added an additional revenue of $284,607. "Where we're unique is that we're directly related to what many people see as part of their own identity. You don't find this in *Time* or *The New Yorker*. Who would walk around with a *Newsweek* tie-clip or a *Life* golf putter?" quipped Hefner. Fast becoming a millionaire, he sought an additional status symbol and traded in his convertible Cadillac Eldorado for a white Mercedes-Benz 300 SL.

Hefner was not super-Midas, however. The idea of publishing his own humor magazine had been germinating in him for years, and in 1957 he published *Trump*, originally to be called *X*, edited by Harvey Kurtzman, one of the founders of *Mad*. It was a well-produced, satirical magazine, but because it originated from New York, Hefner could not exercise the total control (he was always referring to the necessity of having "tc," as he called it, over everything he did) he believed was necessary for its success. The magazine was distributed by American News Company. ANC was one of the largest newsstand distributors in the country, but they were also in great financial trouble, a fact of which Hefner was unaware when he signed the distribution contract. Shortly after the premiere issue of *Trump* was delivered to the newsstands in January, ANC went out of business, and for a period of approximately ninety days, until other distribution arrangements could be made, not only *Trump* but many of America's periodicals were seriously affected, their circulations stymied. This mishap plunged the magazine desperately into debt, almost before the first issue was off the stands. One more issue was published—March 1957—before Hefner blew the whistle, but not before he realized a loss of $95,000.

In 1959, Hefner decided to test his talents as a jazz concert entrepreneur and began making plans for one of the most ambitious jazz festivals ever held. Hefner was hardly a stranger to jazz. He listened to it constantly and had been a sympathetic follower almost all of his life. Hardly an issue of *Playboy* was published without an article on jazz or a personality profile of a musician. Hefner usually listened to jazz while he worked, and it was not unlikely to hear the sounds of Kenton, Brubeck, or Ellington emanating from his office.

The city of Chicago was sponsoring a Festival of Americas that summer, in connection with the Pan-American Games, and invited *Playboy* to hold its jazz spectacular in Soldier Field as part of the Pan-Am event. Then, after a joint press conference was held announcing the event and Hefner had signed more than $100,000 worth of contracts for the talent scheduled to appear, city officials unexpectedly withdrew their invitation and permission to use the field. The explanation given was that the jazz festival might harm the cinder track to be used for the Games. Hefner was incredulous and indignant, especially when he began to suspect that the real reason for the cancellation was the pressure brought to bear against *Playboy* because of its "reputation." In an interview in *Chicago's American*, the Very Reverend Msgr. John M. Kelly, editor of the Catholic *New World*, told a newsman that it was he who had brought the matter of *Playboy*'s reputation to the attention of the Park District, the Pan-American Games Committee, and Mayor Richard Daley. "Playboy is not a fit sponsor for such an event. The quality of the magazine is such, in my opinion, that it should not share in the sponsorship of any part of the Pan American Festival."

Soured but unflapped, Hefner rented the somewhat smaller but more expensive Chicago Stadium and defiantly held the spectacular there. Jazz buffs from all over the country and the world attended, and after the five scheduled performances were finished, nearly 70,000 people had listened to the giants of the art: Stan Kenton, Duke Ellington, Count Basie, Dave Brubeck, Oscar Peterson, Miles Davis, Dizzy Gillespie, Louis Armstrong, and Ella Fitzgerald, to name just some of the legendary names that performed. It was the most successful meeting of musicians in the sixty-year history of jazz.

Hefner thumbed his own nose at Chicago's blue ones, while handing a check for $101,476 (opening night proceeds) to the Urban League, although he suffered an overall loss on the concert of $40,000.

Had the concert been held in Soldier Field, Hefner would have probably broken even, but conversely, *Playboy* received immense national publicity (over 200 reporters attended), publicity which would have cost ten times Hefner's loss if he had attempted to purchase it.

Toward the end of 1959, Hefner decided to host his own television show, *Playboy's Penthouse*, his motivation to reach a wider public with the Playboy "story" than was possible by other forms of promotion. He also hoped to overcome his image problem: to prove to people—mainly potential advertisers—that the magazine was not just a dirty book and that he was not Beelzebub incarnate.

The show was a potpourri of talk and musical entertainment that took place on a set designed to resemble the type of swinging bachelor pad featured in the magazine. The tuxedoed Hefner, in this case, was the bachelor-host, and viewers were urged to join the party that took place in his penthouse each week. "Good evening," said Hef. "I'm Hugh Hefner. Welcome to the party." Celebrities dropped by, and gorgeous looking girls, many of them Playmates, adorned the show.

Since Hefner is not an actor, his performance was lifeless, overly nervous—a cardboard caricature of a playboy. He didn't know what to do with his hands; he provided himself with a pipe, even though he had never smoked one before, and the prop became a real addition to his way of life. He sucked madly and loudly at the tobaccoless pipe whenever he was on camera and having difficulties. On his first show, he had Spectorsky as a guest (also Lenny Bruce, Rona Jaffe,

Ella Fitzgerald, and Nat King Cole), and though Spec, because of his television background with NBC, was more than capable of trading quips with anyone, Hefner was not. The result was that Spectorsky came off as the suave publisher-playboy that Hefner was trying unsuccessfully to be. He never invited Spectorsky to return.

Everyone suggested to Hefner that he hire a professional actor as host, but he adamantly refused. Years later he commented on that decision in an interview with Joe Goldberg:

It never hurt the show, if one understood clearly why the show existed. It might have hurt it in terms of its pure flow and technical competence and entertainment value, but since the purpose of the show was to reach a broader audience and let them know what we were all about and what *Playboy* was all about, the more personal we made it, the more successful it would be in doing that. If we brought in a very sophisticated host—the best in the world, Cary Grant—and created this thing, all it would really prove was that we had taste or we had enough money to buy someone who had taste. But if we did the thing ourselves, and the viewers could meet us as a human being every week, then hopefully they would begin to discover, those people who did not read *Playboy*, well, son of a gun, this guy isn't a dirty old man, young or old. Little by little, a slow eroding away of any misconception of what *Playboy* was really all about. Now that was the purpose, and remains the purpose, of the TV show.

The show ran for twenty-six weeks and cost well over a quarter of a million dollars to produce, though some income was generated as a result of its syndication. (At its height, it was aired in thirty cities in the U.S. and Canada.) Hefner felt, however, that the show had accomplished what he had set out to do with it: improve *Playboy*'s image. "It's difficult to pick out any single thing that we've done that's more valuable," he averred.

To cope with his pursuit of tycoonism, Hefner had a specially designed office constructed on the top floor of the

Playboy headquarters at 232 East Ohio. It also served as a bachelor apartment and, like the Mansion, enabled him to stay in one environment for days on end, without ever venturing outside. The office contained a wall of electronic sound equipment; modern furniture by Herman Miller, Knoll, Eames; opaque, oriental-type screens that blocked out a view from the street; and an adjoining bath, small kitchen, and bedroom. A separate entrance to a side street made it possible for him to come and go as he pleased, on those rare occasions when he did leave the building, without being seen by overly curious and possibly gossiping employees. His only physical exercise, except for what went on in the bedroom, was a daily balancing act that he would perform on a bongo board, while dictating directives to his secretary. He and Victor Lownes each rented an apartment on the top floor of a charming brownstone on one of Chicago's most distinguished thoroughfares, Astor Street, but Hefner never could find the time to move in. He failed to spend one single night in his new apartment and eventually sublet it.

Due mainly to his losses with *Trump* and as a result of a short, national recession which affected *Playboy's* advertising projections and newsstand sales (from a customary 80 percent sale to an all-time low of 56 percent). Hefner was forced for a short time in 1957 to stop drawing a personal salary. All top executives were given a 25 percent salary cut, and some employees were laid off.

Hefner believed that this first major "rainy day" period for *Playboy* would be a short one. He contended that his business was a sound and growing operation and that his cash shortage was merely temporary, one that would abate quickly. His analysis would prove to be correct, but for the moment he needed a short-term loan of a quarter of a million dollars to tide the magazine over until sales regenerated.

Hefner was astounded and embittered when his bank, the American National Bank and Trust Company of Chicago, refused to grant him the loan. He had given that institution millions of dollars of business each year and had been dealing with them from the magazine's inception. To add to the sting, the bank's officers, wary that *Playboy* had overextended itself, decided overnight to arbitrarily rescind a previously arranged credit line of $100,000, a decision which took a pressing situation and ignited it into a crucial one. It sent Hefner into a rage. "It was made with neither depth or accuracy," he wrote to the bank's president. "It was a mistake." Offering to sign for the note personally, in addition to assuming the corporate obligation, did nothing to reverse the bank's decision.

Though other banks and loan institutions were approached, none would lend Hefner the money he needed. For a short time the future of the magazine was in doubt, though never in actual jeopardy. Eventually, he was forced to put up 50 percent of the stock of the company to Empire News as collateral for a ninety-day loan of $250,000 and at an interest rate that Hefner described as exorbitant.

Though there were a few weeks of concern on Hefner's part as to whether he could repay the money, he claimed that he never seriously doubted that it would be forthcoming. The newsstand sales for the next two issues increased steadily, as did the advertising lineage, and the debt was liquidated in its entirety within the ninety-day period, and the terms of the loan renegotiated. If a new basis had not been arranged, Hefner stated that it might have cost him "many of millions of dollars." It still cost the Playboy corporation $50,000 and a mandatory renewal of *Playboy*'s newsstand circulation contract for a period of ten years. Empire took its $50,000 interest in shares of stock in the corporation in lieu of the payment owed.

Hefner learned a bitter lesson from this incident which greatly affected his business philosophy, one that he would follow throughout his career. It was exemplified in cutting back on his own salary and also in his constant reinvestment of almost all of the profits back into the corporation. *Collier's* had failed due to the exact opposite operational procedure: large amounts of money were drawn out as profits and virtually no funds were ploughed back into the business. Hefner learned that during a period of rapid growth as much money as possible should be earmarked for elevating *Playboy* to a position where it would experience the security of a solid corporate foundation. And as a safeguard against a repetition of such traumatic financial emergencies, he began building a cash surplus to meet as many eventualities as possible.

In addition to his provident, near conservative business posture, Hefner employed another technique repeatedly: the combination of his pursuit of individual pleasures with specific promotions or editorial features. For example, the large amount of money he expended in having his office-apartment designed and furnished seemed trivial when compared to the attention his quarters received by the media. Articles about Hefner usually referred to his posh office; the fact that such an office existed helped to generate more stories and pictorials in the general press. The office was also used frequently for articles that appeared in *Playboy* itself, as a model of the ideal work-play environment for the cosmopolitan executive that the magazine so energetically advanced.

Gradually Hefner's life-style and the very ambience of *Playboy* became inexorably intertwined; whether it be a party he hosted, a wardrobe he purchased, or a secret resort he discovered, the end result was a synthesis of the personal and the promotional.

To the public, Hefner was the playboy that the magazine kept describing, and this personal image, largely genuine though sometimes apocryphal, eventually became a crucial element in helping him elevate his corporation to the level of success it has ultimately attained.

It was not only *Playboy*'s readers who identified with Hefner, however, or who longed to live the type of urban, sophisticated, and sensual life that was implied as his routine. Often *Playboy* executives and editors and many of its writers, photographers, artists, printers, advertisers, suppliers, and others who came in contact with the *Playboy*-Hefner life-style also frequently bought the fantasy of the Good Life. Working for or doing business with *Playboy* became an instant status symbol, and to many, direct contact with Hefner himself assumed the importance and prestige of a papal audience.

Hefner became more and more "unavailable" to all of those who were trying avidly to reach him. Most of his mail was acted upon and answered by others: Lownes took all the promotional offers, Spectorsky handled most editorial matters, and Robert S. Preuss, the Cagney-like accountant who had been Hefner's roommate at school and who had joined *Playboy* as business manager and controller, became intimately involved in all of the many business offers and deals that were presented to *Playboy* almost daily.

None of this diffusion of responsibility meant that Hefner was abandoning control of his operation; he still insisted on approving the most minute editorial detail, and any business decision approaching near-major importance was submitted to him before action was taken.

Hefner labored over the editing of the magazine and demanded such slavish dedication to perfection from his editors and contributors that he made Captain Ahab appear benign. Every item that finally saw print in *Playboy*, from the color of the lower eyelash of Little Annie Fanny to a misplaced semicolon in an article on abortion, was agonized over by Hefner. A memo dated January 8, 1958 to Spectorsky from Hefner, for example, of a review of the book *How to Succeed with Women* contained the following subtle observation:

The first sentence of the review of *How to Succeed with Women* has me thoroughly puzzled and yet I'm sure this was read and re-read and proofread, so it must be correct. Shouldn't it read, "The hip, hilarious series *has.* . . ." Doesn't the word "series"

136

take the singular, the same as *group* or *collection* or any similar noun? I recognize that the word "series" can be either singular or plural, but it is hard for me to understand how it can be used in the plural here. . . . I would be interested in the fine line that made this plural.

Words, colors, cartoons, and photos were all given the special brand of Hefner diagnostic approval or condemnation, and *Playboy* was not printed until he felt it was perfect in every aspect.

Because of this rigidity, Hefner became the magazine's most effective bottleneck, and when an article, feature or detail touched upon an area in which he had some personal interest, the changes, editing, and revisions went on interminably.

Before *Playboy* ran a personality profile of Frank Sinatra, one of Hefner's favorite superstars (". . . he is the absolutely perfect man for a profile by us," he said in a memo to his staff), written by the late Robert Reisner, it was rewritten by Richard Gehman, rewritten twice again by Jack Olsen and finally rewritten two more times by Hefner himself. All this had to be done before he felt satisfied enough with it to send it to the printer, desperately late and as a result costing thousands of dollars extra in overtime. And when Jules Feiffer submitted his cartoon-story, "The Lonely Machine," Hefner accepted it, but not without first sending Feiffer a nine-page, single-spaced typewritten memo on how it could be improved, suggesting everything from rearrangement of panels and the revision of dialogue to the reworking of the drawings themselves. Feiffer complied and was thankful for the lesson: "Hefner is the best cartoon editor in America," he said.

Fiction was the only area where Hefner relinquished his control, allowing Spectorsky the right not only to purchase it without approval (with the exception of very large contracts, such as Ian Fleming's short novel, *The Man With the Golden Gun,* for $45,000) and with hardly ever a critical Monday-morning memorandum. It soon became obvious to the staff that not only did Hefner have no interest in some of the great short stories that were being published in his own magazine, but when asked his opinion of some of them, he usually indicated that he had never read the piece. The reason for this disinterest could have been a combination of Hefner's faith that Spectorsky could function better as a fiction editor than he, being too busy to become involved in fiction, and, simply, his dislike of reading it. Some people have described Hefner as bibliophobic, and though it's true that he reads not more than a few books a year, he is a voracious reader of magazines and newspapers.

Hefner was proud of his other skills, however, not only as a copy editor, but also in his ability to generate ideas for new articles and features month after month. He has also given his staff credit for their abilities. In his diary he noted that he had brought his own writing and editorial skills to *Playboy,* and added to them the equal or greater talents of others. He felt this combination created the most successful magazine of his time.

Not all of Hefner's editors shared his high regard for his own editorial aptitude. Ray Russell, perhaps soured by the fact that he was passed over for the job as editorial director, was particularly outspoken about what he considered to be Hefner's lack of editorial skills and told a reporter that Hefner's use of words had the "sophistication of Dennis the Menace." When Hefner heard about this remark (long after Russell had left *Playboy,* though he was still freelancing for it), he shot back a four-page letter to Russell defending himself and displaying a sensitivity that has a refreshing quality to it. The following are excerpts from that letter:

I really don't mind the "sophistication of Dennis the Menace" crack, but attempting to create the illusion that I was not personally responsible in large part for the early editorial excellence of *Playboy* is really hitting below the belt. When you worked here . . . we had our occasional disagreements about writing style, word usage, and that sort of thing—and if, as boss, I always won those disagreements, it certainly didn't make me believe that I was always right. But right or wrong, I *had* to trust my own judgement about words, phrases and style, as well as ideas, point of view or over-all subject matter itself. And whether I was right or wrong, whatever *Playboy* became editorially was what I felt it ought to be. And your suggestion that I am sadly lacking in writing and editorial skills, but fortunately had good sense to hire others of talent to do the job, is really a bit of subjective bullshit. . . .

It may somehow feed your ego to think of me as sort of the illiterate Mike Todd of publishing, with a flair for promotion and graphics, while casting yourself in the role of the fellow who gave *Playboy* its early stamp of editorial excellence, but we both know that I was very personally involved in all the text in the magazine during those early years, and that I didn't let go of any specific editorial part of the magazine until I was completely convinced it would carry itself, in the way I wanted it, without my continuing personal attention. It was this very reluctance to let go of specific editorial parts of the magazine, which caused so much of the falling behind in deadlines, so no one with any memory at all can seriously suggest that I was not personally in-volved—to the fullest extent—in the actual editing of *Playboy*, all through those beginning years.

You may have felt, as you once stated, that when I edited your copy—changing a word, or a phrase, or an entire paragraph —that I invariably replaced a fresh and telling word with one that was dull and lifeless, and I may have felt that your reactions presented a writer's understandable pique at having any part of his "beloved prose" altered, but we both know that I was very much involved, and the slightest intonation that I was out front taking bows and waving to the members of the press, TV and radio, while talented ones really turned out the magazine in a back room, is fantasy of the most extreme form.

Yes, I may occasionally misuse a word. Most of us do. And for an editor, I'm not exceptionally well read. Despite what you apparently like to believe, my ability as a writer goes a bit beyond copy for, "Alone with Lisa";* and my ability as an editor goes quite a way beyond my ability as a writer. Ken Purdy's article, "Hypnosis," in the February 1961 issue, offers a pretty good example of both capabilities, since I took a very uneven and confused first draft, and thoroughly rewrote and edited it into its final, excellent, I think, form.

After making a reference to its being difficult "to feel either warmth or friendship—to feel anything at all, in fact, except hurt or anger," toward Russell, Hefner warned him that if he valued his friendship, he had better think before he speaks to reporters the next time. In a separate explanatory note to Spectorsky and Kessie, with an attached blind carbon of his letter, Hefner stated that "it is bad enough when a guy lashes out at you for no particular reason, except to appear smart in front of people, but when you get a shot from someone closer to you, it is really a drag. I guess I'm just getting tired of people who, as human beings, take more than they give back."

---

* A trite and saccharine story in the December 1957 issue of *Playboy* of a shy Playmate written—but not by-lined—by Hefner.

CHAPTER 8

"We have reached a state of maturity in this country where our courts and literary critics agree that any subject is permissible, and any situation can be described, if it is done with taste and care."

HEFNER's failure to read the fiction in his magazine occasionally lead to complications. There is a possibility that had he carefully perused a piece of fiction called "Bus Story," written by novelist Calder Willingham, which appeared in the July 1962 issue, he might have elected not to publish it or at least been prepared for the insuing furor it caused. The story sparked an immense controversy that temporarily rocked Hefner's position with his readers, advertisers, and distributors.

"Bus Story" tells of a brutal encounter between a seventeen-year-old girl and an older man who sits next to her on a long bus ride. She's a virgin and he's a sexually cynical, almost psychotic, cad. During the night, while all the other passengers are sleeping, he manages, by way of slick talk, lies, and playing on the girl's inexperienced vulnerability, to remove her panties and finger her to orgasm. When the bus stops for a dinner break the next day, he violently deflowers her in a back room—some might describe the process as rape—and then coldly contemptuous to her now-defenseless need for comfort, catalogs her statistics in his little black book and treats her with ruthless disdain.

Though the synopsis of the plot, while admittedly depressing, can hardly be considered outrageously shocking, it was Willingham's description of the sexual scenes that incensed the Comstockery:

Harry had spread his raincoat over his and the girl's laps like a blanket. He held her wrist in an iron grip with his left hand. "Oh, please," whispered the girl. "Don't anymore." In a futile effort at escape, the plump buttocks that straddled his wrist lifted again from the seat, gluteus maximi contracted and firm. He held fast, middle finger uplifted and hand spread as if supporting her; then a strained trembling in mid-air, and helpless soft descent. "Oh, this is so wicked," she whispered. . . .

Even now, lying on the bed with Harry half across her, the girl obviously did not realize exactly what was happening. Nervous and frightened though she was, nevertheless she responded to his kisses, as she had done on the bus. Two minutes later, not more than five minutes after they first entered the little bedroom, her dress was high above her waist and suddenly it dawned on her that an incredible thing was about to happen. It was practically happening! What could she do?

"Tom, please," she whispered. "We can't."

"Move your knees," he replied, in a strange voice.

"I can't! Please!"

There are times to be tender and there are times to be just a little bit rough. This was a time to be just a little rough. Left forearm heavily across her breasts and left hand gripping her shoulder so hard she winced, Harry used his knee like a wedge, gray eyes hypnotic above her. *"Open your legs,"* he said in a cold, harsh and vicious tone. Lips apart and eyes empty with shock,

142

the girl did as she was told. A moment later, hands limp on his shoulders, a gasp came from her. Then, another gasp. . . .

Actually, the story is perceptively written and by today's standards of what is publishable sexually, it might even appear somewhat corny. But a large segment of people other than *Playboy* editors felt it was, at the very least, in poor taste. For some it went beyond the bounds of morality; for others it breeched what they considered to be the limits of legality.

Though there were some favorable reactions, hundreds of readers wrote to the magazine complaining that it was "disgusting" or that reading it had made them "sick." The advertising community, and hence *Playboy's* advertising department, protested to Hefner that he had gone too far: the Ford Motor Company and Hart, Shaffner, and Marx were just two of the corporations that threatened to withdraw any further consideration of *Playboy* as an advertising medium.

John M. Tyson, Jr., a vice-president of Batten, Barton, Durstine, and Osborn, sent Hefner a strongly worded letter indicating that both his clients and his agency firmly contended that "Bus Story" was "absolutely nothing but a dirty story in print."

The president of Independent News, Paul H. Sampliner, then principal newsstand distributor for *Playboy*, reported that a number of newsstand wholesalers simply refused to carry the July issue because of "Bus Story" and though he would "defend the story publicly on all fronts, I must take issue with it privately." That issue of the magazine had been banned from Fort Dix, New Jersey as being unfit reading for the military men stationed there, Sampliner pointed out indignantly.

The attorney general of the state of Iowa, Evan Hultman, had the July issue of *Playboy* banned from sale in all places throughout the state and in a personal letter to Hefner said he believed that the story "violated every standard of moral decency and was of the type that appealed to the maladjusted and perverted within our society." He strongly warned Hefner that "this type of material contained within *Playboy* magazine will not go unnoticed and will not be permitted to come into this State unchallenged."

Even Preuss complained to Hefner that circulation had dipped for the July issue and he was concerned over what effect this story would have on the entire future of the magazine. A late-night meeting was held including Spectorsky, Preuss, Hefner, and *Playboy*'s corporate attorneys to determine what their next action should be. Hefner admitted that he had not read the story before it was published, but that he would, of course, personally support Spectorsky in his selection of it.

It didn't matter, however, that he was unfamiliar with the story, Hefner contended. First of all, he believed in the judgment and sense of his editors, and secondly, he stated, he was against any type of censorship; though the advertisers and agencies and distributors and readers could not legally stop him from publishing his magazine, by their actions they were in effect doing just that. He did eventually read "Bus Story" but felt, as does Supreme Court Justice William O. Douglas, that it is not necessary to read any particular work to determine its obscene content; if one is opposed to all types of censorship, then it matters not whether the material is "pornographic."

Though Hefner believed the arguments of the would-be censors to be synthetic and their threats without substance, he realized that if just a few advertisers began to withdraw from *Playboy*, others might conceivably follow the pattern. Much finesse, persuasion, talent, and energy had gone into securing many of the prestige advertisers that were in the same issue as "Bus Story"—the P. Lorillard Company, British Motor Corporation, American Tobacco Company, Triumph sports cars, Gordon's gin, American

Honda Motor Co.—and Hefner was loathe to do anything that would jeopardize these relationships.

He composed a reasonable rebuttal statement that was sent to all the people who wrote to him and suggested to the advertisers who still disagreed that they permit him to meet with them personally and talk directly about the situation. This was one of the few times that Hefner agreed to meet directly with his advertisers. For the most part, he was inaccessible.

After pointing out the dangers of censorship and the fact that Willingham's book *Eternal Fire,* from which "Bus Story" was extracted, had received rave reviews (". . . must be mentioned if one is to speak of greatness in American fiction" [*Newsweek*]), Hefner stated in *Playboy:* "Nothing excuses the printing of trash, but we must all recognize that "trash" describes the quality of writing in a story, and not the theme or plot of it. No particular aspect of personal experience, no idea, no situation is in itself taboo or objectionable. We have reached a state of maturity in this country where our courts and our literary critics agree that any subject is permissible, and any situation can be described, if it is done with taste and care."

After publishing supporting letters from such science-fiction literary lights as Theodore Sturgeon, who described "Bus Story" as "erotic realism" rather than pornography, and William Tenn, who claimed somewhat overenthusiastically that its publication made him feel "proud" to be an American, the controversy began to abate. When it was finally realized that publication of the story would not turn men into uncontrollable sex fiends roaming the streets raping the fair and the innocent, and that the very existence of the story in the midst of our society wouldn't corrupt the American populace nor affect its pocketbooks by selling it less products through the advertising medium of *Playboy* magazine, the whole *megillah* was finally forgotten, and no specific legal action was ever taken against Hefner for its publication.

145

Playboy's reputation as a magazine for publishing articles other than those that titilate, however, began to grow, and readers were beginning to receive an education in areas other than just sexual. Seventy-five percent of most issues was devoted to editorial features (as opposed to advertising), making *Playboy* one of the most generous magazines in the country as far as the ratio of editorial-to-advertising is concerned. It is not uncommon now for *Playboy* to spend over a quarter of million dollars for the artwork, photos, and text for a single issue, and a large percentage of the material is nonsexual in content. The January 1970 issue consisted of the following features, many of them classic magazine pieces by some of the world's foremost writers:

Playboy
January 1970

Feature	Cost
1. Cover	$ 1,200.00
2. Playbill	1,892.15
3. Playboy After Hours	4,090.00
4. Interview: Raquel Welch	3,072.30
5. "Thomas in Elysium": fiction by Irwin Shaw	10,500.00
6. "Classic Comebacks": modern living	2,812.16
7. "A Recluse and His Guest": fiction by Tennessee Williams	4,500.00
8. "The Most Unforgettable Swordsman": humor by Art Buchwald	3,600.00
9. "The Americanization of Vietnam": article by David Halberstam	3,300.00
10. "Roman Revel": modern living	13,551.28
11. "For Christ's Sake": opinion by Harvey Cox	2,700.00
12. "European Fashion Dateline": attire by Robert L. Green	7,349.11
13. "That Was The Year That Was": humor by Judith Wax	2,875.00
14. "Bring Us Together": articles by U.S. Senator George McGovern ("Reconciling the Gen-	

erations"), Cesar Chavez ("Sharing the Wealth"), Julian Bond ("Uniting the Races"), and Tom Wicker ("Forging a Left-Right Coalition")   12,475.13

15. "The Good, the Bad & the Garlic": satire by Harvey Kurtzman   19,341.72
16. "Charmed by a Snake": humor by Mort Sahl   2,600.00
17. "Crook's Tour": fiction by Graham Greene   7,671.19
18. "Sunny Girl": playmate of the month, Jill Tewksbury   9,780.97
19. *Playboy*'s Party Jokes: humor   1,125.00
20. "Playboy Plans a Duplex Penthouse"   10,185.00
21. "Points of Rebellion": article by Justice William O. Douglas   4,400.00
22. " 'Beauty Trap' Beauty": pictorial   1,939.90
23. "The Past as Future: A Nonlinear Probe": opinion by Jacob Brackman   7,088.00
24. "The Mourner": fiction by Bruce Jay Friedman   3,800.00
25. "Zinsmeister & the Eighter From Decatur": humor by Jean Shepherd   4,600.00
26. "Marco Roly-Poly Meets the East": humor by Robert Morley   2,700.00
27. "Our Besieged Bill of Rights": article by The Hon. Arthur J. Goldberg   4,000.00
28. "Vargas Revisited": nostalgia   1,882.70
29. "Morocco—Man at His Leisure": by Leroy Neiman   3,401.95
30. "The Girl & the Shark": ribald classic   1,100.00
31. "Alphabets Noires": humor by J. B. Handelsman   4,500.00
32. "Little Annie Fanny": satire by Harvey Kurtsman and Will Elder   9,750.00
33. Other features, cartoons, etc. under $1,000.00 each   19,920.76
    TOTAL $193,704.32

Hefner continued to live the kind of existence where "working hard and playing hard" became standard operating procedure. The pursuit of women consumed a tremendous portion of his time and was constantly vying for his attention with his role of editor-publisher. "Romance is one of the most important motivations in my life, to an extent that nobody really knows or understands," he once told me, his voice taking on a seriousness that convinced me he was sincere. It is intriguing to take a glimpse at the types of women that Hefner has become involved with since starting the magazine and separating from Millie. They have all been young, in most cases marvelously pretty, and nothing short of voluptuous. In addition, almost all of Hefner's girl friends have worked for the magazine, and many have been centerfold Playmates. In fact, Hefner has made a ritual of meeting and usually dating the twelve Playmates who come to Chicago each year to be photographed by *Playboy*.

The girls are met at the airport by a limousine and proceed to be treated like royalty. Hefner is given a copy of their schedule and he makes an attempt to meet each girl at least once during the week that she spends at *Playboy*. Very often, if the chemistry is right, the meeting develops into a semipermanent liaison. Hefner has boasted that the girls he has been most attracted to and those whom he has been most successful with are often the same ones *Playboy's* readers select as the most popular Playmates. It is most probable that Hefner has made love to more beautiful women than any other man in history, making the legendary Casanova appear diffident and shy by comparison.

But aside from the relationships he establishes with multitudinous females, Hefner has always had one favorite girl at any given time, a practice dating back to his high school days. Soon after starting *Playboy*, Hefner went with a young and insouciant Chicago charmer, a bosomy girl who worked in *Playboy's* personnel records department. When that relationship began to deteriorate for no apparent reason, Hefner sent her on a trip to Europe, picking up all of her travel expenses, naturally, while he began to establish a rapport with another favorite, a teenager named Joyce.

When Hefner first met Joyce in 1958, she was an eighteen-year-old model from Miami, Florida, desperately looking for work in Chicago. A stunning girl with black hair and dark eyes, she greatly resembled a less ethereal Jennifer Jones. Hefner first made a cover girl of her in the July 1958 issue and then uncovered her—in the December 1959 issue—as a centerfold Playmate. Until the mid-1960s, Joyce continued to appear in the pages of *Playboy*—her picture appeared over two dozen times—and it seemed that Hefner was attempting to make her a special brand of *Playboy* "star," much the same thing William Randolph Hearst did with Marion Davies by giving her so much exposure. After Hef's divorce from Millie, Joyce optimistically thought that her relationship with him would eventually lead to marriage. Apparently, marriage was the last thing he had on his mind. He told Paul Krassner: "I don't want my editors marrying anyone and getting a lot of foolish notions in their heads about 'togetherness,' home, family and all that jazz," perhaps applying this philosophy to himself as well. On other occasions, however, Hefner has elaborated on his sentimental feelings toward mariage. In a letter to Cleveland Amory complaining about being misquoted in Amory's column, he wrote: "I confessed to being a romantic and a sentimentalist, which I consider to be synonymous with our magazine's view of the world (or our playboy's view, if you will). I never said, and cannot understand how you could have thought I said 'romance and marriage are . . . deadly enemies.' What I said was, that unfortunately romance and marriage are not synonymous, and that marriage without romance is a sad, sad affair. You've turned it into an anti-marriage statement, that I never made." Nevertheless, Joyce eventually abandoned all hope of ever marrying Hefner and finally left him, though they have remained close—though geographically distant—friends.

Cynthia, a green-eyed, eighteen-year-old redhead who was known for her customarily audacious décolletage, became a receptionist-secretary for *Playboy* at about the same time Hefner was ending his relationship with Joyce. Both girls were friends for awhile, and then Cynthia slowly stepped into what she apparently considered the highly coveted position, the queen consort of Hugh Hefner. She felt flattered that Hefner had singled her out, since he had so many women to choose from. It strengthened her self-image, something she needed desperately, and she fell deeply in love with him. Cynthia adorned the cover of *Playboy* five times, and like her predecessor, appeared constantly in other pictorials and advertisements—in many of them she was half nude. She never agreed to become a Playmate, probably due to some irrational lack of confidence in herself: her body (38-22-36) and face were of the type that Hefner usually selected for the girl in the centerfold. Cynthia was seen with Hefner whenever he appeared in public, and she, too, believed their relationship would eventually develop into a permanent one of the marital kind. Most of their time together, however, was spent in Hefner's apartment. They watched Charlie Chaplin movies and listened to Jeanette MacDonald and Nelson Eddy records. "I don't know how real it was," she said in an interview in *Life*, "but it was beautiful just sitting there sighing."

Contrary to rumors, Hefner's relationships with women have all been fairly typical affairs with the exception of the fact that they all contain the May-December element.

"For one thing, I simply find them more attractive physically than women my own age," Hefner said of the teenagers he has become involved with. "There's also something nice about an affair that's the first serious relationship in a girl's life; it permits you to recapture your own early romantic responses. It's a way of holding onto your youth and the enthusiasm you first felt about life and love."

Though he's often been criticized as regarding women as objects, merely accessories to the good life along with the right sports car, stereo, and penthouse apartment, Hefner contends that those adversaries who hold this view "miss the whole point of what *Playboy* is all about."

Hefner is a sensitive romantic, as all his girl friends will attest, and though he usually remains in control, he is, according to them, a thoughtful, generous, and sympathetic lover. He told interviewer Larry DuBois in the twentieth-anniversary issue of *Playboy:* "More than wealth and power and whatever other primary motivations most men have, what lights my fire is my romantic relationships with women." He has always been direct about his embargo on remarriage. "I have the advantage of being preceded by my reputation, which announces that I'm not apt to be getting married in the near future and that my life-style isn't apt to dramatically change as a result of any new relationship. So, in most cases, a girl has different expectations with me than she might with another man, and that makes it easier for me to avoid disappointing her."

It should be pointed out that Hefner made these statements in 1973, more than fifteen years after starting the relationships heretofore mentioned, and that his "reputation" as a confirmed bachelor had not yet been established in his own mind and not to mention the minds and hearts of Betty, Joyce, and Cynthia.

Eventually, Cynthia began to understand that although she found being Hefner's mistress a fascinating position, it wasn't leading her where she wanted to be. Occasionally they would argue. She retaliated against Hefner's "devouring her words" by running around his office stepping on layouts, photos, and cartoons. "Trampling his work was a great outlet for me," she told *Life.* "It seemed like I could destroy it. He was furious."

Despite their contretemps, Hefner promoted her to assistant cartoon editor, a position which she carried out with a certain amount of flair as she developed a friendly rapport with many of the country's leading cartoonists. Her name showed up once in a cartoon by John Dempsey as "Cynox

Maddthia," and Alberto Vargas used a photo of her as a model for one of his voluptuous pinups that appeared in the April 1966 issue. Hefner was her direct boss—he functioned as *Playboy*'s cartoon editor—and that was one of the major reasons Cynthia was given the job as his assistant. She would screen the hundreds of unsolicited cartoons the magazine received weekly, make a selection, and bring them to Hefner for his approval. They worked more closely together, and she didn't have to report to anyone else, a previous source of strife among his executives and employees. She took advantage of her position in any event, ostentatiously arriving at the office late in the afternoon and usually leaving early, and sometimes not appearing for days on end. Most of the time in her office was spent absentmindedly twirling her hair while staring into space. She rarely deigned to talk to other employees, and when she did, it was in a breathless, Marie Wilson whisper of attractive confusion. No one, not even Spectorsky, felt he could fire Hefner's girl friend, so her eccentric hours were tolerated.

Cynthia became more and more bewildered about her position at *Playboy* and by the manner in which the other employees reacted toward her. Basically they liked her, but she could never really believe it. "I really don't know how I feel," she told author Studs Terkel in an interview he did of her, under an assumed name, in *Division Street: America*. "I'm nice and cordial but people sense something about me. I don't know, maybe I don't like them. Maybe I feel I'm above them."

She became especially perplexed by her ongoing affair with Hefner and began consulting a psychiatrist. Hefner and she finally stopped their relationship, though she continued working for the magazine for some time. "I can't afford to quit," she once told me, "because then, if I do, I won't be able to afford to continue going to the 'shrink.' Someday I'd like to be able to figure out what went wrong with my relationship with Hef." Cynthia was replaced by

Mary, a regal-looking, Grace Kellyish blonde with a delightfully abandoned laugh, who started working for *Playboy* as the "Door Bunny" at the Chicago Playboy Club and finally transferred to the magazine's personnel department. She was intelligent, friendly, and, by attrition, acted as Hefner's hostess and Woman of the House, a role she performed with efficiency and good taste. They lived together for over five years, and all of Hefner's friends and associates predicted eventual marriage. A playpen was set up in Hefner's apartment for his not-so-small Saint Bernard puppy whom Mary christened "Baby," with her and Hefner acting as "mommy" and "daddy." But Hefner would not be tempted into the real thing. Like the other women before her, Mary also exited when the fact that there was no hope of marriage became evident. For a short while after she moved out, Hefner tried courting her but finally gave up. She married a surgeon six months after leaving him.

In 1961, Hefner became involved in his third publishing venture, *Show Business Illustrated,* and though it was certainly more successful and ambitious than *Trump,* the two publications suffered from two of the same problems: Hefner's failure to choose an editorial staff he could work effectively with and his inability to free himself from his day-to-day Playboy tasks so that he could find the time needed for a new venture.

Though the idea for a show-business magazine had intrigued Hefner for years, it was Frank Sinatra who served as his catalyst. In the fall of 1960, Sinatra was Hefner's houseguest, and the two men talked of starting a show-business newspaper—more graphically attractive and less industry-oriented than *Variety*—to be published out of Hollywood. Hefner was not certain, nor was Sinatra, that they could establish a workable and nonexplosive arrangement which could accommodate their supercharged egos, but after their meeting Hefner was convinced his own next magazine venture would be a consumer magazine on show business, and, as he noted in his diary, it would have all the fun, the drama, the color, and the excitement of show business itself.

He approached the publishing of this new magazine in a considerably more relaxed fashion than he had when he began *Playboy* seven and a half years earlier, and that complacency could very well have been one of the major factors behind the troubles the magazine finally experienced.

When *Show Business Illustrated* rolled off the presses for the first time in August 1961, it carried a cover price of fifty cents, making it, at that time, the most expensive biweekly magazine in publishing history. The first issue carried some fifty pages of advertising and offered advertisers a guaranteed circulation of 350,000.

Hefner imported a staff of professionals from New York to Chicago. They included Frank Gibney, who had been with *Life* and *Newsweek,* as *SBI*'s editorial director and assistant publisher and Leonard Jossel, who had been art director for the book division of Time, Inc. and assumed the same position at *SBI*.

Hefner issued a memorandum of editorial style and procedure to his new staff, some extracts from which follow:

SHOW BUSINESS ILLUSTRATED will bring all the thrills, the excitement, the humor, the pathos, the color and glamour of show business right into the home in the very pages of the magazine itself. Excitement is the word—excitement in words and photographs and art and design. . . . We'll have a Show Business Beauty in every issue, but we musn't count on this alone for sex content. An additional pictorial feature of some kind should be included in almost every issue that has some kind of girl flavor or aspect to it. It doesn't necessarily have to have any nudity, but it should have meaningful sex impact . . . show business at its best is a wonderful fairyland (and I'm not referring to any of the sexual leanings of its inhabitants), a world of make-believe, of colored lights and tinsel and sequins—as sophisticated and corny in the same moment as Rodgers and Hart's first song hit, "Manhattan," that permitted the incredibly wonderful imagery and internal rhyming that takes place within the song.

Though it appears that Hefner knew exactly what he wanted editorially, he had difficulty in gaining acceptance of his ideas by his new staff, his main insurgent being Frank Gibney.

Gibney claims that he moved to Chicago to take over *SBI* with the understanding that he would be given total editorial control. He soon discovered, much to his horror, that Hefner refused to accept the role of rubber-stamp publisher and that he and Hefner had irreconcilable differences in their approaches to what they thought *SBI* should be. Gibney was a Yale man and author of several books: a confirmed intellectual. He considered Hefner to be an unsophisticated and unschooled Midwesterner. Gibney told writer Calvin Tompkins of *Look:* "I wanted to intellectualize *Show Business Illustrated.* Hefner wanted to use his *Playboy* techniques and make everything breathless. The two concepts just didn't go together." Curiously, Hefner claims that after the first issue came out, he never became intimately involved because he just couldn't take time away from his seven-day-a-week marathon entanglement with *Playboy.* "There weren't any other hours left. I found that I just wasn't sleeping anymore."

Conservative advertisers who were afraid to take a chance on buying space in *Playboy* because they considered it too risqué initially bought into *SBI* but were enraged when —from month to month—Hefner continued to introduce more and more photos of girls with their chests uncovered. Cancellation of space contracts began to trickle in as a result.

Circulation for *SBI* began to dip with the second issue. The staff could not give Hefner the editorial expertise he sought and demanded, and he began to tamper with the personnel. Eventually he started firing people *en masse.* Others began to leave of their own volition because they felt, like Gibney, that Hefner would not give them the editorial responsibility commensurate with their position.

The old journalistic, show-business bromides began to

appear in the pages of *SBI:* four-color pages of dancers at Las Vegas; not-so-in-depth profiles of Alexander King, Frank Sinatra, and Marlon Brando; and hackneyed reviews of less than profound movies, together with stills of censored footage from European films.

SBI also had an energetic competitor: A.&P. heir Huntington Hartford's *Show* magazine began at about the same time as *SBI.* It had one advantage over *SBI* right from the start in being published directly from New York City and therefore being more in the throes of the entertainment business. Joe Goldberg, in his book *Big Bunny,* points out:

Although neither Hefner nor Hartford felt himself in competition with the other (the difference in approach can be exemplified by feature articles in the first issues: *SBI* had Joe Hyams on Frank Sinatra; *Show* had Kenneth Tynan on Orson Welles), the world of journalism sensed a battle and manufactured a rivalry. Questioned about Hartford by *Time,* Hefner answered, "it's no serious problem. I don't think Hartford would be too worried if I decided to put out a chain of supermarkets."

Eventually, Gibney and Hefner decided to part company, with a vivid amount of bitterness on the former's part. "Hughie always reminded me of a corrupt Methodist trader who sold liquor to the Indians, and felt he ought to just *taste* each brand first."

Hefner called upon Spectorsky, Art Paul and Vince Tajiri in an attempt to save the magazine. Though they made a valiant effort, it was too late. After six months, over $1.5 million had gone into the editorial and promotional sides of the magazine, and the public was simply not taking to it. Hefner, however, was just beginning to experience renewed confidence in the possibility of editorial excellence for *SBI.* In an interview in *The Wall Street Journal,* he said:

After eight issues of wandering and wobbling, the magazine is showing life. Our editorial approach is going in the right direction. With any meaningful upturn in circulation, *SBI* could go into the black this fall.

After nine issues, the circulation had descended from 350,000 to 250,000, and the return on initial subscription renewal efforts were dismal. Subscribers were simply not sending in their checks for $4.00 for another year.

A Pollyannish attempt was made to turn *SBI* into a monthly. An editorial stated that the change would allow the staff

time for a deeper look into the realm of the performing arts and to give to our pages finer pictures and graphics by which to gratify the discerning eyes of our entertainment-oriented readers . . . with what we hope is modest confidence, we believe *SBI* will be an even more satisfying and perceptive illustrated guide book to the fascinating world of show business.

The gesture, though it reduced costs, failed to either improve the content significantly or raise the readership a trace.

Hefner scheduled a meeting with Hartford in New York to discuss the possibility of a merger of some sort since, contrary to Goldberg's interpretation, they were both competing for the same reader and advertiser. Actually, Hefner arrived in Manhattan with a multimillion-dollar nightmare on his hands and flew back to Chicago with all of his problems neatly—almost magically—solved. He perceived correctly that Hartford really *did* dislike the competition, less for business reasons than for the desire to have the entire show-busines limelight to himself. Hartford was also aware of Hefner's growing reputation as one of the country's leading publishing entrepreneurs and knew it would appear to be a coup if he could "defeat" Hefner in the battle of the show-biz mags. Hefner sensed all this, and he also knew that Hartford had more money than he, so he began his discussions with an ingenious psychological ploy: he attempted to buy *Show* magazine outright. Eventually he turned the negotiations entirely around; Hefner ended up selling *SBI* to *Show*, which is exactly what he wanted to do. *The New York Times* of February second carried the following story:

The competitive fight between Huntington Hartford, President of *Show* Magazine, and Hugh M. Hefner, Publisher of *Show Business Illustrated*, has been won by Mr. Hartford.

Mr. Hartford announced late yesterday that arrangements had been completed for his magazine to absorb *Show Business Illustrated* for an amount in excess of $250,000. Both magazines started in the fall of last year. Mr. Hartford said the April issue would be the last issue of *Show Business Illustrated*.

It is understood that Mr. Hartford's main interest in acquiring the magazine was to obtain its backlog of stories and its subscription lists. Mr. Hartford said the transaction would not change editorial plans to turn *Show* into a "magazine of the arts" beginning with its April issue.

Hefner was delighted and not so secretly proud in making the deal, judging it a shrewd horse trade. Hefner considered the sale of the editorial inventory, subscription list, and outstanding advertising contracts "a lot of money for some bits and pieces"; he received $250,000 in cash, $60,000 in advertising credits (so that he could advertise *Playboy* in *Show*), and $200,000 in relief by not having to carry through on the rest of the year's issues to *SBI* subscribers. In addition, he kept a copy of the subscription list which had a market value to direct mailers of well over $100,000. "If that doesn't show good business sense," he said in a letter to his bank, "I don't know what does."

Years later, he made an attempt at being philosophical about his first major failure in publishing in an "Impolite Interview" in *The Realist:*

The thing that went wrong was a business thing and for that reason, because it was a business mistake far more than a creative one, it was not a terrible kick in the head for me emotionally. We blew a couple of million that I would rather not have blown, but fortunately the operation was strong enough so that it didn't hurt us. And I have no better use for the money that we make than to do other things we get involved with which are not based purely

158

on whether or not they are going to make "X" amount of dollars; they are done for other reasons, because they are things we want to do.

Though it's true that *SBI* foundered because of its atrocious financial condition, the real reason that the circulation continued on a steady decline had nothing to do with "a business thing," as Hefner states, but rather because of the poor editorial image the magazine was projecting. If Hefner is to be faulted for *SBI*, it cannot be in the initial concept or in the promotion, both of which were sound, but in his total lack of insight in selecting editors with whom he could not establish a rapport, and his underestimation of the time it would take to build the magazine into a viable editorial product, and hence, a success.

Show business—its personalities, its haunts, its glamorous permutations—has always enthralled Hefner's imagination, and though he failed with *SBI*, one other of his show-business ventures became an almost instant success while simultaneously establishing what has become a genuine American mythos: The Playboy Club.

In the late 1950s, Victor Lownes often frequented a private key club called the Walton Walk, located on Chicago's Near North Side, not far from the Playboy offices. As a member of the club, Lownes would occasionally invite guests and on a few occasions sometimes convinced Hefner to abandon his work and join him.

They liked the concept of a private club, and over drinks (bourbon and Pepsi for Hefner, extradry martini for Lownes), they talked of the possibilities of starting one of their own where they could hang out and perhaps get closer to a greater number of women. The promotional and business justification seemed such a natural step, they felt it was virtually incumbent on them to go into the club business.

The readers of *Playboy* had been reacting to the magazine almost as though it were a house organ for a fraternity and had assumed common-law proprietorship of the magazine's pages. A club where members/readers could meet, perhaps enjoy a hearty drink, good entertainment, and succulent food, all served by pretty girls, in a setting reflective of the mood, taste, and attitudes displayed in *Playboy* magazine could be a success, Hefner and Lownes agreed, if they were correct in their estimate of the strength of the readers' identification. As it developed, they were not quite accurate in their judgment of the *Playboy* reader, but they were successful nevertheless.

The owner of Walton Walk was Arnold Morton, a highly aggressive but congenial young man who had been in the restaurant business all of his life and came from a family of restaurateurs. He also shared with Hefner and Lownes two uncontrollable passions: the accumulation of large amounts of money and the constant quest for attractive women. The three men decided to join forces: Hefner to supply the capital and the use of his magazine; Lownes to summon forth his promotional talents and experience with entertainers; Morton to use his proven abilities as a successful "saloonkeeper," as he liked to describe himself. A corporation was formed, called Playboy Clubs International, and a formula established for stock ownership among the three: Morton received 14.4 percent, Lownes 13.5 percent, and Hefner 20.6 percent. The remaining 51.5 percent was placed in the name of the HMH Publishing Co., of which Hefner owned some 75 percent of the shares.

An editorial in the August 1960 issue somewhat self-consciously stated that the establishment of a Playboy Club was a way

of recognizing the need, on the part of urban men of taste and sophistication, for a private club that is as unique and entertaining as *Playboy* itself. The Playboy Club is dedicated to projecting the richly romantic mood, the fun and *joie de vivre*, that are so much a part of the publication; as *Playboy* has gained a reputation for being the smartest and most sophisticated of journals, so the Playboy Club will be similarly known as a gathering place for those who appreciate this side of life.

The first Playboy Club was opened in Chicago in February of 1960, directly across the street from Morton's Walton Walk. Lownes initiated the idea of calling the girls "Bunnies," consistent with the rabbit symbol used on the cover and all through the inside of *Playboy*.

Bunnies were cast rather than hired, and they were made to feel they were not just waitresses but a part of show business; tutorage in method acting was given each girl, in addition to a vigorous training program on poise and beauty care. Before starting work they were also given extensive familiarization with the food and drink served at the club. The Bunny's manual teaches her such things as how to light a guest's cigarette without obstructing his view of the lady at his table and to identify 143 bottle brands, including 31 brands of scotch, 16 bourbons, and 30 liqueurs. All the girls were striking looking and most were extremely full breasted. Many were Playmates or models for *Playboy*. The Bunnies' costumes consisted of a tight, formfitting garment, similar to a one-piece bathing suit, which made their breasts ooze seductively from their garments. They also wore a white collar, black bow tie, French cuffs, spiked heels, a set of satin rabbit ears on their heads, and a white cotton "tail" on their behinds. To maintain at least an illusion of accessibility, married Bunnies were forbidden to wear their wedding rings. Paradoxically, Hefner was apparently also aware of Dorothy Parker's archaism that men don't make passes at girls who wore glasses; those girls who did and who would not or could not switch to contact lenses were not hired.

Playboy-observer Norman Mailer offers this memorable picture of the Bunnies in his book, *The Presidential Papers:*

The bunnies went by in their costumes, electric-blue silk, kelly-green, flame-pink, pinups from a magazine, faces painted

161

into sweetmeats, flower tops, tame lynx, piggie, poodle, a queen or two from a beauty contest. They wore Gay Nineties rig which exaggerated their hips, bound their waists in a *ceinture,* and lifted them into a phallic brassiere—each breast looked like the big bullet on the front bumper of a Cadillac. Long black stockings, long long stockings, up almost to the waist on each side; and to the back, on the curve of the can, as if ejected tenderly from the body, was a puff of chastity, a little white ball of a bunny's tail which bobbled as they walked . . . the Playboy Club was the place for magic. . . .

The decor of the club was made to resemble an attractively appointed townhouse or, more appropriately, a swank club: a British officer's drawing room with wood paneling and large, comfortable chairs but with modern appointments, Mondrian-like stained glass, for instance. The main appeal was, however, the young ladies who were as attractive as Ziegfeld's favorites had been; over the years they have become known as America's version of the geisha girl. There was closed-circuit television so that one could watch for arriving guests and a board which posted the names of those members in attendance on any particular night.

The building consisted of four levels of restaurant-bar-nightclub rooms, and on any given evening, members had the opportunity to move from room to room, watching different entertainment in each and hopefully experiencing a party atmosphere of casual circulation. Since each room had a cover charge attached to the purchase of even one drink, such movement proved to be expensive for the member but highly advantageous for Playboy Clubs International, making it the most profitable club, per square foot, in the world. The formula of attractive and well-presented and packaged wine, women, and song proved to be a smashing financial success: within one year, over 50,000 men joined the Playboy Club (paying either $25 or $50 depending on their geographical proximity to the club), and other clubs were constructed in Miami, New Orleans, New York, and Los Angeles. Hefner related the ambience of the clubs directly to himself: "They represent the communication of my views and tastes and interests relevant to these changing times." In a little over ten years from the inception of the first club, there were over a score of Playboy clubs and hotel/resorts all over the United States and several foreign countries, generating a revenue of some $75 million a year. Hefner and his associates are the only men in the history of the entertainment industry to successfully initiate and operate an actual chain of nightclubs. "What we have is a cult," explained Lownes somewhat callously to *The Wall Street Journal.* "The Rabbit is the father symbol. We could tell them to go right out the window and they would follow our advice."

Perhaps it was this spellbinding grip on Playboy's members or just an inhibition concerning *Playboy*'s epidermal spreads that disturbed some of the Windy City's citizenry. Though Chicago had had key clubs of all types for over twenty-five years and Hefner was already one of its captains of industry, during the first week the Playboy Club was open, the corporation counsel of the city of Chicago announced such clubs were illegal, and Hefner had to temporarily open the club to nonkeyholders as well. Since the position of the corporation counsel had no real basis in any actual law, it was reasonably assumed by Hefner that, like the jazz festival incident, the action meant that some city officials didn't approve of the magazine or of Hefner's other operations for that matter. Hefner confirmed the legality of his Playboy Club in district court and—when the city foolishly appealed the decision—in the court of appeals as well. After two months he was back in the keyholder-only business.

At first, it was difficult for members to discern exactly what the clubs were all about. A large segment of the readership believed that any girl who posed in the nude—as much as the reader enjoyed viewing her—was, in reality, a high-class prostitute; ergo, since they employed girls who appeared undressed in the magazine, the Playboy clubs must be the harbingers of national brothelism or at least the start of a mystic cult of concubines.

Hefner had anticipated all of this and was prepared for it. A look-but-don't-touch policy was established, and the Bunnies were strictly forbidden to date key holders, as indicated in this confidential directive:

Personal Information: Bunnies may not give out their home addresses or phone numbers at any time in the club for any reason and may not give out information on *other* Bunnies.

Dating of Employees: Bunnies are forbidden to date *any* employees of the Club. This rule applies to floor manager, office personnel, bartenders, musicians and performers.

Dating of Keyholders and Guests: Bunnies are not permitted to make dates with keyholders, guests, or any other persons visiting the Playboy Club. Any Bunny who arranges to meet or be met by a keyholder, guest or employee of the Club either on or off the Club premises will be immediately dismissed. If a Bunny is asked for a date by a patron, she should advise him, in as polite a manner as possible, that Bunnies are not permitted to make dates with people that they meet at the Club. As stated above, she must also advise him that she is not permitted to give out her home address or phone number either.

To enforce the no-dating rule, Playboy hired the Willmark Service System, Inc., an investigation agency, to "shop" the Bunnies; i.e., to send their investigators to the clubs in a willful attempt at entrapment. If the Bunny agrees to a date with the investigator (unaware that she is being spied upon), she is fired on the spot. If there is any question of a Bunny being dishonest, she is offered a lie-detector test. If she fails to take it, she is fired. "We don't necessarily believe every rumor," said Lownes, "but we do feel an obligation to protect ourselves."

164

As a result, members who came to the Club steaming for erotic adventure were forced to lapse into voyeuristic dalliance, since the Bunnies were not even permitted to sit at a keyholder's table.

Hefner established the touch-me-not rule in the clubs for several reasons, but the most obvious was the protection of his liquor license. In his January 1974 interview in *Playboy* he put it this way: "One critic described the Clubs as 'a bordello without a second floor.' If we permitted members to manhandle the Bunnies, we'd have the equivalent of that second floor, and you don't need a vivid imagination to see where that would lead. The policy was established for the protection of the Bunnies, and we've continued it at their insistence."

Nevertheless, at first there were other reasons why the Bunnies were not permitted to date customers, and it becomes clear when you read again the directive forbidding dating of employees *of the Club*. It says nothing about dating the magazine's executives and staffers; this is the most compelling reason why the rule was instituted.

Some twenty or thirty *Playboy* executives and editors had a field day when the clubs first started and established a not-so-small harem consisting of the eighty Bunnies who worked at the Club. Hefner and his executives dated the girls, partied with them, and often slept with them. Those on the inside of *Playboy* could always have "the pick of the crop," as one staffer described it. Bunnies who were off duty were almost command attendees at all of Hefner's parties and "fuck-ins."

There was another subsidiary benefit that developed as a result of the clubs: they served as perfect conduits for Hefner in producing a constant inventory and flow of Playmates for his precious centerfold.

In more recent years, *Playboy* has greatly relaxed its strict control over the Bunnies. Hefner insists that the company doesn't attempt to police the Bunnies' personal lives but tries to keep them separate from the people they meet at the clubs.

Perhaps it was the unprecedented interest in the Bunnies as potential prostitutes that produced rumors of a connection between Hefner's clubs and the Mafia, especially since the Chicago Playboy Club is in the heart of what is considered syndicate turf. Ovid Demaris in his book, *Captive City,* foolishly links the two due to the fact that such known gangsters as Sam Giancana, Joseph Di Varco and James Allegretti, among others, were discovered to be Playboy keyholders. There is as much deductive logic here as saying those men were members of the American Red Cross (which they might be), and, therefore, the Red Cross is Mafia connected.

Demaris cited as further "proof" of gangster infiltration of Playboy Tony Roma, an executive for the Playboy operation, stating that he had connections with a Capone-mob bootlegger and other Mafia friends and associates. Roma, who claims he's a street-fighter from way back, but no hoodlum, was outraged.

It turned out that Demaris, either through ignorance or guile, had mistaken Roma for someone else entirely. This was the second time around for Roma. One of *Captive City's* early collaborators, Ed Reid, managing editor of the now-defunct *Brooklyn Eagle,* launched an editorial attack on Roma in New York some years earlier, but his charges were all directed to another Tony Roma—a notorious ex-convict. Having suffered unrelenting attacks from Reid and the *Eagle,* Roma sued for criminal libel. Realizing that he had made an error, Reid dug deeply into Roma's background hoping to uncover anything that might remotely be used to defend his case, but he came up with nothing. The case was settled out of court.

It has been suggested that one of the reasons the Mafia has adopted a hands-off policy toward the Playboy enterprise is that they are afraid that Hefner could retaliate against any strong-arm tactics by resorting to a counterattack, citing names on the printed page of his magazine.

It's common knowledge that some of the concessions (such as laundry, garbage disposal, etc.) used by the Playboy clubs have been owned by companies that are listed by the Chicago commission on organized crime as having owners and managers with long police records, but what Demaris failed to point out when stressing this as more evidence to indict Playboy, however, was that it is virtually impossible in the hotel-restaurant-nightclub industry to be serviced in certain areas of Chicago by a company that is not on that list. In many instances, these companies verge on being monopolies. Hefner has insisted upon and adhered to a policy which dictates that any firm with which Playboy has been doing business be dropped if and when it is identified by responsible authorities as Mafia dominated or connected.

Extortion and strong-arm tactics have never been used against Playboy, and as a former high-level executive of Playboy Clubs International, with constant occasion to see and hear classified information about the operation of the clubs, I never once found any shred of evidence that Playboy and the Mafia were any more than just aware of each other's existence. To my knowledge, not one cent of Mafia or gangland money has ever been invested in any Playboy club or hotel or any other Playboy operation, nor has any protection money ever been paid or given by Playboy to the Mafia.

Several years ago, the federal government, as part of a thorough investigation into possible hoodlum involvement in legitimate businesses in Chicago, painstakingly analyzed the financial records of the HMH Publishing Co., Playboy Clubs International, and Hefner personally. After completing the audit, it gave Hefner and all his operations its imprimatur, having found no ties whatsoever with organized crime. Mere rumors of hoodlum involvement in gambling in

Las Vegas had served to dissuade Hefner many times in past years from opening a Playboy club in that city, though a casino there would clearly have been lucrative. Only after the arrival of Howard Hughes did Hefner feel he could pursue the opportunities that existed for a Playboy club in Las Vegas or elsewhere in Nevada.

There have been attempts, however, to get Hefner involved in the Mafia. Shortly after the clubs had begun in the early 1960s, Hefner was approached at a private party by Marshall Caifano, a Chicago mobster known locally as "John Marshall." A convicted bank robber and extortionist with over thirty-five arrests on his record, Caifano talked to Hefner about possibly investing in the Playboy operation. Hefner stalled him and tried to sidestep the question but Caifano was persistent. Finally Hefner told him that he never discussed business at a party and that if Caifano was truly interested, he should call for an appointment and they could discuss the possibilities more formally.

Two days later, Hefner received the dreaded call, and the two men met privately in Hefner's office. To imagine Hefner's true emotional state is comparatively simple: Caifano was one of the nation's most feared gunmen, a man who had been a prime suspect in more than ten murders. Caifano reiterated his desire to become a Playboy club investor.

"Look John, I really don't know what business you're in," said Hefner. Caifano, smiling embarrassedly, answered, "Well, gambling." Hefner continued: "You people have your enemies and we have ours. It really doesn't make any sense for the two of us to become involved." Hefner literally held his breath, trying to look and act as nonchalant as possible. "I guess you're right," said Caifano. "Thanks for your time." Caifano quietly accepted the decree, left the office, and Hefner never heard from him again.

The only incident to ever blemish Playboy's reputation took place when the New York City club was being constructed and a license to serve liquor was being sought.

In May of 1960, Arnold Morton was approached by a Chicago public relations man, Ralph Berger, who allegedly said that he knew the chairman of the New York State Liquor Authority, seventy-three-year-old Martin L. Epstein, and would "put in a good word for you on your license."

Morton was taken to meet Epstein who, according to Morton, set the price for a license at $50,000 and suggested that a separate deal with L. Judson Morhouse, then New York State Republican Chairman and advisor to Governor Nelson A. Rockefeller, would have to be made in order to secure the license. Morton paid the $50,000 to Epstein. Berger allegedly told Morton that Morhouse requested a payment of $100,000, in addition to an option to buy $100,-000 worth of *Playboy* stock and the rights to operate a chain of gift shops in all the Playboy Clubs.

Hefner, in consultation with his top executives, decided that the situation was a blatant attempt at extortion. He had $4 million invested in the New York operation—63,000 people had paid $25 for their Playboy keys—and he was being denied his right to a license by the official who had the authority to grant or deny it. Hefner, Preuss, Morton, and Lownes flew to New York and paid a visit to the late Manhattan District Attorney Frank Hogan's office. They complained of being blackmailed for $150,000.

A grand jury was formed, with the Playboy officials testifying under immunity of prosecution. Morton, in response to an allegation that perhaps he had bribed Epstein because Playboy was so desperate to secure a license, responded, "I felt I was being blackmailed. I didn't think I was bribing a public official."

Berger was ultimately convicted and sentenced to one year in prison. Epstein was never brought to trial due to reasons of health. B. McKenna, the prosecutor in the case, stated to the press that he thought Hefner and the other Playboy executives deserved high credit for providing the evidence that eventually resulted in the conviction and removal from office of the S.L.A. authorities involved. "Corruption had reached such a level in that agency that one could hardly obtain a license to sell liquor without paying off officials of the New York State Liquor Authority. Throughout our investigation and subsequent trials, the Playboy Club officials cooperated fully. Their testimony was crucial in indicting and convicting public officials and the Chairman of the New York State Republican Party. Any reprisals against the Playboy Club or its affiliates for their cooperation in our investigation would be a disservice to the cause of law enforcement."

Officials in Governor Rockefeller's office also commended Hefner and the others for "coming forward." Playboy was awarded its liquor license in December of 1963.

CHAPTER 9

"I wanted to become more inaccessible."

WITH the Playboy clubs prospering and *Playboy* itself making the largest circulation gains of any magazine in the country, Hefner discovered that his hectic pace was beginning to enervate him. His office/apartment was not functioning at all as he had planned: he had time only for work, and since he slept in his office so often, his work was always there as a testament to his procrastination. He felt imprisoned.

Arlene Bouras, *Playboy*'s copy chief, remembers coming to the office on Saturdays to catch up on her work and finding Hefner there, puttering around in bedroom slippers and pajamas. "He acted as though the whole office building was his home and though I'm sure he was happy—as my boss—to see me working overtime, I always felt as though I was intruding as an unwanted guest in his castle."

Hefner realized that he had to have a place of his own,

and immediately after his divorce from Millie, he began looking for an appropriate bachelor pad. "I wanted to become more inaccessible," he said, in what would become one of the gross understatements of the century.

The dwelling that he found and how he transformed it and absorbed it into his life-style and what effect it had on his life as it became one of the most famous houses in the United States has already been discussed. There are a number of opposing views on the possible sybaritic philanderings that might or might not occur at Hefner's house, however, and as the following stories will relate, the ultimate appraisal must be left to the reader's imagination.

After Gloria Steinem did an article on Hefner in *McCall's* several years ago, she traveled the New York literary party circuit telling a story about a visit Jules Feiffer paid to the Mansion. Feiffer was asked by a senior Playboy executive if he would like a Bunny brought to his room. According to Steinem, Feiffer accepted the offer and the girl soon arrived. Fifteen minutes later—again according to Steinem—the executive called back. "Well, how was she?"

Feiffer was furious when he heard the rumor and stated that nothing even remotely similar to that had ever happened to him. Hefner told DuBois, "My male guests usually know me well enough to be aware that whatever happens in the house is a matter of individual initiative and the personal preferences of the people involved. The sort of impersonal exploitation suggested by the story in *McCall's* is completely foreign to me. It's simply not my style."

When the Rolling Stones were on their 1972 American tour, they were Hefner's guests at the Mansion for five days of almost nonstop partying, much of it self-inspired, but with the cooperation and endorsement of Hefner, as the world's most congenial host. Robert Greenfield, in his book on the Stones' tour, *S.T.P.*, described the final night at the Mansion:

172

So it comes as no shock to Hef that the Bunnies like to get loaded and fuck. Everyone likes to get loaded these days. The counter-culture's greatest contribution to America was to point the way to unbridled drug use. As the party gets more intense, it's obvious that ladies are being passed hand to hand like good joints, going off first with one person, then another. Some of the braver dears are walking right up to S.T.P. [Stones Touring Party] honchos and saying, "Joy tells me you're a bitch. Dominate me!" and there's nothing you can do with a macho challenge like that but respond, and quickly. One S.T.P. dude finds out about that "sheik thing," which he describes as being able to fuck six or eight women in one night, do it and then forget it, and start all over again because it's a brand new trip. . . .

Some of the girls have giggled and leaned over to Hef . . . and asked if it's okay if they could . . . and he said yes . . . so they've gone about inviting the inner circle of grooviest people . . . to do a little number in Hef's private bath. . . . So by the time the Roman Bath comes up, no one knows what to expect. Hef and all these superstars and shiny ladies . . . the Mansion roof might come off. Everyone that's been invited goes down through Hef's bedroom to this great pool of a bathtub that can hold as many as twenty-four people. The water's all fragrant with special oils and a little of the special stash is going around and everyone's waiting for Hef to slip out of his robe and get into the swim.

But it's so late in the evening and everyone is already so multisatiated that nothing happens. Nothing more than a friendly dip, with some pleasant conversation and lots of eyes, watching eyes.

Hef clambers out when he's had enough and goes back to his round bed with his two ladies for the evening. He flicks on the videotape recorder to watch a film and orders something to eat, and when the bathers troop back on their way upstairs, there is Hef, the gentle ringmaster, sitting between two pneumatic ladies, smoking his pipe and watching late night TV, like the most charming parody of what life must be like in the suburbs.

There was only one other incident, to my knowledge,

that ever had the possibilities of developing into a full-scale, genuine, union-label orgy at one of the larger parties, and that was when the cast of *Hair* decided to go skinny-dipping in the underground pool. A few of the other guests joined in, but all that occurred was an occasional grope, much fun, and some swimming.

A totally different happening takes place virtually every week when Hefner is in town: the Sunday movie. Hefner selects prints of first-run movies, occasionally before they are released or perhaps during the first week of their national distribution, and screens them for a relatively small group of people. About twenty or thirty regular guests, mostly employees of *Playboy*, have a standing invitation. Certain celebrities who happen to be in Chicago are also invited; on any given Sunday, there are usually one or two movie stars, famous writers, or sports figures.

Guests begin arriving at about 6 P.M., dressed informally. They have drinks from the ever-open bar, make reluctant, only rarely sincere attempts at conversation, kibitz a game of pool in the game room, or occasionally take a swim. Hefner is never present for these stiff, often uncomfortable preliminaries.

At about seven, an elegant buffet dinner is served, and guests sit randomly at the large dining table, at cocktail tables, on cushions on the floor of the main room, or at places of their own devising. Hefner still has not appeared to share the repast with his guests. The clearing away of the dinner plates by the silent, almost invisible, and invariably excellent house servants signals that it is time for the film to begin. But it can't begin, of course, until the host is there.

Hefner sometimes keeps his assembled guests waiting for hours before appearing, but usually, at about 8 P.M., the door to his apartment opens and Hefner steps out, often dressed in paisley pajamas and a yellow silk robe and usually accompanied by his then-current special girl. His arrival is staged and timed by the projectionists and technicians stand-

174

ing by, almost at though he were an actor. As he descends the steps into the main room, the movie screen begins to lower, and the lights all over the great room start to dim.

By the time he reaches a special reserved chair in the center of the room, the screen has totally descended, the lights are out, and Leo the Lion begins to roar at the precise second Hefner settles in. Hefner sits in his chair—which is a huge, deeply upholstered affair with a matching ottoman, making the whole thing something like the size of a bed—like Henry VIII on his throne, his good lady of the moment snuggling up to him for the duration of the film.

Guests sit on their choice of the other chairs which are spread about the room in quasi-theater fashion. Some are lucky enough to commandeer one of the long, plush sofas; others elect the floor, with a cushion or two.

Next to Hefner's chair, on the left-hand side, is another throne, an exact duplicate of Hef's. This is also reserved, and there is a certain mystique about who does and doesn't sit there. Very often it is either Shelly Kasten or John Dante, two old friends of Hefner's, one a present *Playboy* employee, the other recently resigned. Anti-intellectual, nightclub types, John or Shelly will sit in the companion chair, either alone or with a date. Hefner's offhand comments—whether mundane or profound—are always answered with the invariable Kasten chorus: "Love ya, baby!" When Hefner's brother Keith worked for *Playboy*, he had first choice on the other chair. Now Hefner's teenage son David, who has recently begun to work for *Playboy* part-time, proudly sits there, next to his father.

There is apparently a curious, unspoken rule which says that only those to whom Hefner somehow silently communicates his approval or beneficence can have the pleasure—or honor—of sitting next to him. No visiting celebrity is ever asked to sit next to Hefner; rather, he or she is escorted by a servant, secretary, or public-relations man to a high-level chair directly behind him. This is true even when the companion throne chair is empty. If someone new, who doesn't know the rule sits in that chair, he is told immediately by one of Hefner's assistants that it is taken.

On occasion, there has been a game of one-upmanship between Kasten and Dante over the seating arrangement. Dante once arrived early on a Sunday afternoon, before Hefner had surfaced, and took his position—together with a comely Bunny—in the left-hand chair. When Kasten arrived with his date, he saw that Dante was claiming squatter's rights to the chair. Kasten turned around and left the Mansion immediately, rather than be seen sitting anywhere other than next to the King. From that point on, each man would arrive earlier and earlier in the day on Sunday, scurrying to claim the valued chair as his own. Eventually, they solved the problem by both agreeing to arrive without dates and consequently shared the chair equally.

The *Playboy* hierarchy—one that matches the royal intrigues of the Old World—is a function of one's proximity to Hefner. To be seen putting a hand on Hefner's shoulder or be spotted in quiet conversation with him carries immense prestige for a status-hungry executive. And that status is intimately related to the chair-on-the-left. Upper-level Playboy executives who have been attending Hefner's Sunday movies for years would not dream of sitting there unless beckoned to do so by Hefner. Somehow, they never are.

Because Hefner is constantly attempting to gain more control over his personal life, one must assume that he is perfectly aware of the weekly jockeying for position by his guests and the manipulative display of egos for which he is indirectly responsible. What he is saying, in effect, to the celebrities, to the editors and executives of Playboy, to all who enter his presence is that he will tolerate no Falstaffs. One has the impression that if he deigns to talk to you, it is through what he considers a sublime benevolence. The protocol is that of true royalty: no one, except Hefner's closest intimates, talks to him first. His guests in this miniature duchy

176

only speak when first spoken to. One editor who had been with the magazine for nearly seven years told me that Hefner had never exchanged as much as a word with him, and though he had been at the Mansion nearly every Sunday for years, he was certain that Hefner did not know who he was.

Because the Sunday movie scene is such a star trip, with everyone in the room aware of the Hefner *persona* at all moments, many people who have standing invitations have stopped attending. In my almost five years of regular Sunday Mansion-going, I never saw either Spectorsky, Morton, Tajiri, or Preuss there. Art Paul came only rarely. When pressed for a reason why they prefer not to socialize with their employer, they state that even though the Sunday soirées are purely social, Hefner maintains the position of control, keeping everyone else in a distastefully subordinate role.

Others, like myself, had a masochistic obsession about being present each week, a senseless display of *hauteur* combined with a peculiar and irresistible curiosity concerning the degenerateness of the personalities—including myself—in attendance.

Despite the almost unbearable tension, an invitation to the Mansion, tendered to Playboy editors and executives, was a highly prized status symbol, jealously guarded by those who achieved it and fiercely resented by those who were ignored.

For many, the Mansion became as difficult to enter and understand as Kafka's surrealistic castle. There was no apparent logic or consistency concerning who was invited and who was not. A few vice-presidents of the Playboy corporation were, mysteriously, never invited, while the receptionist or file clerk working in that ostracized executive's department might very well appear on the guest list. Whenever inquiries were made to Hefner's assistants or secretaries as to whether a particular person could be invited, it was impossible to determine who was responsible for the final decision, when

177

it would be made, or what the criteria were. It seemed unlikely that Hefner himself would become involved in passing judgment on each name, yet one never knew . . .

Stanley Paley, one of *Playboy*'s editorial film experts, a distinguished Hollywood scenarist and story analyst, who was imported to Chicago specifically for the purpose of bringing professional expertise to *Playboy*'s growing film interests, was probably the only person on the staff who had a legitimate business reason for attending the first-run Sunday movies. He waited almost a full year, however, without any explanation, before receiving The Word that he could attend. Meantime, his secretary had been invited every Sunday.

One young junior editor was incensed and almost insanely jealous at never being invited, since some of his peers unaccountably were. For years, he would wait on State Street almost every Sunday, a block from the Mansion, until he spied someone en route there who would agree to take him along. When they reached the lobby, he would stand out of range of the inspecting television camera, and then, once the door was buzzed open, he would dash through with his benefactor. Once inside he would somehow meld with the small crowd, and no one thought to ask him to leave.

Now, perhaps to avoid that very ploy, two of Hefner's assistants sit at a desk in the lobby each Sunday afternoon, accompanied by a uniformed guard, and check off each visitor's name against an attendance list.

A female editor, Julia Bainbridge, who was officially invited, once arrived with her husband and was humiliatingly turned away by the faceless voice through the television speaker: "I'm sorry. Only male guests are permitted to bring females. Since your husband's name is not on the list, we cannot allow him to enter." To give the rulemakers due credit, that policy has since been changed.

The snubbing that takes place at the Sunday soirées is incredibly blatant. Business types rarely talk to editors. *Playboy* magazine staffers are aloof toward Playboy club people.

All take their cues from Hef, who rarely talks to anyone except Kasten or Dante. A bevy of young and bored-looking Bunnies-Playmates-models and aspirants, all sleek and slender except for enormous breasts and a variety of elaborate hairdos, usually sit together, talking to no one—even themselves—filing their long nails and primping continually. Attempts by any of the men present to begin a conversation usually bring a monosyllabic rebuff, even when the man in question is a celebrity of some note. These vacuous Lolitas would rather sink into narcissistic celibacy than to be seen considering any other than their leader's phallus; they wait dutifully for a smile—even a raised eyebrow will do—from Hefner, while studiously ignoring everyone and everything else. Hefner allows them to attend every Sunday, apparently to stack the room and impress the visiting stars and because it probably boosts his own ego.

As one of Playboy's own comedians, John Barbour, once crudely put it: "Hefner keeps himself so surrounded by 'brown noses' that he has to take weekly treatments at a proctologist."

Perhaps the strangest aspect of this carefully adhered-to snobbism is the way it affects those stars and celebrities who attend. Courted and complemented enough to draw them to the Mansion when they visit Chicago, these famous people are then given to know the extent of their relative unimportance. With the rare exception of certain show-business greats who are known to be particular favorites of Hefner's—renowned and otherwise—respected personages are generally left totally to themselves during most Sunday afternoon-evening sessions. No one speaks to the guest during the cocktail or the dinner hours until, probably as a relief, some appointed staff member materializes at his or her lonely elbow to lead the way to the chair behind The Chair, for the screening of that week's film.

As Hefner enters the room from his apartment, he will first have been briefed on the day's guest list. Walking quickly to his chair, he may occasionally deign to nod to the by now cowed guest; even more rarely, he may stop to speak a word or two. (This invariably produces a murmur among the throng. Many of the regulars have not, until that moment, even noticed who is present.) Then Hef takes his seat, the lights dim abruptly to blackness, the film begins, and the guest is left to ruminate on the true levels of importance of those assembled. In the minds of the disciples, there is only one god.

CHAPTER 10

"I found that I had built a marvelous machine, but far from being master of that machine, the machine was ruling me."

As of the summer of 1963, *Playboy's* circulation was topping two million. A book division was selling tens of thousands of copies of such titles as *The Bedside Playboy*, *Playboy's Party Jokes*, and *The Playboy Cartoon Album*. Playboy clubs were operating in Chicago, Miami, New Orleans, New York, Phoenix, and St. Louis, with others under construction. This phenomenal growth meant even more work for Hefner, additional executives and employees for him to deal with, and increasingly pressing decisions with far-reaching effects for him to make every day.

He was also working on an editorial feature, "The Playboy Philosophy," which was originally initiated to answer some of the magazine's and his own critics. ("I'd rather be damned for what I believe, than have people damn me for what they *think* I believe.") The Philosophy developed into a fascinating, sometimes pretentious, but thoroughly scholastic and well-documented, twenty-five-part, three-year monologue, running a quarter of a million words. Maddeningly repetitious, covering censorship, sex and the law, birth control, abortion, drugs, and divorce—the whole absurdity of a puritanical sex code—Hefner would spend inordinate amounts of time and energy both researching and writing. It was, in effect, a living statement of the beliefs, insights, and prejudices of Hefner himself, and hence, of *Playboy* magazine.

Hefner's main thesis was that our society had too long and too rigorously suppressed what he called "healthy heterosexuality," and since its growth had been stunted, perversion flourished in its place. "You get healthy sex not by ignoring it but by emphasizing it," he wrote. He's right, of course.

If a man is released from repression, he maintained—and he attacked organized religion as one of the principal retarding agents—he will instinctively pursue a healthy life in sex and business. "Sex can become, at its best, a means of expressing the innermost, deepest-felt longings, desires and emotions," he wrote poetically in one of the early parts of the Philosophy. "And it is when sex serves those ends—in addition to and apart from reproduction—that it is lifted above the animal level and becomes most human."

Hefner really enjoyed the hours of work he put into his ideology: "The Philosophy is the most satisfying thing I've gotten involved in since the whole operation began," he said. The monthly installment proved to be one of the most controversial and widely read features the magazine ever published, generating thousands of letters of response—both positive and negative. To inspire even more reflective and authoritative letters, he issued a 25 percent discount on subscriptions to *Playboy*, for clergymen only, hoping that they would subscribe, read the magazine, and write letters to him.

182

They did all three, in the thousands, making *Playboy*, ironically, one of the most popular magazines among the religious community in this country.

But the rest of Hefner's duties continued to increase. Each mail delivery from the *Playboy* offices, hand-carried by messenger twice a day to Hefner's apartment in the Mansion a few blocks away, almost sent him awash in a sea of minutiae. What was demanded of him by others and the work load he insisted upon for himself became too much to cope with on any sensible level.

He began refusing all telephone calls, not only from outsiders, but even from his top executives. Bobbie Arnstein, his secretary, would constantly have to explain: "I'm sorry, but Mr. Hefner does not receive telephone calls unless he specifically originates them himself." He did that rarely. He worked mostly at night because it created a psychological moat around the house, keeping him from being badgered by any number of people.

He would systematically lock all the doors to his apartment, leave sacrosanct orders not to be disturbed for any reason, and stay in there for hours, days, even weeks on end attempting to cope with the morass of layouts, papers, and memos spread over his bedroom and study, all of which kept his 100-million-dollar corporation operating. Even some of the servants who worked in the Mansion wouldn't see him for months at a time.

He would feed belts into his dictating machine as if it were addicted—three secretaries carry on a twenty-four-hour relay race of eight-hour shifts—issuing memos and directions pertaining to the smallest detail of his organization. Here is a sampling:

To: Michelle Altman (assistant cartoon editor)
The backside on the girl in the Interlandi cartoon is a little oversized, but not so much as to warrant a redrawing of the cartoon.

H.

To: Bobbie Arnstein

Please get word to all the girls in the House, plus all of the Bunnies in the Chicago clubs, that Anthony Newley will be my houseguest here Wednesday and Thursday, and we would enjoy having as many of the girls hanging in in the evening, and after work, if possible. . . .

H.

To: Bob Preuss

I'm sure you know that *Playboy*'s policy of always giving its executives attractive working space is a very conscious, calculated thing—based upon a principle in which I firmly believe—which is, that a man produces more for his company if he has the feeling that he is being properly respected and given a prestige area in which to work. It is not a matter of guilding lilies—simply the feeling that when you invest in a man, you get the best from him with more than simply salary. In other words, the small additional investment in truly adequate, executive space is calculated to pay for itself many times over in a short time, because an executive with a high morale is one who is most apt to prove highly productive.

I want you to personally, immediately check out the space situation with all of our key personnel and make a point of personally reassuring those who do not now have adequate space that they will have as quickly as it can be arranged for. Then see to it that it is arranged.

I don't want to feel that simply because I'm not over there these days that fundamental policy approaches to our personnel tends to erode, break down or disappear. These policies—like the problem of office space—have never been an accident. They are a part of an overall attitude that I want continually conveyed in *Playboy*'s approach to its employees. We took this approach in the early years, when we really couldn't afford it; we certainly don't want the same approach breaking down now, when there is no possible economic reason for it.

H.

To: Jean Parker (office manager)

It is my understanding that the switchboard is supposed to go on at 8:45 each morning. On Friday, March 13, it was not on yet by 9:00 A.M. and an attempt to rouse someone at the office by dialing MI2-1000 got me no response whatever.

H.

To: Bob Preuss

This is to confirm what I've already indicated verbally to you on our Jamaica trip: Please instruct the manager of the Jamaica hotel that, starting immediately, the shops in the hotel are to no longer stock copies of any of the girlie magazines—the *Playboy* imitators: *Rogue, Dude, Gent, Escapade, Play Dates, Caper,* etc.

The only men's magazines they are to stock, other than *Playboy,* are *Argosy, True,* and *Esquire.*

H.

Letter to:
Premier Fidel Castro
Havana, Cuba

Dear Premier:

PLAYBOY Magazine is interested in publishing an interview with you by our cartoonist-correspondent, Shel Silverstein, and photographer, Larry Moyer. Any cooperation shown them in this regard, or in the obtaining of the general feature they are doing for us on Cuba will be very much appreciated by this publication.

You have our assurance that any interview granted will be published in a way that fully reflects any and all of the answers and statements you care to make. Mr. Silverstein will be pleased to submit the full text of the interview to you or to your representatives to check the accuracy of his notes. If it meets with your permission, we would like to record the interview on tape so as to insure the complete accuracy of all statements and answers given.

Thank you in advance for every cooperation that you are able to show.

Sincerely,

Hugh M. Hefner
Editor-Publisher

To: Jack Kessie

We can stop worrying about "pros" in our French prostitution

185

story. Pro is listed as a regular word in the unabridged Webster and pros is shown as the plural.

H.

To: Jack Kessie

In the future, pick the Letters To The Editor on the basis of their interest value. Do not feel obliged, a la *Time* Magazine, to give both sides and to include a lot of stuff that is negative about the magazine. We assume that most of our readers dig us, so we don't have to include lots of letters calling us homosexuals or sex nuts. However, neither do we want a long list of empty, pointless letters that say only how swell we are. That is what makes the letters dull. *Pick the letters, as I said, for their interest value and for what they do to continually build the image of the magazine.*

It isn't necessary to run comments about the Playmate unless they are interesting ones. If we do run Playmate letters, and it is perfectly o.k. to do so, let's limit them to two to four. We ran about a column's worth on Joni Mattis, which is not a good idea.

H.

As he thought of them, Hefner would often hurriedly jot down on a small memorandum pad the tasks he knew he had to do. The trivia that he became entangled in seemed endless. Here is a typical selection from four sheets of the same pad:

—Invite director of film to party
—PR man to Chicago on Wednesday, re. party
—Spec—re. magazine article to send to Dave Alpert
—Miss Universe Contest
—re. Playboy Newspaper (include Bunny Ball Club & June obscenity charge, plus June sales figures)
—Bob Preuss—re. checks for lawyers
—letter to readers re. State Liquor Authority scandal
—Nancy—get me last cabaret decisions
—get background on St. Louis TV scene and letter to Catholic paper re. N.Y. Playboy Club
—change things to fit that court's decisions re. club operations

186

—thanks to Sam Raphaelson
—letters to Playmates
—letters to Sharon Hugery
—Art Paul on "Forum" heds [sic] (type style)

Hefner's memoranda to his staff were immediately recognizable since they were typed on gold-colored paper while everyone else at Playboy issued their memos on pink paper. When a Hefner memo was delivered by messenger, the sight of the gold paper visible through the holes in the gray interoffice envelope brought the recipient an inevitable rush of recognition; the communiqué would instantaneously take precedence over whatever else was being done at the moment.

Hefner's directives were always to the point, often abrupt, sometimes pedantic, but never cruel or patronizing. They underwent subtle transitions as they passed through his assistants, however, and the typed, formal transmissions always had the depressing immediacy of Caligula ordering mass suicide rather than a polite request to do another layout revision or delete a sentence. The main reason that Rosenzweig was such a valuable assistant to Hefner was that he had the ability to transmit Hef's directives in a diplomatic and professional manner which left the receiver feeling almost honored that the editor and publisher had taken the time to tell him what to do.

It was not infrequent for a staff member to receive a two- or three-page single-spaced memo on anything from the placement of a photo to the editing of a proposed "Playboy Advisor" answer. Don Myrus, former head of Playboy's book division, claims to possess the world championship Hefner memo: forty single-spaced pages—39,000 words—on what should be done to develop his division. Myrus also claims another Playboy distinction of sorts. In his last two years of employment, he met with Hefner three times in meetings devoted to the business of the book division, each meeting progressively breaking the company record for length:

twelve hours, eighteen hours, twenty-six hours. According to Myrus, the meetings were bearable for both principals because while Myrus sipped Dom Perignon champagne, Hefner popped amphetamines and swigged from a bottle of Pepsi. The seeds for Myrus' ultimate departure from the company were laid in the twenty-six-hour encounter, a meeting which proved to him that he had moved too close to the King.

During the times of Hefner's reclusive entombment, the corporation would often seem to be on the brink of disaster, for he still insisted on approval of so many minor details, and his key people could not get to see him for discussion. Executives, hopeful for a brief meeting with him, would often spend the day in his secretary's office, waiting for Hefner to make a brief appearance so they could corner him for vitally needed approvals. Even though Hefner was the self-confessed bottleneck, he would not tolerate a missed deadline or an uncompleted project. He expected his staffers to work around him, and, if necessary, get materials to him months in advance so that he would have enough time to study them. Hefner paid high salaries; the demands he placed on those who worked for him were in proportion to the money they received.

Spectorsky was once forced to send Hefner a telegram requesting a meeting and this when the two men worked on the same floor of the old Playboy building, their offices only thirty feet apart.

I once had a desperately pressing topic to discuss with Hefner, concerning a specific layout he wanted to see before it went to press. The deadline was already past by several days. Memos requesting a meeting and calls to his assistants and secretaries were unsuccessful. In desperation, I constructed a large sign, four feet by four feet, that said: "HEF, I MUST HAVE A BRIEF MEETING WITH YOU ON LONDON LAYOUT. FRANK" and hung it outside the glass doors that separated his apartment from the rest of the Mansion. I had the meeting the next morning.

Once, a layout for *Playboy* was so desperately late—Hefner had not returned it approved—that Preuss took matters into his own hands and sneaked into the apartment with a master key while Hefner was sleeping, in order to retrieve it. Hefner awoke and almost literally kicked Preuss out, warning him that he would never tolerate such an intrusion again. Years later I asked Preuss how he had reacted to Hefner's ruthless ingratitude. "I got the layout—that was the important thing—and the magazine was out on time," he answered dutifully.

Despite the unusualness of Hefner's method of operation and what ultimately developed into outrageous procrastination on his part simply because he was so incredibly overworked, the Playboy empire continued to grow.

His assistants were placed in a constant state of frustration and anxiety as they received hundreds of calls and memos each day from *Playboy*'s editors, lawyers, art directors, promotion people, accountants, etc. asking for Hefner to return something that had been sent to him weeks before and which still required his approval or signature.

The people at Playboy headquarters on Michigan Avenue were always suspicious of Hefner's Mansion assistants (Was Hefner really asleep? How could he fail to answer my query?), while the Mansion people seemed incredulous, pompously indignant sometimes, that staffers at headquarters could not follow Hefner's sometimes-vague directives. Spectorsky often described the situation as bureaucratic warfare between the "Michigan Avenue Mafia" and the "Mansion Nostra."

In 1970, the Reverend Malcolm Boyd, frequent contributor to *Playboy* and a friend of Hefner's, spent weeks at the Mansion and in the Playboy Building gathering information for an essay about Hefner that appeared in his book,

189

My Fellow Americans. His description of the animosity between Hefner's Mansion personnel and the rest of the organization is astute:

Visiting the Playboy Building, one felt great waves of feeling —envy, hostility, love and anguish—constantly, washing against The Mansion. "It's a damned mausoleum," an important magazine aide complained. "That huge English mead hall. Those gigantic works of art and coats of armor. And most of the people there are corpses and zombies. Oh, I know there are some who are really great, enjoyable, stimulating, but in that atmosphere they encapsulate themselves in a shell of shiny armor. You can't get to them; they're a slick sophisticated shell. Nobody quite touches."

Why did these men in Hefner's own organization speak so critically of him? Partly out of frustration, I thought. *They* worked hard for the magazine too, yet had not made millions of dollars or achieved world fame. Also they were obviously smarting under hurt. The Master paid them well and gave them editorial freedom, but he had left them behind, or at least outside his private life. They could observe it inside The Mansion, from time to time, when they were invited to a large party or a movie screening, but his life was clearly his own business. It lay well beyond the pale of their superficial involvement in it. They compulsively had to show an outsider such as myself that they did not care. In this gesture, of course, they revealed the aching care they suffered. All these pent-up feelings of theirs came through to me between the lines of what they said.

Whenever Hefner made his appearance in Bobbie Arnstein's office, located above his apartment, she would grab him and present him with her capsulized interpretation of dozens of urgent messages:

Bobbie: "Spec says he *must* have a meeting with you and Art Paul on replacing Vince Tajiri as head of the photo department. The situation is deteriorating, he says."

Hefner: "O.K. If it can't wait until our scheduled meeting next month, set something up for the end of the week."

Bobbie: "Arnold Morton says he's found a choice piece of property for a possible Playboy Club in Las Vegas. He wants to show you the plans and photos, and discuss the whole thing with you quickly, before he loses the option to buy. You have a scheduled meeting with him next Wednesday."

Hefner: "Call him and see if we can put it off until then. Call Preuss and Lownes and make sure they're at the same meeting also—whenever it is."

Bobbie: "The advertising department has to know whether you will accept this full-page ad for wigs for men. They want to run in the July issue. Ad closing is tomorrow."

Hefner: (After briefly studying ad) "Tell them that I have no objection to a standard toupee ad if it's done in good taste—but this ad is not. Tell them to go back to the company or agency and have them re-do it—if they're interested in being published in *Playboy*. Tell advertising, in any event, that they ought to present the ad to our executive committee and get their thoughts on it. I'd consider another point of view, perhaps."

Bobbie: "Keith called and said that 'you know who' was passing out LSD to Bunnies at a party he gave the other night. Keith thinks someone should wise him up."

Hefner: "Call him yourself and tell him that I heard about it and that, even though he knows that I would never interfere with his personal life, if there were any legal problems developing out of this, it could be very bad for us. Point out to him that it could end up getting the girls into a psychological mess, also. Tell him I was *very* upset when I heard about it."

Bobbie: "Murray Fisher says he's run out of subjects for *Playboy* interviews and needs your approval—quickly—to get going for the August and September issues. He's sent over a list of possible people:"

Hefner: "O.K. Read them off."

"Cesar Chavez"—"Yes"
"Jimmy Breslin"—"No"
"Herbert Marcuse"—"O.K."
"Averell Harriman"—"Yes"

191

"Prince Charles"—"Yes"
"Jacqueline Susann"—"No"
"Gamal Abdel Nasser"—"Yes"
"Tiny Tim"—"No"
"Buckminster Fuller"—"Yes"
"Earl Warren"—"Yes"
"Steve McQueen"—"Yes"
"Ronald Reagan"—"Yes"
"Bob Hope"—"O.K."
"Mendel Rivers"—"Yes"
"S. J. Perelman"—"No"
"Buddy Hackett"—"No"
"Robert Heinlein"—"Yes"
"Adam Clayton Powell"—"No"
"Walter Reuther"—"Yes"
"Lewis Mumford"—"No"
"David Brinkley"—"Yes"
"Robert McNamara"—"Yes"
"Vanessa Redgrave"—"Yes"

Hefner: "Tell Murray I'm not really impressed with this list. If we have to go with some of these—it's okay—but I'm not particularly enthusiastic about any of the names here. How about Arthur C. Clarke, Sidney Poitier, John Wayne, Barbra Streisand? Tell him to check *those* people to see if they'll grant an interview."

Bobbie: "The art department must have your approval today on the Vargas cartoon for July."

Hefner: (Starts circling things on cartoon as he studies it) "I was going to say, let's cheat a little and do something with the feather. But wait a minute, I'm terribly confused: the feather . . .the toe . . ."

He quickly exits, without warning.

Bobbie: "But wait, Hef, I don't understand your corrections! And call your mother!"

But it's late, it's late: Hef has a very important date. He scurries down the spiral-staircased hole and is swallowed up by his own fantasy world; the artists will have to determine, on their own, what must be done with the Vargas feather and toe.

On occasion, Hefner claims that his retreat from the outside world in the mid-60s was, for the most part, inspired by a conscious decision to create his own special environment and, in fact, doesn't really represent a lapse into seclusion. "Magic is the answer," he says concerning keeping the avenues of communication open, referring to his electronic input of television, films, radio and a constant barrage of books, magazines, and newspapers. "Physical insulation isn't the same as psychological isolation," he maintained in his *Playboy* interview. "A private world that manages to minimize wasted time and motion actually permits greater attention to individual interests and matters of greater importance." At other times, however, he will admit that he was becoming an actual recluse and that he was suffering from a "hardening of the emotional arteries."

But when he is compared to Howard Hughes, probably the world's most famous recluse, Hefner claims that though they both have chosen to live in self-contained, separate physical worlds, the comparison ends there: "Hughes has purposely cut himself off from all contact with other people, and the Playboy Mansion was conceived as an environment in which I could more readily *enjoy* the company of others." Hefner said that the Mansion had worked out so well in providing for his every whim, and perhaps serving as a catalyst in bringing many of the most renowned people in the world to him, that going out of it seemed to be a useless exercise. "What the hell was I supposed to go out for?" he asked rhetorically.

Hefner's vision of himself as a multimillionaire, with enough money, women, and power to feed the egos of several hundred people for a lifetime, undoubtedly made him feel immensely fulfilled within the personal universe he had created. Yet if one were to peel away a few layers of Hefner's surface, it would become clear that these declarations of self-satisfaction are mere rationalization; for, in reality, Hefner was actually highly pressured, constantly overworked, and often melancholy.

By the late 1960s the business had grown so large (and was still growing phenomenally) that Hefner was forced, finally, to delegate responsibility and authority to his key executives, even though he begrudged relinquishing the most minor aspect of control. By his own admission, he was losing "hundreds of thousands of dollars" because of his bottleneck methods; others claim the figure was more likely in the millions. By allowing others to take on his chores, he saved his business; he may also have saved his own life.

Because he had been so inexorably involved with every phase of *Playboy*'s operation, Hefner now had the sinking feeling that once he allowed others to make the decisions, the entire mechanism would plummet out of control. Advertising revenue for 1969 was over $32 million; the December issue alone that year sold 5,624,000 copies—at $1.50 each— and almost $4 million in advertising. Over twenty Playboy clubs and hotels were in operation, and the entire Playboy empire was grossing over $100,000,000 a year.

"I found that I had built a marvelous machine, but far from being master of that machine, the machine was ruling me," he finally admitted to Calvin Tompkins. His health was in serious jeopardy, since it had been literally years since he had had any physical exercise (despite the fact that he has a pool in his home, Hefner has a fear of water and doesn't swim), and his consumption of Desoxyn was increasing to well beyond the danger level as his tolerance for it soared. His cheeks hollowed even more deeply; his weight dropped drastically, from 175 to 135 pounds; he rarely ate; his teeth began giving him enormous problems and pain because of his malnutritive diet and his overconsumption of sugar-laden soft drinks. His doctor warned him that if he continued neglecting his body at the same pace he had, continually assaulting it with drugs to keep himself artificially stimulated, he'd never reach the age of fifty.

I asked Preuss at that time how he foresaw the future of *Playboy*. He answered fatalistically: "We *could* continue to grow as we have been doing, but who really knows what will happen when Hefner dies, and he *will* kill himself if he doesn't start taking care of his body and stop those goddamned pills. He's only a little past forty—a young man! He's theoretically on top of the world with the rest of his life still ahead of him, and the idiot is going to blow it all!"

His mother was very concerned about his health, noting that he looked "gaunt, almost a skeleton." She took a snapshot of her son and showed it to him when it was developed: "See? You look ghastly. You'd better be careful," she warned.

Hefner soon discovered that after letting go of the reins of control, which he'd held onto so messianically for almost fifteen years, it was not as bad as he'd thought it would be. The company didn't collapse. The magazine *did* get published on time. Circulation and profits did continue to grow. When he stopped writing his Philosophy—an act that stimulated his staff to genuflect in gratitude, since they assumed it meant he would become more accessible—he stated that he would eventually put the entire series into book form, when he reached his sixties. Apparently he then had hopes that he would get his life in shape so that he could live that long.

He began to reevaluate the pattern and structure of his life and decided that "what worked very well for me earlier in the decade wasn't satisfying any longer." There is also the possibility, though he probably wouldn't admit it, that he had simply begun to become bored with the actual process of day-to-day editing, the business problems, the thousands of photos he was forced to study, the endless memos that he felt compelled to write, and the meetings that sometimes would last for fourteen or sixteen hours.

He stopped taking pills—"cold turkey," as one of his

aides described it—and within a week he was already feeling better and increasing his weight. He began working out on a slant board and exercise bicycle and started to reverse the drastically rapid aging process that he had been experiencing.

But he was irritable when it was suggested that doctor's orders had been the catalyst that made him cure his habit: "I didn't stop because the doctor said stop. I stopped because I thought, wait a minute: everything is so good, let's keep it good for as long as we can."

Perhaps the most cogent reason for Hefner's emergence was the obvious one he offered himself: "I wasn't free." Hefner began a systematic effort at weaning himself away from the Mansion, to get himself out and going, so that he could help improve his physical condition and simultaneously bolster his psychological perspective. Plans were made to start a new television show, *Playboy After Dark*, to be taped in Los Angeles. "I knew that would force me out of the house and into new areas of activity," he confessed. Off came his pajamas and bathrobes, and on went $15,000 worth of Edwardian suits.

At the very first taping of the show, Hefner met Barbara Klein, a five-foot-three, green-eyed, eighteen-year-old UCLA coed and former beauty queen from Sacramento, who was working as a TV model in her spare time. In addition to a spectacular body and an Ultra-Brite smile, Barbi—as she became known—had a fresh, spirited quality about her; just months prior to meeting Hefner she had been a high-school cheerleader and a Miss Teenage America contestant in her hometown.

Hefner was immediately attracted to her and after the taping session invited her to join him and a few others from the show at a local discotheque. He asked her for another date, and at first she was hesitant. "I've never been out with anyone over twenty-four," she responded. "That's okay," quipped Hefner. "Neither have I."

They began dating, and six months later she was living with him at the Chicago Mansion. Barbi remained Hefner's "constant companion," as the magazine described their relationship, for over five years. She started as an extra on the television show, but after meeting Hefner she served as an unofficial hostess each week. Curiously, she is the only woman, other than Millie, with whom Hefner has had a somewhat permanent relationship that did not work directly for the Playboy organization. Barbi did appear, however—with her name changed to Barbi Benton—on three *Playboy* covers and surfaced seminude, showing off her unforgettably healthy and sexy body, in a pictorial in the March 1969 issue. They have been living together—on and off—since they met, and in an interview on *The Tonight Show* in the spring of 1974, Barbi said she thought Hefner would be "ready" for marriage in about four years. "When I'm ready, he'll be ready."

Playboy After Dark ran for twenty-six weeks and was a considerable creative improvement over *Playboy's Penthouse*; it received some remarkably good ratings, though like its predecessor it also lost money, while simultaneously elevating Hefner's celebrity status. "He set out to make himself instantly recognizable to the public, just like a movie star," said Victor Lownes. "And he succeeded. He was envious of the recognition that the stars get. He needed it. People now stop him on the streets and in restaurants and ask for his autograph. No other publisher in history has enjoyed the recognition that Hefner has. Henry Luce or William Randolph Hearst were not physically recognizable to the public."

Hefner was, as always, the undaunted optimist about *P.A.D.* "I know how good the show is," he reported to *Time*. "It's better than the Johnny Carson show or the Joey Bishop show and I do a better job hosting than Ed Sullivan does."

In order to remove any objections he might have to airline scheduling while flying back and forth between Los Angeles and Chicago—and so that he could travel in the most comfortable and efficient way—he purchased, for five and a half million dollars, the world's most opulent jet plane, and perhaps, with the possible exception of Air Force One, the country's most famous flying machine. One of his top executives stated that there were a number of reasons behind the plane's purchase; it was acquired partly as a status symbol, partly as a highly publicizable gimmick, and partly because of his reclusiveness, "a paranoia that makes him not want to travel on public transportation." And to make it as distinctive as his Mansion and his magazines, he proceeded to have his DC-9 designed so that it would be the most original-looking plane ever manufactured. Even *Newsweek* relaxed its usual deprecation of all that is Hefner's to dub it "the most mind-boggling display of sensual opulence ever assembled in a flying machine."

It is the only all-black jet in the world: "The only logical color was black. That made it unique and added a touch of elegance." One splash of white was added, however; on the tail is emblazoned the all-pervasive Playboy rabbit. "My big black mother in the sky," Hef cynically calls it. It seats thirty-nine and sleeps fifteen (or sixteen, if two are in Hefner's large bed at the rear of the plane).

There is a custom-equipped galley to provide multi-course gourmet meals. One can have Château Lafite-Rothschild 1964 served with lobster *fra diavolo*, for example, or a score of other classic dinners. A 16-mm movie projector has been installed for showing films in Cinemascope. There is a living-conference–room area that has a swing-out bar and a 100-square-foot discotheque. Hef's private compartment is furnished with an elliptical bed (complete with a huge "bed belt" that is strapped from one end to the other during take-offs and landings) covered with a bedspread of Tasmanian opossum pelts, a light table for viewing transparencies, and a contour-molded desk with a concealed dictating machine and typewriter. A skyphone installation allows communication with the cockpit and other compartments as well as with the ground. The large adjoining bathroom also contains a full, step-down shower.

The plane has been stretched to accommodate larger gas storage tanks, giving it international capability. In *Playboy* Hefner stated that "the plane is a logical extension of the concept behind the house. . . . Whatever time is spent in transportation isn't wasted, since I can do anything aboard the Big Bunny that I do in the Playboy Mansion. Well, almost anything. We don't have a swimming pool or a bowling alley on the plane."

To Hefner, his spectacular jet plane was like having a new toy, and it immediately helped to demolish his hermetic ways. To the world, it was the airborne answer to Aristotle Onassis' yacht, *Christina*. *Time*, *Life*, and *Newsweek* all did stories on the Big Bunny, and just as reporters and feature writers had flocked to the Mansion for articles, now they came to view the amazing black airplane: Satan's chariot.

Hefner decided that the plane, unlike the Mansion, could take the mountain to Mohammed; he made plans for his first international tour, to display the craft to the world and possibly capture what he thought would be tremendous publicity, based on the immense interest already shown by the media, and to signal his intention to permanently end his self-imposed exile.

I believe that the real motive force behind the trip was Barbi Benton. It was, in essence, a gift to her, not just of the trip but of himself, since she knew he was going only to please her. Hefner had been out of the United States only twice before in his entire lifetime: in 1959 he went to the Cannes Film Festival accompanied by Joyce Nizzari and in the mid-1960s he attended the opening of the London Playboy Club. On both occasions he had sorely missed American cooking and was reported to have been bored and anxious to get home. He speaks no foreign language.

Hefner, Barbi, Shel Silverstein, John Dante, Leroy Neiman, Nelson Futch, Alexas Urba (Hefner's ever-present photographer), several other friends, and an entourage of servants and assistants left Chicago on July 28th, their first stop London. When the plane touched down at Heathrow Airport, Hef and his group could not believe what they saw: 300 people were waiting to greet them and view the plane—all, however, reporters and photographers. This intense publicity was to follow Hefner wherever his tour went. During the month-long journey, they flew to Nairobi, where they traveled on a photographic safari, and to Tanzania, to view the spectacular animal migrations across the Serengeti Plain.

At Rabat they were the guests of the interior minister of Morocco, General Mohamed Oufkir, at his private palace. They cruised the Greek islands and spent time sightseeing and wining and dining in Rome, Venice, Malaga, Munich, and Paris. And all the time, photographers, journalists, *paparazzi*, and the just plain curious gaped and wondered about the big black plane and its equally strange-looking inhabitants.

Hefner dined at the famed Maxim's in Paris, saying he enjoyed a great and romantic evening there. Someone pointed out that, ironically, the rarified assemblage at Hefner's table, with the exception of Hefner himself, was born under the sign of Pisces (Hefner's sign is Aries). The rapport between Hefner and his group was confirmed by the fact that those two signs are supposedly compatible.

Hefner's valet, Jodie MacRae, had spent the whole afternoon at Maxim's showing the world-famous chef how to prepare Mr. Playboy's favorite meal, fried chicken, which it seems almost sacrilegious to order in a restaurant of such gastronomic reputation. "I was pretty horny for some home-cooked chicken," explained Hefner, reinforcing the beliefs of those who consider him a social primitive. Maxim's apparently recovered from the blasphemy, since a short time afterward they attempted to sell the restaurant to Hefner.

Though Hefner still talks fondly of his overseas trip, four years have elapsed without his taking another, and it could easily be another four, or more, before he again ventures overseas. "Places hold no interest for me," he says. "Visiting the most beautiful or historic spot in the world would hold no meaning for me unless it were shared with someone I cared about."

Hefner does admit to considering an extended trip to the Orient sometime in the near future, though mainly for business reasons. Japan has been eyed by Playboy executives as one of their principal targets for future international development.

There was another gesture that Hefner made in the summer of 1971 which may, at least in part, have indicated his love for Barbi, though a number of growing business involvements were also somewhat responsible: the purchase of Playboy Mansion West.

Barbi was reared in California and went to school there. Her parents still live in Sacramento. For these reasons, she vastly preferred California as a place to live. She also wanted to break into the movies (she had had one part in the unsuccessful movie, *What's a Nice Girl Like You Doing in This Business?*), and as a result started spending more time in Los Angeles. This situation was agreeable to Hefner when he was doing the *Playboy After Dark* series, but after the last of the shows was taped, he did not welcome any prolonged separation from Barbi.

Playboy Productions, a division Hefner had created in 1969 to produce motion picture features and television specials, operated out of Los Angeles and was beginning to come into its own. Hefner wanted to continue to expand his interests in motion picture production, and that fact, combined with wanting to spend as much time as possible with Barbi in an environment that would make her happy, led him to buy his second home: a $1 million, thirty-room Xanadu in Holmby Hills, just a block and a half from Sunset Boulevard. It also made sense from a corporate point of view, because it gave *Playboy* new promotional material and a lavish new showcase in which to display Hefner, the company's living trademark.

He had decided that his house in California, like the one in Chicago, would have to be more than just another house. It would have to stimulate a scene for celebrities and be a pop-happening house that would turn the media on; but he wanted it to be a virtual reflection of the new Hefner, and he wasn't quite sure what that was.

It soon became apparent that Holmby House, with probably the most magnificent grounds of any California house outside of Hearst's San Simeon, would serve to attract movie mogul and star alike. Hefner quickly began to dominate the Hollywood social scene with his flair for flamboyant entertaining. To the press, Hefner issued the following statement: "We felt the organization needed West Coast corporate headquarters in much the same way that one was needed in Chicago. We visualize such a headquarters serving as a business and social catalyst for our West Coast activities, in the same way as our Chicago Mansion."

Built in 1927, the elegant, English Tudor–style house was first owned by Louis D. Statham, a physicist-industrialist and well-known amateur chess player. The building is situated on five and one-half magnificent landscaped acres. Statham and his wife spent little time there and eventually sold it to a private social club. For the four and a half years before Hefner bought it, it served as the unofficial hospitality residence for the city of Los Angeles, housing such guests as the kings of Thailand and Sweden and a number of prime ministers and ambassadors.

As with all of his possessions, Hefner is his own most enthusiastic fan. He fell immediately in love with the place and could hardly wait to get there after his plane touched down at the Los Angeles International Airport. "Wait'll you see the grounds. Just wait!"

He loves to give personal tours of the house and grounds himself, something he never does in his Chicago palace. "I don't think anything I could say could adequately describe it." Yet he tries: "The main building was inspired by a mansion in England called Holmby House; it's built of stone, with slate roofs and leaded windows. The grounds are handsomely landscaped, with rolling hills, a variety of trees, plants and flowers and what is reputed to be the largest redwood forest in Southern California. We added a tennis court and a swimming pool with adjoining ponds and waterfalls, and introduced exotic varieties of fish, birds and animals as a finishing touch. It isn't as large as the Chicago Mansion, but it's even more impressive because of the elegance of the architecture and the grounds. There's a separate guest house, a greenhouse and a game house, with an outdoor bar and buffet dining area done in the same stone as the main building. But the most popular spot on the estate is a grotto we built as a part of the pool, that can be entered by swimming through a waterfall, and includes an elaborate series of Jacuzzi baths that are enjoyed more as a center of social activity than for their therapeutic value. In short, the West Coast Mansion is a veritable Shangri-la, and rumor has it that you really do start aging perceptibly after leaving the grounds."

Since moving in, Hefner has stocked his grounds with an incredible array of wildlife, including a pair of doves given to him by Barbi on St. Valentine's Day. There are squirrel monkeys and another, larger species called wooly monkey swinging and chattering through the trees; flamingos, cranes, and peacocks strutting the grounds; and on the terraces, a pool of hundreds of mottled Japanese carp. Large, kaleidoscopic-colored flowers are everywhere, redolent with sweet-smelling perfume. Black, gray, and white jackrabbits which are thoroughly tame hop unhurriedly across the back lawn. All manner of parrots and other tropical and exotic birds, including an ostrich and a condor, flit, flutter, and fly about the grounds, as large an aviary as can be found in many public zoos. Hef even has a pet llama which graciously strolls the well-tended lawns. Indeed, because of the large number and variety of wildlife, Hefner had to register his home with the city of Los Angeles as an official zoo.

The house has a decidedly English-country flavor inside. One enters a large, balconied reception hall with perfectly polished floors; stone, wood, and glass are everywhere, and a dramatic, curving double stairway of hand-carved oak is perfect for grand descents. There is a formal dining room which has a huge baronial table and twelve blue-velvet-covered chairs, and the charming, green-accented breakfast room has a fountain and is studded with dozens of peregrine plants. The immense living room houses a collection of alabaster eggs, a handsome chess set and table, a Picasso lithograph, and in addition to a grand piano, there is an Aeolian pipe organ built into the wall for Barbi to play. In the air, one catches the scent of leather, oak, and Hefner's "Mixture 79" pipe tobacco.

In the small but adequate library, Hefner gives interviews, watches television, relaxes with friends, plays backgammon on a beautiful, custom-built cocktail table. In what some people indicate is a search for family as described in the philosophy of Wittgenstein, Hefner plays board and card games of all types: bridge, gin rummy, pinochle, poker, Monopoly, Risk, Yahtzee, Scrabble, Clue, Sorry, Life, Millionaire, Movie Moguls, Dealer's Choice, and chess. The sessions go on continually and can last for twenty-four hours at a stretch, Hefner giving as much time and interest to his games as he once gave to his business. He feels that his constant game playing is both an outlet for the acting out of games that he might ordinarily play in life and also a genuine escape. "I have to watch myself with games," he says. "I become so absorbed in them, I could almost do nothing else."

Some of his executives believe he has already reached that stage, in contemporary analogy to Marcel Duchamp, who gave up his art for chess. Like Poe's analytical man in

204

Murders in the Rue Morgue, he is constantly absorbed with all manner of conundrums, enigmas, and hieroglyphics. Hefner's love for games seems delightfully obsessional: he has competed in international backgammon tournaments (with Prince Alexis Obolensky as his partner) and has recently started a swank, private club in Los Angeles called "Pips" simply to play backgammon in sumptuous surroundings. And no little, metal top hats, thimbles, or terriers can be found as tokens in his Monopoly set. He has replaced these with perfect full-color metal miniatures of himself, Shel Silverstein, Barbi, and all of his regular Monopoly coplayers, which they move about on his specially built $1,000 Monopoly table. For years he was a truly addicted Risk player. The object of the game is to conquer the world.

Also in the library is a larger-than-life epoxy bust of Barbi, done by sculptor Frank Gallo, which stands on an oak table near the leaded windows. A large, framed, ethereal photograph of Hefner and Barbi—he looking spectacularly handsome in a white-vested Gatsby suit, wearing a white fedora, and she splendid in a ruffled, flowing gown—standing in front of his spired Holmby House during a blue dusk graces one wall. On another wall is a framed epigram, needlepointed by Barbi, in mock though somehow poignant humor, stating:

BE IT EVER SO HUMBLE
THERE IS NO PLACE LIKE HOME.

Occasionally Hefner will call a high-level meeting with some of his top executives on the operation of both his mansions, temporarily abandoning discussion of high finances and the Playboy empire. The following is an extract from a tape recording made during a meeting with Hefner, Rosenzweig, and Hefner's troubleshooter, John Dante:

Dante: Arnold picked up a bottle of wine from lunch and presented it to us as $15 a bottle. Do you want fine wines and a look of a millionaire's mansion or do you want cheap wines?

Hefner: I specifically want fine wines but I don't want them used for *everyone's* lunch.

Dante: But there was another incident with wines, at the Board Meeting.

Rosenzweig: This type of wine is only served during what is called a special luncheon for important people.

Hefner: That's okay. I just think that not all of the staff should have expensive wines every time.

Dante: Okay, just the important events.

Hefner: We want to take a look at both Chicago and Los Angeles as part of an overall look for additional ways of cutting down unnecessary expenses. This goes for everything: eliminate fat and reduce costs. Plus . . . we don't seem to be getting the kind of controls and services in Los Angeles that I would like. We seem to be hiring people who are either untrained or who put white pepper in the salt shakers or bring empty sugar containers. They don't know how to do anything, like make banana splits.

As with the Chicago house, Hefner has transformed Playboy Mansion West into not merely a showplace but a *salon de célébrité*. He already had many friends in show business, but as he became a producer of feature films, his position in the movie industry and his status among the stars soared. His new house now epitomizes, more than anyone else's, the great salons of heyday Hollywood. Burt Lancaster, Groucho Marx, Peter Lawford, Linda Lovelace, Warren Beatty, and Sammy Davis, Jr. have all joined the growing brigade of stars constantly and lavishly entertained by Hefner. At the same time, the interest generated in *Playboy's* readership by his new abode shows that Hefner's instinct for promotion has not deserted him. *Playboy's* readers still identify closely with his realizations of his own fantasies.

As in Chicago, Hefner shows movies on Sundays to a large group of stars, starlets, sports figures, and pretty faces, but he is much more relaxed and informal there than he is in the Midwest. Often he'll appear wearing a terrycloth jump suit; he seems less concerned about his physical appearance, allowing his hair to become thoroughly disheveled and occasionally not shaving. Most times, however, he still wears the uniform which has become as famous and as studied as Castro's tailored fatigues: yellow silk pajamas, maroon velvet bathrobe, and blue velvet slippers with a gold monogram indicating to the world who he is (lest they forget): H.M.H. He treats Mansion West as if it were truly his home, and he becomes a graciously warm host. The Chicago Mansion has begun to represent the business side of his life; it is an institution that has somehow gotten away from him. California has succeeded in giving him the social life he now values so deeply, one which perhaps he always wanted and which he could have had in Chicago only after a total divorce from the business that obsessed him there.

Hefner's involvement in movies dynamically increased after moving into his West Coast home. His first film, released in late 1971 and directed by Roman Polanski, was Shakespeare's *Macbeth*, which had received tremendous advance publicity. Hefner's decision to do the film was not a particularly popular one among his key executives, and he received several exhortations to reconsider. In a memo to him, Spectorsky warned that Polanski would go way over budget ("He'll lead us down the garden path and leave us there," he wrote), and Preuss and others were also pessimistic. As it turned out, they were right.

The $1 million budget quickly turned into $1.5 million and ended at $2 million. In addition, the completed film was delivered almost a year late. Hefner still had confidence in it and in Polanski's judgment as a director, however. He felt that *Macbeth* was an excellent vehicle to indicate to the audiences, critics, and Hollywood at large that Playboy Productions was interested in making serious films, not just erotic frivolities. The publisher from Chicago and the director from Poland became even closer friends than they had been before, and Polanski often spent time as Hefner's guest at one Mansion or the other.

On Hefner's forty-fifth birthday, April 26, 1971, he

hosted a small party at the Chicago Mansion at which several movies were screened. Polanski, in London at the time, still working on the filming of *Macbeth*, sent over the latest rushes for Hefner's approval and comments, and these, too, were screened that night.

The scene of the witches boiling up their poisonous, prophetic brew was one of Polanski's most striking interpretations. Not only did he use very old and truly hag-like women, he had them play the scene in the nude. As Hefner and his friends watched the scene for the first time, they could feel the horror and loathing that audiences would later share.

"Bubble, bubble, toil and trouble," they chanted, hovering around their obscenely smoking cauldon.

Suddenly, all of the ghastly, naked, droop-breasted women walked to the front of the cave, linked hands, looked straight at the camera, and, their old voices cracking and croaking, burst into song: "Happy Birthday to you, Happy Birthday to you, Happy Birthday Hugh Hefner, Happy Birthday to you!"

Perhaps Polanski should have left this practical joke in the film that was finally released. Though criticized for its use of gore and violence and for the fact that it was an obvious psychological purging or reenactment of the murder of Polanski's wife, Sharon Tate, it was hailed as an artistic *succès d'estime* and was voted the best motion picture of the year by the National Board of Review of Motion Pictures. It didn't draw large audiences, however, somehow failing to capture the public's fancy, and the film lost $1.5 million.

Despite the commercial failure, Hefner let it be known that he did not regret having produced the movie. "The film business is always a crap-shoot in which only a small percentage of films make money, but it's a calculated risk I'm happy to take, because on a long-range basis, filmmaking is going to be an increasingly important form of expression as society moves beyond the print era, and I want to be personally involved in Playboy's development of expertise in that field."

Though Hefner denies it, some financial analysts thought that the loss incurred by *Macbeth* was the catalyst behind the decision that few people—including himself—ever thought he would make: Playboy would go public. When Hefner referred to Playboy, he spoke of it as if it were another human being: "Playboy is a world unto itself, a world within a world. It's inconceivable that I could ever sell the company—it would be like selling a loved one, or myself. It's my own identity, what I want to be and accomplish."

Almost ten years previously, in 1962, there were involved discussions about listing Playboy Clubs International with the New York Stock Exchange, and they even started preparing a prospectus. But Hefner vetoed the move at that time because he felt that the corporation didn't need additional funding and he was loathe to have the public, in effect, telling him what to do. And in 1964, Hefner was approached by J. Paul Getty, who evinced an interest in having Hefner manage Getty's Hotel Pierre Marques in Acapulco and transforming it into a Playboy resort/hotel. Hefner was eager to do business with Getty's billions. In a letter to him, Hefner wrote, "You may be assured, therefore, that any of a great number of directions that might be mutually advantageous in a business alliance of the sort that has been suggested will be viewed with the greatest possible initial interest from this side." Getty's stock holdings, however, took a minor plunge shortly after that, and the two men never got together.

There were additional pressures in the early seventies that made him reconsider going public. Hefner had many long and involved meetings with his vice-presidents about the stock issue before he was convinced to take the step. The company was growing rapidly, but its cash position was, though in no way dangerous, somewhat tight. $50,000,-000 had been invested in Playboy resorts in Lake Geneva,

Wisconsin, and in Great Gorge, New Jersey. Though Hefner believed that both of these resorts would eventually show a profit, he had no guarantee that they would do so in the near future. Further expansion of more clubs and the production of more movies were now out of the question unless additional cash was generated quickly. But there was a more crucial reason for going public. *Playboy* magazine provided about 65 percent of the corporation's sales and 80 percent of its profits. The clubs, resorts, and other ventures produced the rest. The magazine had reached what Hefner and his associates felt was near peak circulation and ad sales, and growth would be slow from then on. Profits in 1970 were up only 8.5 percent from 1969. To avoid any unseen catastrophies to the corporation, such as a successful competitor, it became necessary to diversify.

Hefner took the step, as he says, reluctantly, for the good of the company and because it was the proper way to assure greater growth. There are some financiers who believe that the real reason he went public was the hope of markedly increasing his own fortune. If this stock could double within a short time, for example, Hefner could have easily found himself, had he been willing to sell say 30 percent of his shares, a bona fide billionaire. As it developed, each time the stock market fluctuated one point, Hefner either lost or made seven million dollars. Mostly he lost. A catchall company, Playboy Enterprises, Inc.—P.E.I.—was formed, consisting of all the Playboy divisions and publications. The offering was made in the name of the new corporation.

On November 3, 1971, 1,115,812 shares of stock were offered at a price of $23.50 a share, and by the end of the first day every share was sold, thus releasing about 10 percent of the company for approximately 20 million dollars. Hefner personally sold 300,000 of his shares, reducing his share of ownership from 80 percent to 71.7 per cent, "so it isn't like I'm selling out my control." He retained 6.7 million shares and a salary of $300,000 a year as chief executive officer, the highest annual emolument of any publisher in the world.

The stock was sold at twenty-three times earnings, a high ratio based on the declining condition of the market, and instead of rising as Hefner had expected, it dropped a few points in the days immediately after the opening and then declined steadily until it reached an all-time low of 4.5 —which is four times earnings—in the spring of 1974.

An article in *Forbes* in March 1971 described in true Orwellian fashion what the new, publicly held corporation might be able to achieve in the not-too-distant future, perhaps unaware that most of it was already standard operating procedure:

A young man dressed in Playboy clothes and living in a Playboy-built apartment might choose to read Playboy's book of the month, or peruse Playboy magazine while listening to a Playboy record or radio station, or he might watch a Playboy special on what could only be called the Boob Tube, or listen to a Playboy educational cassette on how to be a gourmet cook. In serious moments he might invest in a Playboy mutual fund.

On his night out, our ideal bachelor might catch the latest Playboy film at a Playboy theater, then take his playmate for dinner, drinks and a floor show at a Playboy nightclub. Come the weekend, he could hire a Playboy limousine and go to—you guessed it—his Playboy vacation home at a Playboy resort outside town. And for summer vacation, he may choose a Playboy tour to Acapulco or Spain (where Playboy would have resorts) or London (where Playboy has a thriving nightclub-casino).

And all these props of the pleasurable life, plus the life itself, could perhaps be insured by Playboy burglary and health insurance.

Hefner's personal fortune was increased by 7.05 million —to an estimated 200 million—as a result of the offering, but those who have held on to their shares have taken, at least temporarily, a severe drubbing.

211

Hefner once indicated to me that he considered his investments in art, made on behalf of the corporation, to be of more substance than some of his stock market ventures. His Franz Kline was purchased for $14,000 and was recently appraised at $80,000. One of his de Kooning's was also bought for $14,000 and is now worth $65,000. His *Nude Reclining* by Picasso, for which he paid $110,000, has skyrocketed to $275,000, and his Jackson Pollock has increased from $24,500 to $110,000.

Hefner's second film *The Naked Ape*, starring Johnny Crawford and Victoria Principal, cost $800,000 and was even unluckier than *Macbeth:* it was a stupid film, poorly directed, and turned out to be a total flop, both commercially and artistically. Though some of Hefner's film advisors begged him to produce what they considered to be two large money-makers, he could not be convinced to become involved with *The Godfather* or *Deliverance*. Both films have made tens of millions of dollars. *Vrooder's Hootch,* perhaps Hefner's last attempt at feature films—other than for television—will be released in the spring of 1975.

Playboy Press has become somewhat more successful than Playboy Productions, with one best-seller—*Cosell*—to its credit, and a possible second with Spiro Agnew's novelty, *A Very Special Relationship*. Hefner denies any advance knowledge of the purchase of the Agnew novel for $150,000, stating that the executives of Playboy Press bought it without his knowing about it. He says he's unhappy about the purchase but must go along with it because the sale was consummated: "The men who are in a position of power in the government are criminals of the worst sort. Why should we be publishing them?"

CHAPTER

*"When, with money and fame, you're put in
a position where most of the rules don't
apply to you, then you find out what kind
of person you really are. That has always
been important to me: to not be changed
by that success and power."*

THERE are so many diverse elements—psychological, sociological, philosophical, personal, financial—that one
is forced to confront head-on in an attempt to sincerely
understand or explain Hugh Hefner that it is almost embarrassingly pretentious to do so. A sign hanging in a Chicago
bar presents the dialectic with as much perception as is probably possible:

EVERYBODY ALWAYS TALKS ABOUT HUGH HEFNER,
BUT NOBODY EVER DOES ANYTHING ABOUT IT.

Nevertheless, over the years, for his critics Hefner has
become an elementary target. It is surprising, therefore,
that the exercise is continued: William F. Buckley, Jr., Nelson Algren, Gloria Steinem, Benjamin DeMott, and Oriana

213

Fallaci are just a few of the literary guerrillas who have aimed their pens at Hefner for being a male chauvinist rabbit, for possessing a lobotomized social conscience and choreographing a continuous psychic molestation and subliminal seduction of society's child. He is accused of exploiting sex by people who, for the most part, would consider it sacrilegious to name *Sports Illustrated* an exploiter of sports or *The New York Times* an exploiter of news. Because sex is so taboo in America, it somehow seems immoral to a broad segment of society that a man can not only earn his living from it but actually make a fortune doing so.

From my point of view, Hugh Hefner is a temperate and sometimes kindly man. In *Playboy* he has shown a highly developed sense of how prejudices hurt people on all levels and what, in lieu of talking, we can do about it. He also has to have a magnificently pure business instinct, since he is one of the most successful publishers in the entire history of the art of communications.

It is my belief that we can extract from the story of Hugh Hefner's life an extraordinary odyssey, the development of an editorial and business genius. Of course the image is tarnished and shopworn in spots, and though it's fascinating gossip, it really has little to do with what Hefner is really like or what he has accomplished.

Is he a playboy? A philosopher? A businessman? An editor? An entrepreneur? Or is he a combination of all these? We expect the real Hugh Hefner to stand up and tell us who he is, and we become annoyed when he constructs a barrier, mostly physical, which is more difficult to penetrate than the repression he attacks in our society. The layers of imagery that coat him so thickly also prevent a lucid glimpse of what he is.

We do know that Hugh Hefner is an authentic phenomenon. At the age of eight he was already editing and publishing his own newspaper; this precocity and singleness of purpose are usually the trademark of the very gifted (and the very determined, which may be a gift of its own). As we can see, Hefner taught himself, in effect, to be exactly what he is today: the editor and publisher of a major national magazine. And he approached his tasks with a slavish industry. "If you look at everything Hef does as a memorial to himself, you get a better understanding of what drives him," Spectorsky cynically observed, and his observation may have been astutely clever: Hefner's career does seem to parallel the skinny young man who gets sand kicked in his face only to become a muscled superman through overcompensation.

But if Hefner had decided back in 1953 to start his magazine on Chicago, or if he had ventured a sports magazine, or a news periodical, or whatever, he would undoubtedly have succeeded equally as well—though he might not have made quite as much money. He is probably the best picture editor in the world today and might have been the only man who could have saved *Life* had he been involved.

He has always possessed—and still does—an unlimited amount of confidence in his own ideas. It mattered not to him whether his concepts were good or bad, sacred or profane; when he had an idea, he saw it through to its conclusion. For twenty years his critics have been unsuccessful at dampening his dream. Values were changing in America in the fifties, and the country was ready for a magazine that brought sex out into the open but without the tawdry, black-garter, backroom sneer usually afforded it by the publications sold under the counter or in sleazy shops with "For Adults Only" signs. With *Playboy* Hefner proclaimed that sex was healthy, desirable, even fun. In *Playboy*, sex was no longer dirty or remote. Hefner, instead of just being a packager of flesh, as he's so often labeled, is actually the Prometheus of what was heretofore considered unprintable or unacceptable; he gave sex back to the people. The Playmate suddenly became the girl next door in Mason City, Iowa or Brooklyn, New York, instead of the model from Marseilles who, despite her nudity, would be a cold and commercial bitch. In an article entitled "Sophistication in America" in *The Nation*, David Cort pointed out that

instead of being an unattainable and in that sense undesirable mannequin, as in *Esquire*, she is the girl next door or at the next desk with her clothes off and looking very well, thank you. One month PLAYBOY's Playmate was the lady author of a story in the magazine. As a male writer, I must protest unfair competition, but as an editor I must applaud a brand-new invention in eroticism which grew out of the free-wheeling, ebullient attitude of its editors.

The nation's males responded by buying out the newsstands. "It was the right idea in the right place at the right time," Hefner has said, and Voltaire would have proclaimed him a genius for recognizing that the time for the idea had come, if for no other reason. Pure sex, presented in a way that the American male had rarely if ever seen it, sold and built *Playboy* in its salad years. As Hefner, the millions of regular readers, and the magazine itself matured, the *Playboy* concept became virtually a way of life. Even if viewed from an entirely negative perspective, *Playboy* has had more effect on world society in the past few decades than any other magazine published during that time. "*Playboy* is like a Rorschach test," Hefner insists. "In twenty years, we will be viewed as one of the major elements of pop culture that influenced our time." And Hefner himself came to stand for the American assault on sexual inhibition.

For the first five years of its publication, Hefner kept his magazine's content and format very close to his original concept. This may leave him open to criticism, in that he failed to present anything other than a flaccid view of society. He wanted to emphasize the spectrum of concerns of a college-educated man in his twenties whose interests and activities were largely urban oriented. He also took seriously —perhaps too devoutly and exclusively —the phrase that appeared on the cover of every copy of *Playboy:* Entertain-

216

ment for Men. The result was that very little material of any social significance found its way into the magazine, and Hefner was attacked as the apotheosis of materialism rather than lauded as a new champion of ethical behavior.

"I know there are many serious problems in our world, disease and suffering and injustice," he said in an interview with a Chicago reporter in 1955, "and there are lots of magazines that give much attention to all these things. And that's good. But the unhappy part of life is not PLAYBOY's field of interest. Our format is based on the good things in life, the fun and joy of living. I don't know whether it will always be this way though. I expect that as I grow and mature, the magazine will grow with me."

Just such an editorial metamorphosis became apparent to *Playboy* readers during the early sixties. The changes, however, were made by addition rather than substitution. Hefner retained the editorial ingredients that were responsible for *Playboy*'s early success, gradually adding more serious content; Hefner's increasing interest in the more primal aspects of life seems largely attributable, ironically enough, to his more severe critics. He was having trouble with the Post Office in the early sixties. Also, the nation's press and academic communities seemed suddenly to have discovered the impact and influence of *Playboy* magazine. Articles about the social, psychological, moral (and even political) significance of *Playboy*'s astonishing growth and success began to appear in the popular press as well as in dozens of journals of social, philosophical, and religious opinion.

"While we've been conscious of the virtues in seeing ourselves as others see us," Hefner wrote in the first installment of the "Playboy Philosophy" in the December 1962 issue, "we've decided to state our own editorial credo here, and offer a few personal observations on our present-day society and PLAYBOY's part in it—an effort we hope to make interesting to friends and critics alike."

217

During the notorious 1968 Democratic Convention riot in Chicago, Hefner, out walking with friends and a few Playboy staffers, was wacked on the behind by a policeman and told to "get home." Hefner contends that this incident really had no effect in radicalizing him—he points to *Playboy's* growing interest in social matters as proof—but after that, *Playboy* began running even more politically activist articles and interviews with such people as Eldridge Cleaver, William Sloan Coffin, Allen Ginsberg, and Jesse Jackson.

Spectorsky, however, wanted no part of what he considered to be an economically dangerous position for *Playboy* to assume. He discouraged his editors from becoming more politically active on the pages of the magazine in an attempt to head off Hefner from the direction he believed he was going. In part, one of Spectorsky's memos stated:

I, personally, feel that it would be a tragedy for PLAYBOY to find its slot in the spectrum of politically didactic magazines ranging from *The Nation* and *The New Republic* to *U.S. News & World Report* and *National Review*. Or in that slick miasma of pretended objectivity as typified by *Time* and *Reader's Digest* (though on the left rather than the right).

We have a unique—and uniquely valuable—thing going here, and I think it is incumbent upon every one of us to be vigilant in preserving it from contamination, however well intentioned.
Finally, I have stated above, as I have often stated, that it is wonderful that we make a lot of money although our primary purpose is not amassing more and more money at the expense of exploiting our public. But I predict that if we depart from our editorial principles to become engaged in party politics, we will suffer financially. And I think that this is going to be true no matter how small the entering wedge in our bastion of good conscience: descending to being politically partisan, no matter how slightly we stoop, is like pregnancy—there's no such thing as a little bit, you are or you aren't.

Spectorsky's ploy apparently worked since the political tone of *Playboy* has still not changed greatly. Hefner continued his social efforts, however, and created an additional section in *Playboy* called "Forum Newsfront," a survey of news events related to social issues raised by the "Playboy Philosophy," from nudity to pornography, from civil rights to women's rights.

Perhaps the best short critique of Hefner's efforts at social criticism was published in the spring 1966 issue of the *Columbia Journalism Review*. It was written by Dr. Theodore Peterson, Dean of the School of Journalism of the University of Illinois.

"To summarize the Playboy Philosophy is presumptuous and difficult," says Dr. Peterson,

but it is hard to assess the stir that the Philosophy has caused without some notion of its content. Much of what Hefner says is a Twentieth Century version of John Stuart Mills' essay, *On Liberty*, including a utilitarian basis for freedom. Underlying Hefner's beliefs is a profound concern for the rights of the individual in a free society. According to Hefner, "When I use the word 'free,' I'm not referring to a society completely devoid of restrictions, of course, but one in which controls are established to serve rather than suppress the common citizen: a society that is unfettered, just, rational and humane, in which the individual and his interests are paramount."

Whatever critics say to the contrary, Hefner is not concerned exclusively with sexual freedom, although that aspect has had the greatest attention. In fact, his first seven installments concentrated on matters other than sex.

Hefner is for free enterprise. PLAYBOY's emphasis on leisure and urbane living, far from being merely sybaritic, is consistent with free enterprise. The magazine motivates men by portraying the good life that is the prize for honest endeavor and hard work.

He is for a wide arena of free expression. PLAYBOY believes that this nation is big enough, strong enough and right enough to give free expression to the ideas and the talents of every man among us without fear of being hurt by any man's individual weaknesses or follies.

Hefner is for separation of church and state. He has no

219

quarrel with those who wish to embrace religion, but he believes that an individual has an equal right to be free *from* religion, as he sees it. By stressing self-denial and heavenly reward, it has kept man from enjoying, without guilt, the fruits of his earthly labors and to that extent it is incompatible with the free enterprise system. By influencing the state to enact legislation that people do not believe in and will not obey, it has contributed to a breakdown in law and order. By encouraging censorship, it has curbed free expression. By equating sin with sex, it has inspired harmful sexual repressions. Indeed, it is religion, not PLAYBOY, that has been anti-sexual; it is religion, not PLAYBOY, that has looked upon woman as a depersonalized object or possession and has continuously associated her with its antagonism toward sex.

Hefner contends that it is important to view PLAYBOY in the context in which it exists and not in the vacuum that it is so often examined. Charges that the magazine is materialistic and dehumanizing and exploitive, without reference to the society from whence it comes, states Hefner, since it both reflects and influences the society in which it exists, are inane and unfair. "Sure we reflect some of the things in society that are not necessarily healthy but at the same time our influence on those things has been a highly healthy, humanizing process."

Hefner has been criticized for even using the word "philosophy" to apply to his point of view. Ignoring the fact that anyone is permitted a philosophy, his critics claim that it is a pretentious notion to apply such a serious tone to a magazine as frivolous as *Playboy*.

The fact that Hefner publishes pictures of nude women is an integral part of his philosophy; it really doesn't matter that he formed this thesis as a rationale, in effect, for publishing *Playboy*. That's what publishing is all about: an editor has a point of view—in his selection and rejection of material, or in a specific recommendation or observation on his editorial page, or in the material he assigns to be written or illustrated—that he wishes to share, for the price of his periodical, with his readers. Those who want to expose themselves to his ideas read his magazine. Apparently, 25 million Americans can relate to what Hefner is saying or offering each month: an alternative life-style with a more permissive, more play-and-pleasure–oriented ethic than the puritanical work ethic that most of the readers were probably raised under. It's an upward-mobile life-style that is an unsubtle seducer of twentieth-century man. As a result, *Playboy* has become not only a Baedeker of *savoir faire,* but one of the great communication powers of contemporary American life.

Aside from advancing a philosophy of "work hard and play hard and enjoy the good life," Hefner has used the pages of his magazine to campaign for an end to civil injustices of all kinds, from prison conditions to outmoded divorce laws, and to instigate more humane laws pertaining to drugs, abortion, homosexuality, and virtually every type of act, whether sexually related or not, which has at one time or another been considered criminal.

While *Playboy* seems to some critics to be overly concerned with fashion, sports cars, and other frivolities, it has addressed itself to such concerns as the environment and racial prejudice. For a magazine that carries the slogan "Entertainment for Men" on its cover, it now has a remarkable social conscience; Hefner has molded it into one of the most honest magazines being published in America today.

But editorializing in *Playboy* is not all he does. Hefner's companies donate $500,000 a year, through the Playboy Foundation, to such organizations as the A.C.L.U., National Organization for the Reform of Marijuana Laws, The Masters and Johnson Research Team, Jesse Jackson's PUSH, and similar groups. In his will, Hefner has bequeathed almost all of his money, stock, and other holdings to the Hugh M. Hefner Foundation, which, like the Playboy Foundation, is interested in crusades and causes.

"We're concerned about sex education, trying to change abortion laws (the present backlash, and the 'suppressive legislation' on sex still on the books in many states)" Hefner explained in his *Playboy* interview.

Whenever people start legislating against "a crime against nature," it really means that they think all sex is bad except coitus for procreation. Sodomy laws are as crazy as drug laws. There are penalties of twelve, fourteen, and twenty years for oral and anal intercourse, whether homosexual or heterosexual, or even between husband and wife. In one case the Foundation handled, a guy had had anal intercourse with his wife; she had given her permission, but he was sentenced to something like fourteen years. We questioned the constitutionality of the law and got him out on a technicality.

As a result of his publishing genius, Hefner is now worth over $200 million dollars personally, though he never knows the exact amount of his holdings, and, as pointed out by William F. Farrell, financial editor of *The New York Times*, has succeeded "to a degree unmatched in American publishing history." As an editor he has proved that magazines can combine a delight in wholesome fucking and a respect for the undraped female body with some of the more serious issues of the day and produce a periodical that becomes almost a friend coming into the house each month.

In addition to his success and his altruism, however, we must acknowledge Hefner's personal faults and idiosyncracies. He has never really been able to maintain any close friendships with men due to his need to exercise control at all times; he ignores the fact that everyone enjoys being the captain on occasion. This insistence on maintaining the upper hand has robbed him of one of the great pleasures of adult life: having a truly close friend. At those rare moments when he feels the need to confide in someone, he will invariably turn to either of two employees, Bobbie Arnstein or Dick Rosenzweig. All of the people he refers to as friends are merely vassals who would think it heresy to demand anything from him that was heroic or profound as one might with a friend, unconsciously knowing that it would never be given. He once said that he would like to hear arguments against always being in control, a state which he continuously attempts to achieve. The simplest point to make, which must be obvious but painful for him to consider, is that constant control rules out the possibility of spontaneity, and spontaneity often leads to a serendipitous method of growth. As conditions change, so will the uncontrived man. The truths that we stumble upon can often be our most valued realizations and our most pungent adventures. Hefner cares not to know anything of this, and it is for this reason that he is in many personal ways years behind the times.

He accepts the Emersonian doctrine that there is properly no history, only biography, and goes about frenetically attempting to secure a place in the recorded archives of the media. Someone once described Hefner as the walking press release or PR man gone amuck, granting interviews to all in a classic example of overexposure. In reality, it isn't his egotistical *Zeitgeist* that craves unlimited publicity as it is his Kafkaesque terror of anonymity. He is obsessed with his own image and immortality. "I'm sure that I will be remembered as one significant part of our time. We live in a period of rapid sociological change and I am on the side of the angels."

For close to ten years he has attempted to authorize a biography to be written—with disastrous results. A number of highly talented and experienced writers have spent months with him attempting to capture the elusive Hefner *persona* on paper. People like Richard Gehman, Miriam Rumwell, Hal Higdon, Don Myrus, Noel Gerson, and George Eells have all tried and failed. Tens of thousands of dollars have been expended and over a half-dozen complete manuscripts have been written, and either Hefner rejects the book after giving it a quick scan or, as is more often the case, his editors read the book first and are then afraid to recommend it to him without an enthusiastically unanimous vote. Usually he asserts that "the real Hugh Hefner is rarely to be found in all of that voluminous material." Hefner rarely reads the entire book himself, even though it might represent over a year of the author's work.

Occasionally an unauthorized book appears, such as Steve Byer's *Hefner's Gonna Kill Me When He Reads This*, which will send Hefner into a quiet rage. Byer, a former Playboy executive (who claims to have made $200,000 a year, though everyone at *Playboy* who should know says the figure exists only in Byer's imagination), became infamous by firing over fifty top people in his first six months of employment. He wrote his book out of avarice after being fired himself. It is a spiteful and petty book, poorly written and conceived, but it caused a stir among other Playboy executives because it named exact salaries and exposed some of the dirty corporate linen. Hefner, in turn, spited Byer; he is emphatic when saying that to this day he has not read the book, but he did read the last chapter in which Byer describes being fired by Hefner. "That story is complete bullshit," Hefner recently declared to me. *"Complete bullshit!* First of all I never fired him! That meeting never took place. Preuss fired him and he sat in Preuss' office and cried about losing his job and begged for another job in the company at a lesser salary. He was a brilliant guy, really, but very sick, as his book demonstrates. That's why we had to get rid of him."

Preuss verifies the fact that he fired Byer and that Hefner's story is correct. Byer was given a check when he left the company on October 30, 1970 for $9,687.50 for signing a contract stating that he would "never, under any circumstances whatsoever, use or disclose to any person or organization *any information*" about Playboy or Hefner, and even though he violated the contract, Hefner decided not to instigate litigation, simply because he knew it would personally promote Byer and his book.

Hefner is acutely sensitive of his public image and how it is treated in print. He believes it is remarkable that so few articles have ever shown what the real Hugh Hefner is like.

"The public holds two popular views of my personal life-style; that it is either one continuing orgy or that it's all very square: Pepsi, popcorn . . . a business. Greenfield points out a very interesting thing: it is the fact that it is closer to the former, than the latter, that makes the latter rather necessary. That's a very accurate perception. The public could not stand to believe the other. You see that coming forth in all kinds of forms. That's where you see 'Hefner is really queer' or 'Hefner mustn't really like girls; he really dislikes them or exploits them' or 'it's just a business' or 'it's just a promotion.' The public needs that. It's too much for them to accept the other way. We have a curious way of handling our heroes in this country: we tear them down."

Hefner's loyalties can run wafer thin with the very editors and staffers who helped put him where he is today. Such great *Playboy* names as Vince Tajiri, Anson Mount, Jack Kessie, and Arnold Morton have all been exiled with the feeble excuse that the corporation had grown beyond them, when in reality they were forced out, given the "executive stiletto," by jealous and ruthless newcomers.

Though Hefner claims he tried to retain the services of these men by all means possible, finally, like Pilate, he has washed his hands of them. Surprisingly they are not as bitter as they should be. This is what they told me:

Jack Kessie: "Hefner has made me a relatively wealthy man. Why should I be bitter? I can tell you that his star is beginning to wane, however."

Vince Tajiri: "Hefner claims that Spectorsky was weak. It was Hefner who was really weak in my case. Wait until I write my book. Then you'll see the animosities come out!"

Anson Mount: "I really still like Hef. He actually kissed me goodbye after I was fired. I feel sorry for him though. His life is an empty one. He's the personification of Edwin Arlington Robinson's *Richard Cory*:

Whenever Richard Cory went down town,
We people on the pavement looked at him.
He was a gentleman from sole to crown,
Clean favored, and imperially slim.

And he was always quietly arrayed,
And he was always human when he talked;
But still he fluttered pulses when he said,
"Good-Morning," and he glittered when he walked.

And he was rich—yes, richer than a king—
And admirably schooled in every grace.
In fine, we thought that he was everything
To make us wish that we were in his place.

So on we worked, and waited for the light,
And went without the meat, and cursed the bread;
And Richard Cory, one calm summer night,
Went home and put a bullet through his head."

Arnold Morton: "Hugh Hefner? He's the sweetest, most selfish man I've ever known."

Though Hefner emphatically contends that business is only one segment of life—admittedly a larger part of *his* life than others—he is so influenced by some of his underlings that he often ignores this crucial realization. The money that he thinks he is saving by these corporate head choppings, even if it numbers in the tens or hundreds of thousands of dollars, can never replace the relationships he is losing. The memory of those men will undoubtedly return to haunt him. But Hefner is armed with his own rehearsed answer, his emotional gambit at the ready, when forced to think of some of these people. In an almost pathetically self-revelatory tone, he once said: "The only thing that means anything to me is *Playboy*. Other things, if they have meaning, are extensions of the magazine." Recently he offered me this sardonic note when I accused him of disloyalty: "You have a great danger with a magazine. It's true with any company but it's very clear with a magazine: just keep your friends around you and grow old together and just watch the magazine go right into the toilet." It is not people that he relates to; his work has become his *idée fixe*, his love made visible.

Like an aging hippie or perpetual flower child, Hefner has devoted his whole adult life to the fulfillment of the romantic dream he had as a teenager; his dream, however, demands an adolescent faith built upon delusion and sustained by ingenuity, traits which he has maintained all of these years. In a film documentary produced by Tony Palmer for BBC, Hefner admitted that "much of what *Playboy* is really all about is the projection of the adolescent fantasies I've never really lost. The boy has been father to the man." And yet he does live a paradisiacal life beyond the wildest imaginings of most men in a culminating fusion of his own separate fantasies and realities.

Nevertheless, Hefner erroneously believes that time can be fixed and that his illusions of omnipotence can be enacted repeatedly forever. "Success is how close you get to fulfilling your childhood dreams," he insists. Since he has been successfully doing exactly that for the past two decades, he assumes that he will continue to be fulfilled forever. Youth, beauty, sensuality, and contentment are all his for all time, he thinks, just as long as he keeps amassing his millions, the vehicle to their attainment and the symbolic affirmation of their possession.

It is crucial that one understand, however, that Hefner is not interested in money for its own sake but considers wealth essentially an instrument that allows him to do the things he likes and have the things he wants even though these "things" comprise a multimillion-dollar annual expenditure—admittedly vital to Playboy's image—in what is one of the world's most extravagant life-styles. "I'm the least business-oriented, monetarily motivated, self-made millionaire of my own personal acquaintance. What I do, I do because I believe in it, and enjoy it; and I never cease to be amazed by the success of it."

And for that reason, there is virtually no chance that Hefner will ever enter the ranks of the super billionaires, simply because unlike a Howard Hughes or a J. Paul Getty, who devoutly wish to increase their personal fortunes by attempting new approaches to making money and by making daring investments, Hefner can only relate to those pursuits he really creatively enjoys. His financial ventures have always been and will undoubtedly continue to be a part of his total entertainment congeries; *Playboy* magazine is the source—it sticks to its last—and all other endeavors are automatically and directly related. And to those who doubt his lack of fixation on money, he offers this, as reported in *Time*: "You know, in the next ten years, I would rather meet a girl and fall in love and have her fall in love with me than make another hundred million dollars."

Hefner's vision of the publishing future of his corporation, however, is eclectic. He has plans for starting a number of magazines (he already owns *Playboy, Oui, VIP,* and the foreign editions of *Playboy*) in the fields of photography, general leisure, fashion, sports, and human identity, in addition to a newsletter of contemporary happenings; he still smiles, but is totally serious, when saying that someday he will also revive *Show Business Illustrated* or a magazine like it, but he claims he has no ambitions to construct a "vast publishing empire," implying that he is satisfied with what he already has and what can be nurtured fairly easily in the forseeable future.

Hefner says there is no chance that he will return to the *Playboy* offices as a day-to-day editor, as many of his executives hope he will, to give the magazine added impetus and flair through his leadership. "I have something more important to do," Hefner said to me recently, sitting in his Los Angeles Mansion. "It's called living."

He seems not to be concerned about other *Playboy* imitators or his chief competitor, *Penthouse* magazine, which started publishing several years ago with the explicit goal of exceeding Playboy's circulation. Hefner claims that it is a "blatant rip-off," and that readers will eventually "see through it." *Penthouse* does seem to be a poorly edited version of *Playboy*, and its lack of originality may be a major weakness. The American public has always been more attracted to an original, whether he be a Muhammad Ali, a Bobby Fischer, an Ernest Hemingway, or a Hugh Hefner, and it is to a "first" that the public has always given its support. "What's happening with a number of these guys is that they didn't grow up wishing they would be magazine editors or publishers. They grew up wishing they were *me*," Hefner stated. "If *Playboy* loses its editorial balls, then it will deserve to be knocked over by a younger, more vigorous magazine in the coming generation. But that won't happen as long as I am alive, I can promise you that."

Whether one is critical or not, *Playboy*, and all that it means, is an essential structure of our time. The fantasy, judgment, and ideology of that system, though it is incorporated in a profit-making business, is a monument to the American ideal of prosperity, a triumph of the rights of a man to publish what he believes. *Playboy* is more than just a magazine; it is a direct conduit to the psyche of America.

Playboy is for the most part the product of one exceptional, eccentric, flamboyant, confused, enigmatic, and brilliant man—Hugh Hefner. Whether we admire or despise him, he is undeniably one of the most influential citizens of our generation.

The paradox of Hefner is that he is a sensitive, charming, relaxed, warm, and forthright *Mensch* when dealing man-to-man, while being a ruthless monomaniac in his business dealings. This confusion propels his mystique to immense, illogical heights. When I asked him whether he could sum himself up, his answer, rife with both desultoriness and sincerity, a masterpiece of antithesis, is probably the most fascinating conclusion I can offer: "I'm a romantic, a sensualist, a humanist and a rationalist. Those labels sum me up as well as any labels can sum up anybody. But I'm also a curious combination of introvert and extrovert, which creates a strange picture. I'm continually being described as shy. I'm not really shy at all. In public situations, I'm very conscious of what has happened to me in terms of my success and if I were an overbearing clod, with the power that I have, I would just be impossible. I'm not a Frank Sinatra who in the middle of someone's restaurant throws spaghetti against the wall. I try to act gently and people are always mistaking me for someone who is painfully shy. But it's important to know that I'm nearly two people: I'm one person when I'm in private circumstances with close friends and I'm another person in a public situation when people are coming up to me asking for autographs, or commenting on things. You find ways of handling those things. You can either handle it in an aggressive, obnoxious way, or you can handle it with a little taste. I have a very strong feeling about the personal corruption that can come with power. When, with money and fame, you're put in a position where most of the rules don't apply to you, then you find out what kind of person you really are. That has always been very important to me: to not be changed by that success and power. It's rather like "Rosebud" in *Citizen Kane*. That sled represented Kane's feelings that under the circumstances he had done rather well. Rosebud represented, then, the other opportunity if he hadn't been given all that money or power when he was a little kid and taken away from his folks. The sled represented the other life he might have had.

"Considering the chances I've had for corruption, I

230

think I'm doing pretty well. I'm in a position, because of my success, to have the opportunity to be a real son-of-a-bitch. I could be a prick and get away with it, as few other people could today, but I'm neither of these things. In my world I'm king."